Grant Me Justice!

HIV/AIDS & Gender
Readings of the Bible

This book is the second in a series of Circle of Concerned African Women Theologians books published by Cluster Publications. The series is on HIV/AIDS and African Women.

The first book in the series
(published in 2003) was

**African Women, HIV/AIDS
and Faith Communities**

edited by
Isabel Apawo Phiri, Beverley Haddad and
Madipoane Masenya (ngwana' Mphahlele)

The third book in the series will be

HIV/AIDS, Women and Religion in Africa

edited by
Hinga T. , A. Kubai and H. Nyanga

Grant Me Justice!

HIV/AIDS & Gender
Readings of the Bible

Edited by

Musa W. Dube and Musimbi R.A. Kanyoro

Cluster Publications

Orbis Books

2004

Cataloguing in Publication Data:
Bible, HIV/AIDS, Gender, Women, Interpretation, Liberation theology,
African women, Africa, Feminist Theology, African Theology, Feminist
Interpretations and HIV/AIDS theology

ISBN 1-875053-46-8 (Cluster Publications)
ISBN 1-57075-600-7 (Orbis Books)

First published in 2004

 Published in South Africa by Cluster Publications
P.O. Box 2400, Pietermaritzburg 3200, South Africa
Tel. & fax: (033) 345 9897, *E-mail:* cluster@futurenet.co.za
Internet: http://www.hs.unp.ac.za/theology/cluspub.htm

Cluster Publications is a non-profit publishing enterprise of the
Pietermaritzburg Cluster of Theological Institutions, aiming to produce good
scholarship and accessible and inexpensive resources for contemporary
theology.

 **Published in the United States by Orbis Books,
Maryknoll, New York 10545-0308, USA**

Founded in 1970, Orbis Books endeavors to publish works that enlighten
the mind, nourish the spirit, and challenge the conscience. The publishing
arm of the Maryknoll Fathers and Brothers, Orbis seeks to explore the
global dimensions of the Christian faith and mission, to invite dialogue
with diverse cultures and religious traditions, and to serve the cause of
reconciliation and peace. The books published reflect the views of their
authors and do not represent the official position of the Maryknoll Society.
To learn more about Maryknoll and Orbis Books, please visit our website at
www.maryknoll.org.

Cover design by Alistair Nixon
Typesetting by Lou Levine of *Stylish Impressions* – (033) 3869584
Printed by Interpak Books (Pty) Ltd, Pietermaritzburg, South Africa

Contents

Part II:
New Testament, HIV/AIDS and Gender

Postscript:
In Dialogue and Solidarity

Contributors

Denise M. Ackermann, from South Africa, is a professor of theology in the University of Stellenbosch.

Dorothy BEA Akoto, from Ggana, is a lecturer at the Trinity Theological Seminary, Legon.

Musa W. Dube, from Botswana, is an assistant Professor of the New Testament at Scripps College and has been a World Council of Churches HIV/AIDS and theological consultant for churches and theological institutions in Africa.

Musimbi R.A. Kanyoro, from Kenya, is a general secretary of the World Young Women's Christian Association.

Malebogo T. Kgalemang, from Botswana, is a lecturer of New Testament at the University of Botswana.

Anastastia Male, from Kenya, is a consultant of Bible translation for United Bible Translations based in Tanzania.

Sarojini Nadar, from South Africa, is a Hebrew Bible scholar at the University of KwaZulu-Natal and works for INATE (International Network in Advanced Theological Education).

Letty M. Russell, from United States, is professor of feminist theology in Yale Divinity School.

Johanna Stiebert, from New Zealand & Germany, is an associate professor of Hebrew Bible in the University of Tennessee, USA.

Preface:
"Reading the Bible"
in the Face of HIV and AIDS

Musimbi R.A. Kanyoro

The latest figures released by UNAIDS say that 58% of all the Africans living with HIV are women.[1] We are in trouble. Things keep getting worse for African women. The book of Proverbs admonishes, "Don't give up and be helpless in times of trouble" (Proverbs 24:10).[2] *Grant Me Justice* is a response to this wise advice.

Women everywhere are beginning to heed the advice given in the wisdom of the Proverbs. Today there are networks and organizations of women who are organizing to raise the visibility of issues related to women, girls and AIDS; to catalyse action to address those issues; to facilitate collaboration at all levels; and, in so doing, to scale up action that will lead to concrete, measurable improvements in the lives of women and girls. The Circle of Concerned African Women Theologians is part of this movement. Our contribution serves to educate our societies, to advocate for justice through theology and Scriptures and to empower women to confront the pandemic through a better understanding of the foundation of their faith as is presented in the Bible.

This book is a resource specifically written by women of the Circle of Concerned African Women Theologians with the Bible as its base.

Justice is the central theme of the book. Some of the following are key concepts that are captured through the analysis of the text of the Bible:

Women are not victims and their vulnerability does not stem from inherent physical or psychological weaknesses

(Luke 18:18, Matthew 15:21-28). These and other texts of the Bible teach us that we must build on women's resilience, persistence and ability to reject injustice. Throughout the whole book, the texts of the Bible continually show that resisting injustice is God's option and it must become our option in the face of HIV and AIDS.

Adolescent girls are at particular risk (Mark 5:21-43, Matthew 15:21-28). Advocacy on behalf of young women and with young women is a prerequisite to forming a future without AIDS. Young women need to be provided with information, skills and resources that will allow them to avoid infection in pregnancy and live full and productive lives. Such skills are the first step to their own healing. Young women who read the Bible today need to have at their disposal other ways of reading the Bible. This book provides a resource written by women for women and about women. It is a base for use in training the younger biblical scholars as well as seminary students, both women and men. It is a valuable resource for group Bible studies and individual reading.

Many women who are infected with HIV or those who are at great risk of becoming infected do not always practise high-risk behaviours (Genesis and the Prophets, John 9). Many women are vulnerable or made vulnerable by external issues, laws and cultures, which regulate low status for women. This is where injustice has to be challenged, and the book looks at some of the root causes of faith-based injustices derived from the reading the Bible.

The Bible stories here also show that the affected people are vital to the process of effective change (2 Samuel 13:1-22, Mathew 15:21-28). The lesson here is that women (people) living with HIV and AIDS have a unique contribution to make in strengthening responses to the epidemic at all levels and in all sectors.

The Bible texts explored here constantly confirm that change is possible (Job, Ezekiel, Mark 5:21-43). The factors making women vulnerable are amenable to change, given sufficient attention, commitment and resources. We can use the same hope found in these texts to apply to the situation of HIV and AIDS and preach commitment, leadership and determination to bring about change.

Hope is to be found in the Biblical stories of wisdom, strength, knowledge and courageous action. Many Bible stories indicate that women are part of the tradition that risks finding alternative solutions to dealing with dilemmas. The Bible contains powerful women's stories of collective consciousness and social transformation. Our experiences as women living in the era of HIV and AIDS are similar to those of the women of the Bible times but they are not homogeneous. Likewise the dilemmas of African women are not homogenous to all women of today. Women's lives are lived in very different contexts, which sharply mark us and define our blessings or our misfortune. Among the differences that seem most significant are those which mark us within the borders of economics, race/culture/caste, geography, generation, sexuality, education, health and physical challenges. The credibility of our story will be measured on how we acknowledge and manage these differences without being trapped into helplessness, powerlessness and patronizing paradigms. Contextual reading of the Bible is a form of rendering accountability to how a particular text impacts on us. It is for that reason that many of the authors have defined "their place" from which they read the ancient text of the Bible. This form of accountability protects this book from mere appropriation of the texts of the Bible and justifies why we impose HIV and AIDS on the text, knowing very well that the stories we are using were not speaking about HIV and AIDS.

At this moment in the history of HIV and AIDS, we know very well that poverty, ignorance and powerlessness compromise many women particularly in Africa and increase their risk and vulnerability. We know that those women who have no access to medication die faster, while those who access and use medication and have care and good nutrition live longer. These facts define both the advocacy work as well as the operational work that we need to be involved in. HIV and AIDS may be considered a new disease, but in reality its effect on women and communities is no different from other tragedies in times gone. A woman bled for years and exhausted all her means, and only Jesus could heal her (Luke 8: 43-56). Her story is in this volume. It is a story, which is woven together in a marvellous way to show healing of a woman juxtaposed with the rising from the dead of a twelve-year-old girl. The message here is clear, that nothing is impossible, not even death has a final say. Facing HIV and AIDS from a faith perspective means finding every possible thread of hope that will keep us from giving in and giving up on ourselves.

Bible stories also model for us forms of resistance sometimes needed in order to bring change. Resisting and challenging culture and cultural practices is one of our most urgent tasks in the face of HIV and AIDS. Women's risk of HIV is increased by cultural and social subordination, the failure to recognize women' s basic human rights and the growing levels of poverty, which expose many women to high risk. Women have to challenge gender norms, which legitimize the inferior status of women. Our fore sisters too felt the need to challenge structures and the status quo in society like we do today. There are many more stories with significant messages for women in the era of pandemic, and we shall need to continue searching the Scriptures for these stories and using them for our times. For example we need to read and reclaim urgently the daughters of Zelophehad (Numbers 26, 27 and 36) in order to address the old age questions of inheritance. Inheritance of women and property is a topical subject when faced with a pandemic. In this story, the five sisters asked Moses to give them their father's inheritance since they did not want their father's name to die out. Moses after consulting God agreed to their request but gave them conditionality. In our age we shall need to be better at analyzing conditionality and we may need to advocate against it.

The distinctive elements in our stories as women are the ability to translate our individual domestic and private troubles into public policy. Making the personal political and the private public has enabled women to break the silence over the sexual abuse of women through trafficking, rituals, rape, harassment and all forms of "domestic violence". We have challenged the concept of violence against women and rejected the privatisation of "domestic violence." This is what we need to do with HIV and AIDS. We have to mobilize and take collective ownership of the pandemic and we can do that by working hand in glove with people living with HIV and AIDS. Making the personal political is critical because we invoke moral judgements on our societies. Fairness, dignity, equity and equality are the terms we have used to demand justice and accountability in regards to women's human rights. HIV and AIDS calls on our use of the same methods and framework. Our social analysis has provided both the therapy we need to heal from our past and also given us the possibility to use our collective power to change our lives and to invest in the future generation of women. This is now an imperative in the face of HIV and AIDS.

Networks of women living with HIV and AIDS today model the heritage of women transforming powerlessness into powerful actions. For example The International Community of Women Living with HIV and AIDS (ICW) is an international network by and for HIV positive women. It was founded in response to the desperate lack of support and information available to many women living with HIV and AIDS worldwide. Its aim is to improve the situation of women living with HIV through self-empowerment and the exchange of information. The ICW invites involvement of other women and invites women living with HIV and AIDS to be members (www.icw.org). Our reading of the Bible has to acknowledge that people affected by illness or other vulnerable circumstances are partners in seeking solutions to those issues. Partnership and solidarity are women's characteristics.

Stories of the Bible often show women working together across borders. When two or more groups of women work together, their efforts empower them to overcome challenges and to become more visible. Visibility is a step towards recognition. In the Swahili language spoken in East Africa, we have a proverb which says that *"asiyekuwepo, na lake halipo"*. It means that the one who is not visible has no share in whatever others get. Help will not come for women unless we are visible. Statistics about women dying or infected do not grant women the visibility I am referring to. Such visibility comes when we know who these women are and why they are prone to HIV and AIDS and what the world is doing about it.

The Circle exists to help bring change to the lives of women in general and African women in particular. This book will meet our objective if it contributes to knowledge, and encourages networking and the collective power women to respond to the feminization of HIV and AIDS. Our task as women is to continue to provide education to communities about the pandemic and to care for orphans, widows and communities. We must seek to educate people about knowing their status and to advocate for medications and support systems for women. We must change biases to address all the root causes of stigma and provide proof to our communities that having knowledge about one's status is critical for preventing the virus from spreading. We must be strong advocates for free or affordable treatment for all people. We know that stigma, illiteracy, poverty and lack of personal decision-making and many other barriers are realities of many women. We must continue working to eradicate these barriers and create conditions for men and women and boys and girls to address their sexuality and change of behavior in the face of HIV and AIDS. These things we cannot do alone. We need the friendship and partnership of many different players, women and men. We need a variety of resources. The Bible is definitely one of the resources that we must use.

As a co-editor, I want to thank all of the authors for their contributions to this volume. I would also like to acknowledge the solidarity that professor Letty Russell has given to the Circle of Concerned African women theologians for many years and specifically for her postscript in this book. Letty's pioneer work in feminist Biblical interpretation has influenced many of us. Finally, I wish to thank my co editor Professor Musa Dube. I met Musa first when I took over the coordination of the Circle in 1996 and she was completing her graduate studies at Vanderbilt. We have worked together as co-conveners of the Circle study sections on hermeneutic and the Bible. Musa had the vision for this book and invited me to work with her. I have been out of University academics for a while and I have began in fact to refer to my theology as social theology. I have appreciated working with professor Dube as one who is connected to the academics and can remember all the rules about academic papers. Together we hope we have read and edited these manuscripts both from a social and academic point of view. We celebrate the fact that we have an opportunity to contribute to fight against HIV and AIDS and we take responsibilities for the shortcoming in the compiling of this volume.

Musimbi Kanyoro
World YWCA, August 10, 2004

Endnotes

1. Report of Peter Piot to the Board of UNAIDS, held in Geneva, June-2004.

2. Quoted from the *Holy Bible*, Contemporary English Version, American Bible Society, 1995.

Introduction

Grant Me Justice:
Towards Gender-Sensitive Multi-sectoral HIV/AIDS Readings of the Bible

Musa W. Dube

The link between inequality, poverty and gender discrimination on the other hand is very strong.... The starting point for an adequate response is the understanding that any bid to halt the AIDS epidemic has to include determined efforts to eradicate poverty and drastically reduce inequalities.
(UNDP & Government of Botswana 2000: 53 & 56)

Gender inequalities are a major driving force behind the AIDS epidemic.
(UNDP & UNAIDS 2001:21)

Introduction: Grant me Justice!

In search of justice-oriented ways of re-reading the Bible in the light of HIV/AIDS, the story of Luke 18:1-8 comes handy. The passage features Jesus telling a parable about persistent prayer to his disciples. But when one reads the story through, one is struck that persistent prayer is equated with action-oriented search for justice. Persistent prayer is not a passive and private affair that we do behind our closed doors, nor is it tolerant of injustice. Rather persistent prayer is the *a luta continua* (the struggle that continues) act of insisting and working for the establishment of justice. Persistent prayer is, therefore, the refusal to live in oppression and exploitation until justice is established. Moreover, the parable ends with a big theological bang when it underlines, with no uncertain terms, that God is a God of justice – a God who grants justice to the marginalized and oppressed. Moreover, this God grants justice to the oppressed in time, for justice delayed is justice denied.

Working within the paradigm of the widow's call for justice, this introduction begins by reading the HIV/AIDS texts in order to highlight that it is a social injustice driven epidemic. The second part of the introduction highlights the gendered face of the HIV/AIDS epidemic and proposes gender-sensitive multi-sectoral approach to the epidemic. Lastly, the introduction returns to the persistent widow of Luke 18:1-8, seeking to walk her walk and to talk her talk in search for justice and healing to, with and for all in this world.

Reading the HIV/AIDS Texts

Little did the world realize, when HIV/AIDS was medically discovered twenty-two years ago, that it would become one of, if not the single most, life threatening phenomenon of our time, leaving nothing untouched. It has so far infected 40 million people, killed 22 million people, orphaned 14 million children and continues to infect five million people a year (UNAIDS 2002:8). By the time this manuscript is published these figures would have certainly changed. During the past twenty-two years of struggling to reduce and finally to stamp out HIV/AIDS, it has become clear that the epidemic is not only "a health issue," but also a "social justice issue," which does not only attack individuals, but also attacks families, communities, nations, continents – indeed the whole world (Nath 2001:4). It is not only about individual morality, but the morality of our social institutions, structures and world. HIV/AIDS has affected cultural, economic, political and religious systems (UNDP& Government of Botswana 2000:9-22; UNDP & UNAIDS 2001:3-4) often exposing their limitedness and accentuating the need for new knowledge and new relationships that are founded on different terms – to be more specific, on *justice for, to and with all*. It calls for a paradigm shift (Dube 2001:42-43; 2002:535-549). In particular, it has become apparent that HIV/AIDS thrives through all forms of social injustice that often leaves people powerless to implement decisions that empower them against the epidemic (WCC 1997:14). HIV/AIDS is, therefore, very much a social justice issue, one that pushes us as a world to seek justice for ourselves, for and with all members of the earth community and in all our relationships, institutions and structures.

The all-embracing impact of HIV/AIDS has been attested by the UN Security Council, which even made it their focus in 2000, noting that it is a threat to global peace (UNDP& UNAIDS, 2001:5). The UNGASS (United Nations Global HIV/ AIDS Special Session) of 25-27 June 2001 once more brought the world to focus their attention on HIV/AIDS. Because of its all-embracing impact, the adopted strategy of counteracting HIV/AIDS is now a "multi-sectoral" rather than health/medical approach (WCC 2001:4; UNDP & UNAIDS 2001:10). The former means that every department, discipline, ministry, government, non-governmental organizations, faith based organizations, community based organizations, the private sector, everyone – all of us – are prompted to contribute towards the struggle against the spread of HIV/AIDS; to contribute towards the provision of quality care for the infected and the affected; to contribute towards the eradication of stigma and minimization of the impact of HIV/AIDS and to confront social injustice, which promotes the disease. This means that the struggle against HIV/AIDS is and must be "everybody's business" (Dube 2003:viii). Accordingly, biblical studies, academic and otherwise, must also take its place in the struggle against HIV/AIDS.[1] Given its impact on all aspects of our lives and its link with social evils, HIV/AIDS challenges biblical studies and all other academic disciplines more than ever to undertake multi-disciplinary approach, to seek dialogue between disciplines that have tended to operate in isolation and to seek ways of uprooting injustice from our institutions, structures and the world at large.

Given that the Bible is an authoritative book, a scripture to millions of believers and many non-believers; it was immediately interrogated in the face of the life-threatening epidemic of HIV/AIDS. Much as questions were put to the

medical science guild, the same questions were also applied
to the Bible, its interpreters and institutions: Questions
such as: where does this incurable illness come from; who/
what causes the HIV/AIDS epidemic; who gets it; why do
they get it and how can the epidemic be stopped/halted
were asked. As the epidemic progressed, these questions
have also applied to the economic, cultural, political spheres
– virtually on all departments of human lives. While these
questions were legitimately asked and continue to be asked,
the answers that were found from biblical texts,
unfortunately, contributed more to the suffering of the
infected and affected than to supporting them or to halting
the disease. Many texts were found that linked illness and
plagues with God's punishment for disobedience and
immorality (2 Sam. 12:15-18; 2 Chron. 21:12-15; 1 Sam.
5:6-9; 2 Sam. 24:15; 1 Kings 14:1-13; Jer. 14:12, 16:4).
The disease was thus held to be sent by God as a
punishment to the immoral and disobedient. Sufferers were
accused of immorality, sexual sins and regarded as those
punished by God etc. These interpretations contributed to
the rise of another vicious epidemic; namely, the HIV/AIDS
stigma, that isolated the infected and affected and brought
communities to be gripped by muted fear. Be that as it
may, it was surprising that while HIV/AIDS can infect any
one, God's punishment was primarily directed to the
powerless with this disease – the poor, women, blacks,
children, homosexuals, displaced people and Africa. It was
surprising that those on the margins of power would emerge
as the 'most sinful' and subject to God's wrath. Such biblical
interpretations were certainly problematic, for instead of
depicting a God who takes sides with the poor, the powerless
and the oppressed (Ex. 3:7-12; Matt. 25:31-46; Lk 18:7-8),
God had finally sent a vicious epidemic to clean out 'the
wretched of the earth.' Both academic biblical and
theological forums have not sufficiently taken up the HIV/
AIDS challenge to help the world with the most useful
paradigms of biblical interpretation in responding to the
HIV/AIDS epidemic.

The readings of this volume seek, therefore, to contribute,
in whatever small ways, towards HIV/AIDS prevention,

provision of quality care, eradicating the stigma, mitigating its impact and confronting social injustice, which drives the epidemic. *Grant Me Justice: HIV/AIDS & Gender Readings of the Bible* seeks to contribute towards this end by highlighting the gendered face of HIV/AIDS and insisting that not only do we need a multi-sectoral approach, but we also need *a gender-sensitive multi-sectoral approach* to the struggle against HIV/AIDS. Undoubtedly gender injustice has been recognized for its role in the HIV/AIDS epidemic, but it is not clear that all sectors have been urged to mainstream gender analysis and planning in their interventions. A gender-sensitive multi-sectoral approach is particularly advantageous; first, because we are all gendered. Second, because it takes on the link of gender construction with other social categories such as class/poverty, age, race, ethnicity, sexuality, thereby taking seriously the social face of HIV/AIDS. Third, a gender-sensitive multi-sectoral approach is particularly useful for it carries with it a transformative agenda of seeking not only gender justice for all people in all their various spheres and departments of life, but also insisting on justice for all members of the earth community – an indispensable approach in the struggle against HIV/AIDS.

Reading the Gendered Face of the HIV/AIDS Epidemic

Research and documentation has found that "gender inequalities are a major driving force behind the AIDS epidemic" (UNDP & UNAIDS 2001:21). HIV/AIDS research has found that "gender-based inequalities overlap with other social, cultural, economic and political inequalities – and affect women and men of all ages" (21). Gender constructions are culture specific and they work together with class, race, age, ethnicity, sexual orientation and international status to expose men and women to various degrees of oppression. But given that gender constructions, in their various culture specificity, almost always dis-empower women in the area decision-making, leadership and property ownership, it is women who are in the center of the HIV/AIDS storm. Due to their ascribed gender roles, women are highly vulnerable to infection; they bear the burden of caring for the infected; they carry the HIV/AIDS stigma and when infected they are less likely to have access to quality care. In all the four concerns of the HIV/AIDS epidemic (prevention, care, stigma and confronting social injustice) women are the hardest hit due to their gendered roles. For example, it has been documented that poverty is quite central to the spread of HIV/AIDS through its capacity to pull many threads of transmission (NCA 2000:6; UNDP & Government of Botswana 2000:11-12, 17, 36-37; UNDP & UNAIDS 2001:1-4; UNAIDS 2002:60-61). But due to entrenched centuries of gender constructions that have alienated most women from property ownership, professional skill development, career advancement, from paid domestic labor, combined with the structurally orchestrated gendered violence, lack of control over their own bodies and lack of decision making powers, women are, in almost all, if not every, society, amongst the most poverty stricken members of our societies.[2] Indeed many feminist studies have highlighted the feminization of poverty (Gebara 1996:218-219) and its continuation in the age of globalization (Garba & Garba 2000:24-27). It follows then that if poverty takes the lead in sponsoring HIV/AIDS, women are at the receiving end of poverty-driven epidemic due to gender constructions that distance them from property ownership, decision making and control over their own bodies. Examining how gender interacts with the famous ABC strategy (Abstain, Be Faithful/Monogamous to your partner and Condomise) will illustrate the point.

Gender inequalities render prevention through abstinence from sexual activity ineffective and expose women to high HIV/AIDS infection. While some, especially religious leaders hold that abstinence is the safest method against the HIV/AIDS epidemic; unmarried women who choose to abstain often find that gendered violence, especially in the form of rape both in the private and public space does not protect them from HIV/AIDS. As a matter of fact, the growth of violence against women, especially in the form of rape, and has grown considerably with the rise of HIV/AIDS (Ministry of the State President 1999:16-25), exposing both girls and women to infection (UNDP& Government of Botswana 2000:29; See also Ackermann's paper in this volume). In the HIV/AIDS hot zones, rape has risen almost simultaneously with the rise of HIV/AIDS (possibly indicating the crisis of loss of control among males due to the epidemic). The gendered face of rape does not only expose women, but also the girl-child and the girl-infant to HIV/AIDS (UNDP & UNAIDS 2001:21-22) such that they cannot be protected by the strategy of abstinence. Research and documentation indicate that men who know themselves to be HIV/AIDS positive either use violence to rape teenage girls in order to cleanse themselves of HIV/AIDS, prefer younger uninfected girls or they use their money power to tempt teenage girls into sexual relationships (UNICEF 2000:11; Seloilwe & Ntseane 2000:30; UNDP & Government of Botswana 2000:26-27).

The strategy of "Be faithful/monogamous to your partner" is also crippled by gender inequalities. Research and documentation indicate that 80% of women in long-term stable relationships who are HIV/AIDS positive were infected by their partners (UNDP & UNAIDS 2001:22). In most cases, women may very well know that their spouses are unfaithful, but they would still not be in a position of insisting on faithfulness, abstinence or protected sex in fear of loosing their economic support (NCA 2000:13-14).[3] Some women, however, may very well be economically capable of supporting themselves, yet they still feel culturally and religious bound to remain in such relationships (Fidzani et al. 1999:37). Moreover, married men who are sexually involved outside marriage, still feel that they have the right to unprotected sex with their wives (Hope & Gaborone 1999b:23; Seloilwe and Ntseane 2000:42). With the HIV/AIDS epidemic, heterosexual marriages have turned out to be one of the most deadly institutions due to its patriarchal distribution of power.

Similarly, protected sex or condomizing is also frustrated by gender inequalities. While it is medically proven that male to female sexual transmission is four times more efficient than female to male transmission, because the mucosal surface area exposed to the virus in women is much larger and the viral load is very high in semen compared to vaginal secretions (WAD 2001:64), this could be easily controlled through protected sex. However, prevention through protected sex, or condom, is often difficult because many women do no have control over their bodies. In many cultures women still do not have a say on how, where and when sexual intercourse will take place (NCA 2000:12; UNDP & UNAIDS 2001:6). It makes little or no difference if women have a condom or not as long as gender injustice and feminised poverty prevails – many women often do not have the power to decide on using it. Further, in cultures that insist on child bearing, condomising can be a contradiction (Molebatsi & Mguni 1999:20).

The area of care-giving, nurturing and nursing is also a gendered role that is associated with women (UNDP & UNAIDS 2001:4-5). Given that HIV/AIDS remains largely an incurable disease, caring for the infected and the affected remains central to the struggle against HIV/AIDS. The burden of care is huge and it could not be left to the hospitals, so home-based care is a central HIV/AIDS strategy. Patients who need intensive care and twenty-four hour care are ferried home to be cared for by their close relatives. This means that most women have to spend time at home doing the physically and emotionally heavy duties of washing, changing, feeding, and talking to the depressed and dying patients. The sick patients may be their own siblings, children, husbands or relatives. The impact is that most women's economic production is heavily cut: farmers cannot go to the farms, small business entrepreneurs can hardly continue. The long run impact is that women will be further closed up in the circle of poverty. But worse, when women are sick, they are not likely to have someone to care for them, nor are they likely to have sufficient money to buy anti-retrovirals for themselves. In fact after a long nursing of their sick partners many widows face eviction on the basis of witchcraft accusation – they are accused of killing their husbands either through infecting or poisoning them. Similarly, research indicates that the burden of caring for orphaned children falls squarely in the hands of women, the girl-child and, particularly, the grandmothers (ASU 1998:26-27; UNDP & UNAIDS 2001:4).

The HIV/AIDS stigma is also gendered. Many cultures, including the Bible, have always associated women's bodies with uncleanness and disease. For example, in some Setswana cultures, sexual transmitted diseases are referred to as "*malwetsi a basadi*," that is, 'women's diseases.' With the outbreak of HIV/AIDS, the association of HIV/AIDS with women was inevitable. Fieldwork research studies indicate that women are held to be "the owners of HIV/AIDS," "*ke beng ba AIDS.*" There are many documented cases of women being accused of bringing HIV/AIDS home either by ignoring the cultural taboos of purity (Fidzani et al. 2000:34) or going out with foreign men (Molebatsi and Mogobe 1999:34-35). This gendered stigmatization of associating women with disease and regarding women's bodies as unclean has not been helped by the national mechanism used for monitoring HIV/AIDS. Although monitoring sexually transmitted diseases among men is one method of monitoring HIV/AIDS prevalence rate, national centers monitor HIV/AIDS prevalence, primarily through pre and postnatal health services for pregnant women who visit the clinic. Since most men do not accompany their partners for these visits, pregnant women are taught of the benefits of taking HIV/AIDS tests for their own wellbeing and that of their children. Women are thus most likely to be the first to know if they are infected. The task of reporting such news back home to their partners has earned many women the label of "bringing HIV/AIDS home" and is some cases, expulsion. For example, when Helen Ditsebe-Mhone, one of the few women who are openly out with their HIV/AIDS status in Botswana, tested positive, "she was forced out of her family" (UNICEF 2000:37).

Towards a Gender-Sensitive Multi-sectoral Approach

These broad strokes of the gendered face of HIV/AIDS and its impact on women underline the importance of mainstreaming gender in the HIV/AIDS struggle. Even more importantly, they highlight the link between gender and other social evils. Fighting HIV/AIDS, therefore, is not, as some billboards and strategies have alleged, as easy as ABC: Abstain, Be faithful/monogamous and Condomise (Dube 2001:42). It is not, as some religious leaders and biblical readers are prone to say, an issue of individual morality or lack of it. It is not, as some have said, an African problem. Rather, it is more about an exposure of our world – the revelations of its inherent injustice that inhabits our relationships, institutions and structures and the imperative need to transform them on the basis of justice and health to and for all.

Given this centrality of gender in the HIV/AIDS struggle and the fact that it works together with social, economic, political and cultural avenues to multiply the spread of the epidemic (UNDP & UNAIDS 2001:21), this book seeks to propose a gender-sensitive multi-sectoral approach to the epidemic in biblical studies. That is, the struggle against HIV/AIDS should not only just be factored in all sectors. Rather, each sector must also mainstream gender planning, analysis and monitoring in their prevention, care, mitigation of impact and the eradication of stigma programmes. A gender-sensitive multi-sectoral approach to HIV/AIDS should factor how gender works with class/poverty, age, race, and immigrant status, sexual and ethnic identity. It should take seriously the feminist paradigms of dismantling patriarchal power of building gender justice in all relationships, institutions and structures. The HIV/AIDS struggle, therefore, needs to take seriously the feminist understanding of healing, which "is spoken of in terms of liberation from patriarchal expectations and roles, abusive relationships, constricting stereotypes, and growth-stifling situations" as, "broken bonds" and as "not only personal but also interpersonal and global" (Hardesty 1996:137). Healing is liberation. It is the creation and maintenance of relationships of liberating interdependence.

This book thus features African women and those in solidarity with them interpreting the Bible in the light of HIV/AIDS. The gender-sensitive multi-sectoral HIV/AIDS readings of the Bible, proposed in this book, are their contribution to the struggle against HIV/AIDS. The writers propose *justice-seeking ways of reading* that affirm life, the right to healing and medicine, the human rights of all, while they counteract the social structures of poverty, gender and international injustice, which are the fertile grounds for the spread of HIV/AIDS. In sum, the book seeks to be part of healing the world by standing up to the challenge of HIV/AIDS as not just a health issue, but also an issue of justice which must be tackled by all disciplines.

Grant Me Justice: A Gender-Sensitive HIV/AIDS Reading of Luke 18:1-8

The parable about persistent prayer is set in a "certain town" and it features three characters: a judge, a widow and God. In a quick Hebraic way of characterization (Alter 1981) the judge is introduced as "someone who neither feared God nor had respect for people" (v.2). The following verse introduces the widow[4] and her interaction with the judge. She is described as someone "who kept coming to him, saying, *'Grant me justice against my opponent'*" (v.3). It is notable here that neither the place nor the characters are given any name. This lack of specificity lends the story some wide application, for it could be in any city of the world: my city, your city; their city. Similarly, the lack of naming of both characters successfully draws the readers' attention to the social spaces that characterize each of them. It highlights the power and powerlessness that each of them holds and wields. The reader is impelled to see the judge as the judge and to remember the social responsibility and standing of the judge. Similarly, the readers are urged to think of a widow's social standing both in the biblical setting[5] and in our current setting.

While the systems of justice differ in many different countries and cultures, most readers will have a concept of a judge as one who serves justice – one whose responsibility is to see to it that justice is served to all citizens and people. Be that as it may, most readers are also aware that many systems of justice have, until recently (in the past fifty years), been unashamedly exclusive, and even downright oppressive. Justice was for the dominant members of the society, while the underprivileged and the marginalized groups such as women, people of low class, foreigners, black races, children, physically challenged people, despised ethnic groups, immigrants, homosexuals, slaves etc. have had to, and still have to, fight to be covered by justice. History strongly indicates that many national system of justice have not always been able to escape social categories of exclusion. The various UN charters and conventions such as the human rights charter; the convention of children's rights, the CEDAW (the Convention of the Elimination of all forms of Discrimination Against Women) and many others are all testimonies of the ongoing struggle to bring justice to cover all people.

Such a struggle characterizes our story in Lk. 18:1-8 as it does in many places of our worlds. The widow, as a woman whose husband has died,[6] was likely to be marginalized by justice on two accounts: gender and class. But given that she is a widow, she may very well be in a worse situation, since she may not have a male guardian who should act on her behalf. The system of justice may not regard her word as carrying any legal weight since she is female.[7] Widowhood in patriarchal cultures that do not allow women to own property or live independently is automatically a class issue. If one does not have a male heir apparent or loses one (Lk. 7:11-17) or a willing close relatives to inherit the widow (Ruth 4:1-10) she may very well have no access to the properties left by her husband. She may, like in the case of Ruth and Naomi, live in the verge of poverty (Ruth 2) until a kind relative is found. Moreover, if we could use the example of Ruth, widow inheritance did not automatically occur. For Ruth, Naomi had to come up with a plan to get Boaz and the nearest of kin to act (Ruth 3:1-18). But their story seems to suggest that an unfortunate widow could find a close relative who wants to inherit the property, but not the widow (Ruth 4:1-6). Some families' reluctance to inherit a widow has led to such desperate acts as when Tamar waylaid her father-in-law, posing as a sex worker in order to become pregnant with a child of the family and be accepted (Gen. 38).

An ancient biblical widow, like many widows in today's societies, was on the margins of society. A widow, therefore, graphically symbolizes the situation of women who live in patriarchal systems. Such a woman is not allowed to have independent ownership and management of property save through her male guardians. Such women may not have legal power to act on their own behalf. Bad as it is, when a husband of such a woman dies, she moves from "bad to worse." While being assigned a new husband was the patriarchal approach to widowhood and an essential aspect of maintaining its gender-exclusive empowerment, it certainly is not a solution. The approach resists recognizing the full humanity of a woman as a full citizen and a person made in God's image (Gen. 1:26-27) who, like Adam, was given leadership in the earth (Gen. 1:28b) and access to the resources of the earth (Gen. 1:29). We need to approach womanhood and widowhood within a paradigm of *justice to, for and by all*. The widow of Luke 18:1-8 leads the way for many women, by persistently insisting, "Grant me justice." She is a justice seeking woman against the oppressive patriarchal structures of her day.

The context of the HIV/AIDS epidemic particularly underlines the need to grant justice to all people rather than relying on widow inheritance, for it hinders prevention, care and continues injustice. For example, a widow whose partner died of HIV/AIDS could pass HIV/AIDS to her new husband. Alternatively, an HIV/AIDS negative widow can be assigned an HIV/AIDS positive partner (UNDP & UNAIDS 2001: 8). The vulnerability of a widow to infection also comes through the stigmatization of a woman's body and alienation from property ownership. In some cultures a widow is held to symbolize death, which, if not cleansed, could easily strike in the family again (MAP 2001:17). Some rituals of widow cleansing (by a designated widow cleanser, who sexually cleanses every other widow in the community) exposes widows to HIV/AIDS infection. In some cases, there is no interest in remarrying the widow back into the family, but there is an interest in inheriting the property of the deceased husband. In such cases, witchcraft accusation is often used to disinherit the widow and to throw her out of her home. Quality care is thus denied to many widows, who have labored long, giving care to their dying husbands. Some desperate widows, like our biblical Tamar, are known to have been forced to turn to sex work (UNDP & UNAIDS 2001:8; NCA 2000:13).

However, there are many cases too when widows do not wish to be re-married in the family or at all, for they seek their own independent space or to make their choices. Such widows need the freedom to decide and to act as full citizens and adult human beings. But when they are denied the right to choose, to manage their property, when they are subjected to witchcraft accusation and dispossession, many widows are sanctioned to death by HIV/AIDS. As one widow put it, "We are not protected against anything. Widows are without families, without houses, without money. We become crazy. We aggravate people with our problems. We are the living dead" (Nath 2001: 3). One cannot overemphasize that the circumstances of widows and women in the HIV/AIDS era highlight the need for justice to be served to all of us.

Grant Me Justice: Transforming Power in the HIV/AIDS Era

The widow in the Luke 18:1-8 comes face to face with a patriarchal system and it is a legal system that does not protect her. If the court did not uphold her word because she was a woman without a male guardian, she disregards this attitude. The text does not say what constituted her grievance. But it underlines her insistence on justice; "grant me justice against my opponent," she repeatedly implores the judge. We can imagine that day in and day out she made it a point to appear before this very unjust judge and to insist on justice to be granted to her. This judge who neither respects people nor fears God, finally grants her justice – but for wrong reasons. Because, as he says, "this widow keeps bothering me, I will grant her justice, so that she may not wear me out by continually coming" (v.5). So this widow has her request met, but not because the judge believes that she deserves justice – but for his own selfish reasons. There are three crucial lessons to be learnt here from her interaction with the judge.

First, those who are in power can be so unbothered about the suffering of the oppressed, so much so that even as the oppressed present their pleas, their voices remain unheeded. Such powerful people are comfortable and cannot relate to the needs of those who are crying, "grant me justice!" To these powerful and comfortable people, the cries of the oppressed and the exploited can wait. And so one often hears the saying: "Change takes a long time. You need to be patient." To those who are sitting on the hot fires of social injustice, exploitation and oppression, there is no time to wait. In fact it is not possible to wait. Together with the widow we persist to say, "Grant me justice," now and today.[8] The social evil that plagues our lives and makes us unhealthy must be addressed now.

Second, the characterization of the judge is quite telling about why some powerful people turn a blind ear to the cries of the oppressed: he "neither feared God nor had respect for people" (v. 2). People exist in relationship to other people, God and to the environment. The text, explicitly describes this judge's attitude towards both people and God as unhealthy. He had no fear for God or respect for people. Perhaps he respected the environment! Accordingly, he is not bothered by the cry of a widow who repeatedly appears before him crying for justice. He had no respect for her as a person. But worse, he had no fear for God. Such people see no reason to grant justice to the oppressed, for they do not care that all people are created by God in God's own image

(Gen. 1:26-27); nor do they know that God is a God of justice, who will hasten to serve justice to the oppressed and exploited.

Third, it is a painful lesson to all liberation activists and justice seekers to note that when the judge finally comes around, he acts not for the sake of the justice, but for his own selfish reasons. He does not want to be bothered and to be worn down by this persistent widow (in some version it says he does not want her to give him a blow, or a blue eye). It only makes sense that such a judge cannot be expected to act differently if another widow came asking for justice the very next day. Suppose a widow who is less persistent comes and makes her plea, would he grant her justice? I think it is only fair to assume that he is likely to ignore her. Neither can we expect that such a judge would speak out in the society and insist that widows and all other people should not be exploited. He did not have a change of heart and mind concerning the widow's right to justice. He did not subscribe to justice. The persistent widow, therefore, may have won her case, but she certainly had not persuaded the judge that widows and all members of the society have a right to justice. She has not changed the oppressive structure.

It is the concluding interpretation of this parable that gives all justice seekers the courage to continue knocking on the halls of power saying, "grant me justice." In interpreting this parable to his disciples Jesus says, "Listen to what the unjust judge says," (v.6). Jesus' statement calls attention of the disciples, but above all it carries undertones of disgust for the acts of the unjust judge. The judge's reason for responding to the widow is despicable. Hence Jesus asks, "And will not God grant justice to his chosen ones that cry to him day and night?" The question is emphatic. Jesus continues to ask, "Will God delay long in helping them?" (v.7). These are rhetorical questions. Both questions underline a God who responds quickly and positively. Then he presents the answer to them saying, "I tell you, God will quickly grant justice to them" (v. 8).

In the interpretation of the parable, the attitude of this unjust judge is compared with God as a just judge. First, we note that the widow is counted among "the chosen ones." She is counted among those who "cry to God day and night." Compared to this unjust judge, God is a just judge. While the judge ignores the oppressed, God listens to them. While the unjust judge lets the needs of the oppressed go unheeded for a long time, God quickly grants justice to those who cry day and night for justice. The message is clear: if the creator God grants justice to the oppressed, which seat of power of this earth has the right to ignore them? Yet it is important to point out that the depth of the meaning of this parable does not only lie in comparing the unjust judge with God as a just judge. It is most importantly expressed in the tone that Jesus uses to interpret this parable. At best it can be summarized by saying: it is totally unacceptable to deny justice to those who are crying, 'grant me justice,' for God listens and grants justice to such people, quickly. No one, therefore, has a right to ask the oppressed and the exploited to wait another day within the pain of their social suffering/injustice. God grants justice quickly.

The interpretation of the parable strongly assures us of a God who is unfailingly in solidarity with the oppressed and exploited. God is a God of justice, the parable underlines. It is this strong expression of God's solidarity with the oppressed and exploited that gives the women writers of this volume the courage to say, "grant me justice," in this age of HIV/AIDS epidemic, a social injustice driven epidemic. The volume opens with Denise Ackermann's article. She reads the story of Tamar's rape with the story of violence against women in the HIV/AIDS stricken South Africa. Ackermann makes efforts to find clues for resistance and hope that could be useful for church praxis. Sarojini Nadar in her paper, "'*Barak* God and Die!' Women, HIV and a Theology of Suffering," undertakes an African-feminist re-reading of the book of Job. She departs from the dominant approach that focuses on Job and his male friends while demonizing his wife. Nadar suggests that reading through the eyes of Job's wife gives us a new starting point from which those infected and affected by HIV/AIDS can begin to talk about God in the midst of suffering. Johanna Stiebert's paper, "Women's Sexuality, Gender and Stigma in the Hebrew Bible," explores the notion of HIV/AIDS stigma with reference to women's sexuality in the light of the Hebrew Bible. Dorothy Akoto, in her paper, "Can These Bones Live? Ezekiel 37:1-12 and the HIV/AIDS Context," examines how hopelessness in HIV/AIDS can be as good as dead. She uses this story to challenge all academic readers to become prophets-scholars of life in the age of massive death.

Turning to the second section, on the New Testament, the search for justice continues. The section opens with my paper, "*Talitha Cum!* A Postcolonial Feminist HIV/AIDS Reading of Mark 5:21-43." Here I read the story of the bleeding woman and the dying daughter as a story that calls readers to rise both from international and patriarchal injustice that makes women and men walk too close to death. Malebogo Kgalemang's paper, "John 9: Deconstructing HIV/AIDS Stigma," interrogates the construction of stigma in general, showing its fractures, and the construction of HIV/AIDS stigma and how it is gendered. Through reading John 9, Kgalemang highlights other biblical perspectives that dispute/resist linking illness with sins and curses. Anastasia Boniface-Malle, in her paper, "Allow Me to Cry Out: Reading of Matthew 15:21-28 in the context of HIV/AIDS in Tanzania," reads the lament of the desperate mother of a demon possessed daughter with the laments of women of Tanzania living in the HIV/AIDS scourge. The focus of her paper is thus on the cry of this desperate mother and the cry of Tanzanian women as they cry for healing and justice in the HIV/AIDS context. This section closes with, my "Twenty-two Years of Bleeding and Still the Princess Sings." In this paper, I return to Mark 5:21-43, reading the story together with an African folktale, the story of the continent and African women, struggling to rise from death – from the colonial age to the global age, to the HIV/AIDS era. It is a story of rising against many death forces; a story in search of justice. The book closes with the opening of dialogue with Western scholars, for HIV/AIDS' call for justice requires networking with all people of the world, who like the widow of Luke 18:1-8 are crying, 'grant me justice.' The latter is represented by Letty M. Russell's paper, "Re-imagining the Bible in a Pandemic of HIV/AIDS." In the spirit of the persistent widow, readers from all walks of life are, therefore, invited to join her quest for justice; to join the cry of many millions of people who are infected and affected by HIV/AIDS – for God will quickly grant justice to all who cry day and night saying, *"Grant Me Justice!"*

Endnotes

1. See WCC. (2001). *HIV and AIDS Curriculum for Theological Institutions in Africa.* Geneva: WCC, as one effort of encouraging the theological guild to respond programmatically to the epidemic.

2. See UNDP & UNAIDS. (2001). *Fact Sheets: United Nations Special Session on HIV/AIDS.* 25-27 June, which points out that "According to recent studies adolescent girls in several African countries are five to six times more likely to be HIV positive than boys of their own age," p.6. Similarly, Madhu Bala Nath, (2001). *Gender and HIV/AIDS: Issues for the Commonwealth Secretariat.* London: Commonwealth, writes that "in some worst affected countries, HIV infected women outnumber men by as much as 16:1 in the younger age group," p.4.

3. Madhu Bala Nath. (2001). *Gender and HIV/AIDS* records: "The women tell us that they see their husbands with the wives of men who died of AIDS. And they ask, 'What can we do? If we say no, they'll say: pack and go. But if we do, where do we go to?'"

4. Giving a general view of widows in Luke, Bonnie Thurston. (1998). *Women in the New Testament: Questions and Commentary.* New York: Crossroads, holds that "widows are especially prominent in Luke and usually appear in a positive, exemplary light: Ana (2:36-38), the widow of Zarephath (4:25-27), the widow of Nain (7:11-17), the persistent widow (18:1-8), the victims of hypocrites (20:47) and the generous widow (21:1-4). The widows are the case in point in Luke's mixed economic community, and it might well be that he highlights widows positively because the Christian communities he knew were slow to admit them for fear they would be a financial burden," p.101.

5.   Given the vulnerability of widows, in ancient Israel a widow had a particular claim to justice (Deut. 10:17-18; 24:17, 27:19).

6.   In the early church, the term widow was also used to refer to women in the order of ministry as attested by 1 Timothy 5:9-16.

7.   Commenting on Luke 7:11-17, a story where Jesus brought back to life a widow's dead child, who was his mother's only son, Bonnie Thurston. (1998). *Women in the New Testament,* holds that, "the point is that this woman is not only bereaved, she has no male advocate and essentially, therefore, no legal identity," p.104.

8.   The theme of 'now or today is the time for liberation' is strongly underlined in the first public sermon of Jesus in Luke 4:16-22, where he startled his listeners after reading the words of prophet Isaiah by saying, "today this scripture is fulfilled in your hearing" (v. 21).

Bibliography

Alter, Robert. (1981). *The Art of Biblical Narrative.* San Francisco: Harper Collins.

ASU. (1998). *The Rapid Assessment on the Situation of Orphans in Botswana.* Gaborone: Botswana Government.

Culpepper, Alan. (1995). "Luke," in *The New Interpreters Bible: A Commentary in Twelve Volumes, Volume 9.* Nashville: Abingdon Press, 1995, pp. 1-490.

Dube, Musa W. (2001). "Preaching to the Converted: Unsettling the Christian Church," *Ministerial Formation* 93, 39-50.

_____ (2002). "Theological Challenges: Proclaiming the Fullness of Life in the HIV/AIDS and Global Era," *International Review of Mission Vol. XCI No. 363,* 535-549.

_____ (2002). "Fighting With God: Children and HIV/AIDS in Botswana," *Journal of Theology for Southern Africa: Special Issue on Overcoming Violence Against Women and Children* 114, 31-42.

_____ Ed. (2003). *HIV/AIDS and the Curriculum: Methods of Integrating HIV/AIDS in Theological Programmes.* Geneva: WCC.

_____ Ed. (2003). *AfricaPraying: A Handbook on HIV/AIDS Sensitive Sermon Guidelines and Liturgy.* Geneva: WCC.

Fall, Yassine. Ed. (1999). *Africa: Gender, Globalisation and Resistance.* New York: AAWord.

Fidzani, N. H. et. al. (June 2000). *HIV/AIDS in the North East District: Situation and Response Analysis.* Gaborone: UNDP Botswana.

Hope K. and S. Gaborone. (Sept 1999b). *HIV/AIDS in Botswana: A Situational and Response Analysis of the Town of Lobatse.* Gaborone.

Gebera, Ivonne. (1996). "Poverty," in Letty Russell and Shannonn Clarkson eds., *Dictionary of Feminist Theologies.* Louisville: John Knox Press, pp. 218-219.

Hardesty, Nancy A. (1996). "Healing," in Letty Russell and Shannonn Clarkson eds., *Dictionary of Feminist Theologies.* Louisville: John Knox Press, pp. 136-137.

Maluleke, Tinyiko S. & Sarojini Nadar. (2002). "Breaking the Covenant of Violence Against Women," *Journal of Theology for Southern Africa: Special Issue on Overcoming Violence Against Women and Children* 114, 5-18.

MAP. (2002). *HIV and AIDS Curriculum Development.* Nairobi: MAP International.

Ministry of the State President. (1999). *Report of a Study of Rape in Botswana.* Francistown: Government of Botswana.

Molebatsi C. & B. Mguni. (1999). *Kweneng East Comprehensive District Plan on HIV/AIDS: Phase 1 Situation Analysis Response.* Gaborone: UNDP.

Molebatsi C. & K. D. Mogobe. (1999). *Ngamiland and Comprehensive Plan on HIV/AIDS: Phase 1 Situation and Response Analysis,* Gaborone: UNDP.

Nath, Madhu B. (2001). *Gender and HIV/AIDS: Issues for the Commonwealth Secretariat.* London: Commonwealth Secretariat, 2001.

NCA. (2000). *The Global HIV/AIDS Epidemic: Understanding the Issues.* Oslo: NCA.

Seloilwe E. & G. Ntseane. (2000). *Situation and Response Analyses on HIV/AIDS in the City of Francistown.* Gaborone: UNDP.

Thairu, K. (2003). *The African and the AIDS Holocaust: A Historical and Medical Perspective.* Nairobi: Phoenix Publishers.

Thurston Bonnie. (1998). *Women in the New Testament: Questions and Commentary.* New York: Crossroad.

Tolbert, Mary Ann. (2000). "Gender," in A. K. Adam. ed., *Handbook of Biblical Interpretation.* St Louis: Chalice Press, pp.99-105.

UNAIDS. (2000). *AIDS: Men Can Make a Difference.* Geneva: UNAIDS.

_____ (2002). *Report on the Global HIV/AIDS Epidemic.* Geneva: UNAIDS.

_____ (2001). *AIDS, Poverty Reduction and Debt Relief.* Geneva: UNAIDS.

_____ (2002). *A Conceptual Framework for Action: HIV/AIDS Stigma and Discrimination.* Geneva: UNAIDS.

UNDP & UNAIDS. (2001). *Fact Sheets: United Nations Special Session on HIV/AIDS.* New York: 25-27, June.

UNDP & Government of Botswana. (2000). *Botswana Human Development Report 2000: Towards an AIDS-Free Generation.* Gaborone: UNDP.

UNICEF. (2001). *Botswana's Children Leading the Battle Against HIV/AIDS.* Gaborone: UNICEF.

Visser, A. & Helen Ditsebe-Mhone. (2001). *Needs Assessment Report: People Living With HIV/AIDS in Botswana.* Gaborone: COCEPWA.

WAD. (2001). *Report of the First National Conference on Gender and HIV/AIDS.* Gaborone: Botswana Government.

WCC. (1997). *Facing AIDS: The Challenge, The Churches' Response.* Geneva: WCC.

WCC. (2001). *HIV & AIDS Curriculum for Theological Institutions in Africa.* Geneva: WCC.

Part I

Hebrew Bible,
HIV/AIDS and Gender

Tamar's Cry: Re-Reading an Ancient Text in the Midst of an HIV and AIDS Pandemic

Denise M. Ackermann, University of Stellenbosch

We were born at the wrong end of the century. We are
the AIDS generation. AIDS hit us where it hurts most.
AIDS came to us and said, 'Now you can't eat *sadza*
and *mabhonzo* and *covo*. Now you can't eat!' And we
said, 'But how can we live without eating?' AIDS said,
'You think this is drop or syphilis? All right. Glut
yourselves and see what happens.... We are the condom
generation.... For some it is no use. For some it is too
late. We are dying like flies. But we live on, clinging to
the frayed edges of our lives with our pathetic claws.
We live on, hiding our despair behind tired smiles....

Shimmer Chinodya[1]

Introduction

"When I was pregnant my partner left me. Perhaps he
was afraid that I was HIV because he was. I only found
out just before my baby was born. I was given
nevirapine. I have lost two jobs. First I was a domestic
worker and then I worked in a laundry. The laundry
boss forced all the staff to be tested. I knew it was
against my constitutional rights, but what could I do?
So I was dismissed unfairly. Last week I was walking
home after looking for a job. Three youths attacked
me. They pulled off my clothes. They wanted to rape
me. The one said: 'A man's got have a woman when it is

raining.' I fought with them. They left me because a car came. They did not kill me because I said that I did not see their faces. But today I am so, so happy. I have just heard that my baby is negative. My child will have a life. God is good." *Thembisa, a 26 year old Xhosa woman.*

"He married me when I was only 18. He knew he was positive. I did not know until my baby was tested. Then I found out that I was also positive. I knew it was him. He married me because I was a virgin. He believed that if he slept with a virgin he would be cured.... I walked out. Now I counsel women who are HIV positive. There is life after infection." *Boniswa, a 35 year old AIDS counsellor.*

"I only found out when I came across his medication. I was devastated. Fifteen years of marriage and two wonderful children and I never suspected that he was leading a double life. What a fool I have been! I thought we were a pretty good family. We go to church, we pay our taxes, we work hard. Now my life is shattered. I waited for a year. I was too afraid to go for a test. Last week I heard the worst. I am positive. My children are still so young. What will happen to them? I wonder where God is in all this? But I know that only he can give me the courage to pick up the pieces of my life." *Judy, a teacher aged 38 years.*

These stories are but three among the myriad of tales that link two of the themes of this paper, namely violence against women and HIV and AIDS. In order to sketch the context in which they are told, I shall comment briefly on the HIV and AIDS pandemic in South Africa. Thereafter, I re-read the story of Tamar in 2 Samuel 13:1-22 in a meditative, literary and canonical manner. This is followed by comments on the gendered nature of the pandemic. The last half of this paper is devoted to the search for clues of resistance and hope in the midst of the "bleak immensity"[2] of AIDS. In a series of theological reflections the text is brought into conversation with the context from which I speak. These reflections aim merely to introduce certain theological themes for the churches in South Africa to pursue as they struggle with their role in combating the AIDS pandemic.

A "Bleak Immensity": HIV and AIDS in South Africa

The AIDS pandemic in South Africa is a complex mixture of issues. Gender inequality, attitudes towards human sexuality (see Khathide 2003:1-9), stigmatization, the scarring and fragmentation of large sections of society, our history of migrant labour and uprooting of communities exacerbated today by increased poverty and unemployment and denial of the cause of AIDS by leading politicians, are all part of the South African AIDS story.

Speaking at an AIDS conference in Maputo, Mozambique in 1990, assassinated African National Congress stalwart Chris Hani sounded this prophetic warning:

> We cannot afford to allow the AIDS epidemic to ruin the realisation of our dreams. Existing statistics indicate that we are still at the beginning of the AIDS epidemic in our country. Unattended, however, this will result in untold damage and suffering by the end of the century (Marais 2000:4).

Today the statistics are a nightmare.[3] According to the latest estimates by UNAIDS and the World Health Organization between 32.7 and 39.8 million people are living with HIV and AIDS. Of these some 70 percent (21.6 to 25.7 million) are found in Africa south of the Sahara. On average the prevalence rate in southern Africa last year was about 25 percent, distributed as follows: 38.8 percent of adults in Swaziland, 37.3 percent in Botswana, 28.9 percent in Lesotho, 24.6 percent in Zimbabwe and 21.5 percent in South Africa. "In the past decade 12 million people in sub-Saharan Africa have died of AIDS – one quarter being children" (Whiteside and Sunter 2000:44). According to the South African Medical Research Council (October 2001), 40 percent of deaths occurring in the year 2000 of people between the ages of 15 and 40, were due to AIDS related diseases. In Gauteng and KwaZulu-Natal, one in three mothers visiting ante-natal clinics is infected. There are no longer *any* South Africans who do not know someone or of someone who has died of AIDS or is living with HIV. Our economy cannot escape the ravages of HIV and AIDS and, without medication administered on a large scale, our productivity and growth rate will decline. Statistics and forecasts are numbing. They cannot convey the suffering of decimated families, the despair of orphaned children, the fear induced by stigma, and the material and physical needs of those who are losing loved ones.

In the face of the escalating crisis, any whiff of denialism on the part of politicians can only exacerbate the tragic consequences of the pandemic. Dr Malegapuru Makgoba, president of the Medical Research Council of South Africa, said recently: "History may judge us, the present Africans, to have collaborated in the greatest genocide of our time by the types of choices – political or scientific – we make in relation to this HIV and AIDS epidemic" (*Weekly Mail and Guardian* 16-21 September 2001). We are, in the words the General Secretary of the United Nations Kofi Annan, facing "a tragedy on a biblical scale".[4]

My contention in this paper is that at heart HIV and AIDS is a gendered pandemic exacerbated by poverty. As such it requires a theological response that is prepared to wrestle with the implications of gender inequity in our traditions and our practices as well as the reasons for continuous grinding poverty in sub-Saharan Africa. Furthermore the question of HIV and AIDS raises profound ethical questions about human sexuality and relationships between women and men. I simply cannot do justice to poverty as a theological theme in this paper other than to connect it to the story of HIV and AIDS, neither can I deal with the question of human sexuality. As I said at the outset, this paper is a preliminary effort to raise theological issues for further consideration. Its intention is to look for possible clues on how the Body of Christ[5] can find its way through the present ravages of sickness and death. Attending funerals every weekend is a numbing task. It is more than numbing when the church as the Body of Christ itself feels amputated as its members fill coffins. There are no dividing lines between the Body and some other reality 'out there'. We too are infected. The church today has AIDS.

Re-reading an Ancient Text: The Story of Tamar, 2 Samuel 13:1-22

This literary reading of the Tamar story is done self-consciously from a woman's perspective. I am a white, South African academic theologian with no expertise in biblical scholarship. I read the bible as does the general Christian reader, from the perspective of faith, seeking resources for life in a context with its own particular problems and challenges. Women have distinctive questions about and insights into the biblical texts derived from our life experiences. Our readings are as diverse as are our needs, our identities and our contexts. We know, however, that the bible, as the source book of our faith, is a powerful means for defining women's place in society and that it has been invoked to justify women's subordination to men. So it is not surprising that our readings are suspicious, critical and questioning as we seek meaning for life. We also, in Teresa Okure's words, "read from this place". "Reading from this place" is about the relationship between the biblical text and the social location of the interpreter. Okure continues:

> By *social location* I understand the sum total of those human experiences that shape the lives of the persons connected with the Bible at three levels: (1) the level of peoples in and of the Bible itself...the primary level; (2) the level of the biblical authors and their respective audiences at various epochs of history, the secondary level; and (3) the level of readers/interpreters of the Bible throughout the course of history up to the present day, the tertiary level.... By *interpreter* I understand simply anybody who reads/hears the text with a view to deriving from it a meaning for life (Okure 1995:52).

My reading of the Tamar text is "from this place", my place, a place in which the "bleak immensity" of violence against the bodies of women and children, now haunted by the spectre of HIV and AIDS, rages on. "My place" is also one that knows that the bible is the book of the church and that believes that in the biblical texts, despite their cultural, social and gendered baggage, it is possible to discern interpretations that affirm God's intention that we may have life and have it abundantly (Jn. 10:10). Furthermore, my reading "from this place" is tempered by an acute awareness of the gendered nature of the HIV and AIDS crisis in which women and children are too often the victims. At the same time it is also a reading that seeks hope and affirmation for life.[6]

The story in 2 Samuel 13:1-22 is well known yet seldom preached.[7] King David's son Amnon falls in love with his beautiful half-sister Tamar. He is tormented (sick) and consults his friend Jonabab, a "very clever man". They hatch a plan. Amnon pretends that he is sick, and at his request David sends Tamar to him to make cakes "in his sight". He refuses to eat the cakes, sends the servants away, and asks Tamar to bring the cakes "into the chamber, so that I may eat from your hand". She does so, he grabs her hand and says "Come lie with me, my sister". She resists: "No my brother, do not force me; for such a thing is not done in Israel; do not do anything so vile! As for me where could I carry my shame? And as for you, you would be as one of the scoundrels in Israel". But Amnon will not listen, he is stronger than Tamar and he rapes her. Once the deed is done, Amnon is "seized with a great loathing for her" and he says: "Get out!" Tamar protests at her treatment. Again Amnon is deaf to her entreaties, calls a servant and instructs him to "Put this woman out of my presence, and bolt the door after her". This is done and Tamar puts ashes on her head, goes away and "remains a desolate woman in her brother Absalom's house". Later we learn that Absalom kills Amnon as revenge for Tamar's rape.

Such are the bare bones of this rapacious tale. Its truths are multiple, conflicting and resistant to being read as a simple story of a rape. It is a text that echoes through the ages and that resonates with women's experiences today in a number of ways. But first to Tamar, a victim of rape, betrayal and abandonment. She is the obedient daughter who pays a price in a patriarchal clan. She does as she is told, she obeys her father and serves her 'sick' brother. When she realizes what is about to happen to her, she cries out: "No, my brother, do not force me; *for such a thing is not done in Israel"* (my italics). The immorality and injustice of the violation is more than just hers. It is a shame on the name of Israel. Her words are honest and poignant. While they acknowledge female servitude, they speak of a moral vision that is tragically in contrast with that of Amnon.

Tamar is not only a victim of rape. She is betrayed by her family, raped and then despised. She is no longer "my sister", but "this woman". Amnon ends up hating her.[8] His love for his sister is a disordered love driven by morbid desire. Once the rape is committed, he is confronted by his own morbidity mirrored to him in the tragic figure of his victim. This he cannot bear and she is "put out" of his presence. She is also a victim of her father's abdication of his responsibility as king and as father. There is no record of him responding to this outrage with an appropriate punishment. In fact, he will not punish Amnon "because he loved him, for he was his firstborn". David does not even react to Tamar's plight personally. The house of David, tainted by David's adultery with Bathsheba, is now fouled by incestuous violence. She is also a victim of her brother Absalom's plans for revenge when she is co-opted by him into concealing them – "Be quiet for now, my sister; he is your brother; do not take this to heart". These words may be understood as consoling. They may also conceal his plans for revenge. He and not Tamar will take the law into his own hands.

> For us it is clear that the process of concealment is being reactivated. This is to ensure that the victim is made silent. The word used to describe Tamar's fate means: abandoned, alone, despised [my translation] (Bal, van Dijk-Hemmes and van Gineken 1984:57).

Finally, she is cast out. We last hear of her as remaining in Absalom's house "a desolate woman". Condemned to a quiet life of despair and desolation, her social and spiritual needs are not acknowledged or addressed and she disappears into the mists of history. In 2 Samuel 14:27 reference is made to Absalom's daughter Tamar: "she was a beautiful woman". Can there be an element of restitution here for Tamar in the next generation of women in the house of David? In summary, Tamar lives in a world where men manipulate and coerce by using their power and in which her life is ruined by events she has no control over. Amnon uses his male power and privilege to destroy. In societies where the silence on sexual violence is not broken, abuse of power is not held accountable. David abrogates the proper use of power and opts for expediency rather than justice. Absalom's wish for revenge is problematic, for it expresses his sense of being offended more than it shows concern for the victim. Revenge is easier to indulge in than sharing the pain of the victim. I agree with James Poling (1991:158) that "The latent message of this story is that sexual violence against women is not about the humanity of women but about power between men". Finally, there is no restitution or justice for Tamar.

The brutal rape in this text speaks stridently into "my place". Rape, incest and violence are endemic in South Africa (Bennett 2000). Human Rights Watch/Africa's *Report on Violence against Women in South Africa* (1995:44) states: "What is certain...is that South African women, living in one of the most violent countries in the world, are disproportionately likely to be victims of that violence". Commenting on the fact that South African women constitute 30 percent of members of parliament, an achievement which places us in the top ten of the world's democracies, Professor Amina Mama (2000) of the Africa Gender Institute at the University of Cape Town continues:

> Yet South Africa is simultaneously topping another chart, as one of the world's most deadly environments for women. Statistical evidence tells us that [in] post-apartheid, South African women are more likely to be murdered, raped or mutilated than women anywhere

else in the democratic world, including the rest of Africa.
Their assailants are not foreign invading armies
demonstrating conquest, or even members of 'other'
racial groups in the still divided post-apartheid locales
of the new nation. They are South African men, most
often the very men with whom South African women
live in intimate relationships.

Unlike domestic violence which cuts across all barriers
(Motsei 1993:5),[9] recorded victims of rape are mostly
concentrated among poor and disadvantaged women in
South Africa (Human Rights Watch/Africa 1995:52). While
acknowledging that all women are potential rape victims,
poor women in this country are more vulnerable to rape
than are those coming from the privileged classes. This is
not surprising, as poor women do not have private
transportation, need to walk long distances and live in areas
plagued by crime, gangsterism, overcrowding and poverty
and, in order to work, are often required to leave and return
home in the dark. Our landscape is strewn with the wounded
bodies of victims (Human Rights Watch Report 2001, Pendry
1998: 30-33, Whiteside and Sunter 2000:58). We have our
Tamars, our Amnons, our Davids and our Absaloms.[10]   So
far the lines drawn from the Tamar text to the South African
context have highlighted abuse and rape. How does the
Tamar story relate to the present HIV and AIDS pandemic?
In order to answer this question I need to backtrack and
explain what I mean by "a gendered pandemic".

HIV and AIDS – a Gendered Pandemic

African theologian Teresa Okure startled her hearers at a
theological symposium on AIDS held in Pretoria in 1998,
by saying that there are two viruses more dangerous than
the HIV virus because they are carriers enabling this virus
to spread so rapidly (Kelly 2000:325). The first virus is the
one that assigns women an inferior status to men in society.
According to Okure, this virus fuels the sex industry in
which young women, themselves the victims of abuse,
become infected with HIV and then pass it on to others,

even to their babies. This is the virus that causes men to abuse women. This is the virus that is responsible for the shocking fact that in many countries in Africa the condition that carries the highest risk of HIV infection is that of being a married women. The second virus that enables the HIV virus to spread at a devastating rate is found mostly in the developed world. It is the virus of global economic injustice that causes dreadful poverty in many parts of the developing world. On societies that are not geared for them are thrust capitalist market economies as well as structural adjustment programmes that are designed to meet the requirements of the developed world rather than those whose need is the greatest. Global economic systems disrupt traditional societies, displace economic and educational infrastructures, and the market demands of such systems make access to prevention and treatment of disease difficult and expensive. It is ironic that international organisations like UNAIDS and the United Nations call on countries to restructure their spending in order to ensure that "national budgets are reallocated towards HIV prevention", when these very countries are most often hamstrung by crippling foreign debt. Peter Piot, executive director of UNAIDS, pointed out that in the year 2000 African countries were paying US$15 billion in debt repayments and that this was four times more than they spend on health or education (Trengove Jones 2001:15).[11] Before moving on from this brief resume of Okure's views, I suggest that the first virus related to the HIV and AIDS pandemic is not only about women's questionable status in society but mores specifically about the disordered nature of relationships between women and men as expressed sexually and emotionally. This notion is also found in my reading of the Tamar text.

It is no coincidence that ninety percent of people infected with HIV live in developing countries. Here, according to Lisa Sowle Cahill (2000:282-283), eight hundred million people lack access to clean water and are wanting for basic health care and perinatal care, primary education, nutrition and sanitation, all of which grievously affect their physical well-being and make them vulnerable to disease. Not only do people living in poverty suffer general loss of health but they are forced to adopt survival strategies that expose them to health risks. Families break up as men seek work in cities where they meet women, themselves under economic duress, who are willing to trade sexual access for a roof over their heads and some financial support. Inevitably less money reaches families back in the rural areas and poverty spirals.

The HIV virus causes AIDS.[12]   But it does not act alone. In southern Africa HIV and AIDS is in reality a pandemic that has everything to do with gender relations (Dube 2003: 93-94) and conditions of poverty. South Africa is a society in which cultural traditions of male dominance, bolstered by a particular understanding of the place of men in the Christian tradition, has resulted in continued inequity for women. Poverty, both in the rural areas and in the informal settlements surrounding our cities, is a further grinding reality. Understanding this unholy alliance should be at the heart of all HIV and AIDS programmes whether located in the churches or in state structures. Gender inequality and the snail-like pace at which poverty is being tackled are the main problems blocking effective HIV and AIDS prevention. By this I do not mean that HIV and AIDS does not have devastating consequences for *all* South Africans, regardless of age, race, class or economic status. Of course it does. But for South African women and children the AIDS pandemic is particularly perilous. While it is cutting a deadly swathe across the educated classes in the 20 to 40 age group, its greatest impact is on the most vulnerable members of society: *the poor, the marginalised and the displaced.* This makes HIV and AIDS a crisis for women, particularly poor women in rural areas and those struggling to survive in shacks on the outskirts of cities (Adams and Marshall 1998: 87-93). It goes without saying that when women are affected, children suffer.

Probing beyond the statistics, it appears that women's vulnerability to HIV and AIDS occurs on a variety of levels: biological, social, individual, maternal and care-giving. For instance, an HIV positive pregnant woman runs the risk of transmitting the virus to her child, either during pregnancy, during birth or after birth through breast feeding (Seidel 1998:65-81). Rural women who have little or no education and who live in traditional patriarchal relationships have scant access to information on HIV and AIDS, and generally lack the skills and the power needed "to negotiate safer sex".

> According to UNAIDS (1997) studies in Africa and elsewhere [show that] married women have been infected by their husbands (as their only sexual partner). Simply being married is a major risk for women who have little control over abstinence or condom use in the home, or their husband's sexual activities outside the home (Tallis 1998: 9-10).

Strategies to deal with HIV and AIDS have failed these women because they insist on preventive behaviour which they, the women, have little power to implement. There is a growing body of well-documented research in the social sciences that shows that women in patriarchal societies are "unequipped for sexual negotiation" (Lear 1995:1311-1323, Orubuloye, Caldwell and Cardwell 1993:859-872). Research on teenage girls found that many experienced their first sexual encounter as coercive Human Rights Watch 2001:27) In the province of KwaZulu-Natal, 72 percent of teenage girls attending clinics related that they had refused to have sexual relations with their partners but were usually unsuccessful at doing so and that attempts at refusal could result in physical abuse, termination of the relationship or financial hardship (Jewkes and Vundule *et al* 2001:733-744; Varga and Makubalo 1996:33).

Women who are HIV positive are at the receiving end of stigma, social ostracism and violence. Countless women in South Africa who are HIV positive have, like Tamar, been the victims of sexual violence, perpetrated within a cultural order in which power is abused and women are used for male purposes. The results? Once their status has been verified, they are often ostracized.[13] Tamar knew what it was like to be soiled goods, a status conferred on her by the abuse of power in a patriarchal order.

Tamar's cry "for such a thing is not done in Israel" is ignored. In a patriarchal system women's cries of distress are insufficiently heard and they often disappear under a veil of silence. Breaking the silence about one's status can be life-threatening. Gugu Dlamini became South Africa's first AIDS martyr when, in December 1998, she was stoned to death for speaking out about her HIV status. HIV and AIDS is nourished by silence in South Africa. The dark mystery that lies at the heart of the pandemic in this country is the stubborn multi-layered silence or what is called 'the denial' by professionals. Until such time as our leaders, like those in Uganda, speak out clearly and unambiguously about the causes and nature of HIV and AIDS, we will continue to re-enact the high risk sexual culture and the silence that enshrouds this pandemic.

Re-reading the story of Tamar I feel affirmed by its truth. This biblical text 'says it as it is'. Women's vulnerability to abuse is unflinchingly portrayed. It speaks truth into 'my place'. While poverty is not Tamar's lot, this text names the evil: our human proclivity for abuse of power. It appears to leave us with little hope. But does it really? Tamar's cry: "For such a thing is not done in Israel" is a cry of resistance. The very fact that this woman's voice is heard in this text in this manner is unusual enough to leave some ground for hope, slim as it may be. The quirky power of scripture to uncover new ways of seeing, to point to less obvious paths and to evoke hope when despair seems the only legitimate reaction can allow clues for resistance and hope to slip through this reading that could assist the churches as they struggle to find a way forward in this present crisis.

The Tamar text: Clues for Resistance and Hope

1. "Saying it as it is"

As I have just said, Tamar's story "says it as it is". Why is this important? There is no prevarication, no avoidance of the horror, no cover up. Miroslav Volf (1999: 28-29) speaks about 'the geography of sin' and 'the ideology of sin'. In the case of Tamar 'the geography of sin' is the scene of the crime in which her violated body is at the centre. 'The ideology of sin' is the context backed by aeons of patriarchal traditions and practices that result in women's status being secondary to that of the male in familial relations. Saying it as it is, is the place to begin. What would it take for the churches to accept responsibility publicly for our role in the promotion and maintenance of gender inequality (the ideology of sin) and when will we make the link between this woeful tradition and the present deadly impact of HIV and AIDS on the lives of women and men (the geography of sin)? Positively put, the churches can begin to deal with the present erosion of sexual morality with its devastating consequences for women and children by esteeming women, our entire being, our bodies, our status and our humanity, in every respect, as well as by speaking out unambiguously about the reasons for the present scourge of HIV and AIDS.

Once the Body of Christ is able to make the connection between power, gender relations and HIV and AIDS within its own infected Body, the question then is: What will it take for the Body of Christ to be a body that can bring hope to those living with HIV and AIDS? Given the existing conflicting models for being church, I suggest that a common starting point is found in our creeds. What does it mean to confess to being "one, holy, catholic and apostolic"[14] church in the midst of this HIV and AIDS crisis?

These statements are made in faith and are integral components of the confession of the triune God. As the church acquires its existence through the activity of Christ, the marks of the church are, in the first instance, marks of Christ's activity. Unity of the church lies in Christ's unifying activity. Holiness is not initially ours but is the holiness of Christ who acts on sinners. Catholicity is really about the limitless lordship of Christ. Apostolicity refers to Christ's mission in the Spirit. Seen in this way these confessions of faith are statements of hope – indicators of the new creation of all in Christ (Moltmann 1993: 338-339). They are also statements of action. If we are truly *one*, we are the church with HIV and AIDS. People living with HIV and AIDS are found in every sector of society and every church denomination. We are all related; what affects one member of the Body of Christ affects us all (1 Cor. 12:26). We are all living with HIV and AIDS. There is no 'us' and 'them'. We dare not forget that inclusion, not exclusion, is the way of grace. If we are *holy,* we are not living some superhuman mode of existence. "Holiness does not require a transcendence of our human condition, but a full utilization of our condition toward the concrete reality of love" (Suchocki 1990:115). Holiness is not withdrawal from the smell of crisis, but engagement, often risky, in situations where God is present. If we are *catholic,* we are in solidarity because we are connected, in communion, with those who are suffering and who experience fear of rejection, poverty and death. If we are *apostolic,* we stand in continuity with the church in its infancy and we strive to live as Ignatius of Antioch put it, "in the manner of the apostles" (See Schreiter 1990: 131). This means that we are true to the heart of our confession, that we are zealous for the Word and that we continuously examine the ideals of the early church and measure ourselves against them. This is nothing new. It is no more than a call to put the words we mouth in the creeds into practice. Clearly we all fall short in this regard. The marks of the church do, however, offer solid, practical guidelines for measuring our actions as members of this one universal Body, a Body infected with viruses struggling to live faithfully.

2. *The power of narrative*

Tamar's story raises the issue of the power of narrative. Human beings cannot survive without a narrative identity. Telling stories is intrinsic to claiming one's identity and in this process finding impulses for hope. For those living with HIV and AIDS there is a need to claim and to name their identities in order to move away from the victim status so often thrust upon them. Narrative has a further function.[15] Apart from claiming identity and naming the evil, narrative has a sense-making function. The very act of telling the story is an act of making sense of an often incomprehensible situation, of a suffering and chaotic world in which people wrestle with understanding and in so doing seek to experience relief.

The stories of people living with HIV and AIDS are not only stories of suffering. They are also stories of triumph, of resistance and of hope as attested to by the stories of the two women of faith told at the beginning of this paper. Stories such as these need to be heard in communities of faith. Churches can offer a supportive and empathetic environment for story-telling in the search for meaning. The stories of people living with HIV and AIDS are individual tales within the meta-narrative of the pandemic. Hearing and engaging with these stories in communities of faith has the potential to draw members into relationship. We all have stories to tell. As our stories intersect, they change. We become part of one another's stories. In this process, we are all changed just like Thembisa, Boniswa and Judy's stories have spoken into my life and the lives of my fellow workers in the AIDS field. Hearing and telling stories begins a process of openness, vulnerability and mutual engagement that challenges stigmas, ostracization and the loneliness of suffering and hopefully leads to acts of engagement, affirmation and care. Most importantly, narrative has the power to break the silences surrounding this crisis and to give it a human face.

The real meta-narrative is *the* story of our faith: the story of the God of Israel acting to create and redeem culminating in the ministry, the suffering, death and resurrection of Jesus Christ. Story telling becomes a two way conversation – hearing stories of suffering and triumph, and retelling *the* story of suffering and triumph in our communities of faith. The intersecting of our life stories with the Jesus story is our ultimate hope.

3.   *Embodiment*

The HIV virus enters, lurks, and then makes forays into the immune system until ultimately it destroys the body. This pandemic is all about bodies. Unfortunately, "in spite of doctrines of incarnation, resurrection, and *imago Dei*, and theories about the ingestion of the very body of Christ in the mass, both the Catholic and Protestant Churches, perhaps especially during some of the modern centuries, have conceived their principal domain as that of the soul and its salvation", writes William LaFleur (1998:41). Thankfully, the Tamar story is a tale about embodiment. This text challenges the recurring Christian refrain that the body is secondary to the soul and that the material is less praiseworthy than the spiritual. Our social reality is an embodied reality. Our bodies are more than skin, bone and flesh. Our bodies encompass the totality of our human experience, our thoughts, our emotions, our needs and memories, our ability to imagine and to dream, our experiences of pain, pleasure, power and difference, as well as our beliefs and our hopes. Our bodies are, in fact, the intricate tracery of all that is ourselves. Bodily *praxis* is the agent and the vehicle of divine reality and the faith practices of the Body of Christ are 'sacraments' of suffering and redemption. The Tamar text opens up the issue of the body and challenges any thoughts of separating soul and body, mind and emotions.

For women and children who are infected the body is at the centre of political, social and religious struggles. This is hardly surprising. The female body has, for instance, been the subject of ridicule, adulation, envy, discrimination, abuse and stigma. The question of stigma is particularly relevant to persons suffering from HIV and AIDS. Ignorance, prejudice, stereotypes, issues of power and dominance all conspire to stigmatize sufferers and in so doing to label them and to distort their true identities. You simply become "an HIV positive", a statistic whose identity is now subsumed in your status. This denies the active, meaningful and contributing lives led by increasing numbers of HIV positive people. Erving Goffman's influential theory of stigma points to the link between stigmas and assumed identities. He asserts that stigmas are specially constructed relationships.

> Historically, stigmas were imposed on individuals in the form of physical marking or branding to disgrace them. In modern societies, however, stigmas arise through social processes of interaction whereby individuals are marked or segregated because of an attribute they

possess or because of something discrediting known about them. Hence stigmatized identities emerge through interpersonal interactions rather than as a psychological reaction to events....The mere existence of stigma ensures that social interactions between stigmatized and nonstigmatized persons are usually uncomfortable, tense, and frustrating (See Eiesland 1994:59-60).

Goffman's work on "stigmatized identities" refers to the disabled. Yet it strikes profound cords in our context. Women who are known to be HIV positive are stigmatized by a large section of South African society. Tamar's cry is a poignant reminder of what happens when stigmas prevail. Fortunately, within the body of people living with HIV and AIDS there is an increasing band of people who are slowly gaining power by defining their experiences and claiming their reality, speaking out and breaking the silence around the disease. There is also a new brand of social activism emerging in South Africa, as bodies march in the streets demanding affordable treatment for HIV and AIDS.

When, on the one hand, the body is seen merely as a vehicle for the soul or, on the other, as some kind of a trap, it has been maltreated, vilified and abused. This is an important clue for the churches to seize in the struggle against HIV and AIDS. Bodies are at the centre of this crisis, sick, poor and too often women's and children's bodies. The Gospel demands embodied acts of care, comfort, support and acceptance.

4.   *Ethical codes*

Tamar's cry "for such a thing is not done in Israel" raises the issue of the ethical codes of a people. She does not only cry out for the protection of her own body, but for the honour of her people. Her people are God's people. In reality, her cry is a cry to God. It is a cry for the integrity of life. It is a cry of resistance against the disordered and morbid nature of Amnon's love and a cry for love expressed in relations of trust and respect.

In South Africa today there is much talk, and very necessary talk, about abstinence, prevention and medication in the face of the HIV and AIDS crisis. The Roman Catholics say abstinence is the only answer. The Anglicans say yes, but if you must, use condoms. There is very little being said, however, about the moral and ethical issues raised by the HIV and AIDS pandemic. So far the churches have not grasped this nettle. The recognition that the Body of Christ is a community of sexual human beings is slow in coming, and centuries of ignoring any matter related to human sexuality is merely feeding the silences around HIV and AIDS. It simply is not good enough merely to preach fidelity and abstinence in sexual relations. This message cannot be heard, understood or followed as long as it is communicated without a properly constructed debate on what constitutes a moral community. Moral choices and moral accountability and a community in which women are respected as equal partners in the church itself are essential to this debate.

What makes a moral community? Christian ethics are communal ethics. How people live with one another, and our faithfulness to God are two sides of the same coin. In Amnon's world the people of Israel received the law, according to Rowan Williams (1998), "when God had already established relations with them, when they were already beginning to be a community bound by faithfulness to God and to each other". Williams (1998) continues:

> When the Old Testament prophets announce God's judgment on the people, they don't primarily complain about the breaking of specific rules (though they can do this in some contexts) or about failure to live up to a moral ideal; they denounce those actions that signify a breaking of the covenant with God and so the breaking of the bonds of faithfulness that preserve Israel as a people to whom God has given a vocation.

In the New Testament Paul deals with ethical dilemmas (for example, Rom. 14 and 15, 1 Cor. 10) by arguing that any decisions taken should be guided by the priority of the other person's advantage, by avoidance of judgmentalism and by acceptance of one another and thus by the ultimate imperative of building the Body of Christ more securely. For Christians, ethical actions flow from involvement in community with God and with one another. Actions that promote the good of another are actions which are designed to be for the good of the Body of Christ.

How can the shaping of a moral community begin? Bernard Brady in his book *The Moral Bond of Community* (1998) has a chapter entitled "You don't have anything if you don't have stories". He writes: "Narratives form and inform our values, our dispositions and how we 'see the world'" (Brady 1998:1). It is indeed possible to argue that narrative is *the* medium of moral communication. What is certain is that narrative is at the heart of our faith, a narrative which "sets up the conditions for the possibility of the moral life" (Brady 1998:22). Instead of a negative ethic of human sexuality which consists only of injunctions on what not to do, people's stories can be countered with other stories – stories from our source book. Once the stories of the bible and from our traditions interact with our own stories, then moral consciousness, the ability to distinguish the "is" from the "ought" and the choices this involves, can be nurtured. Acquiring moral agency does not separate "being" from "doing" or character from decision-making and action. To be a member of the Body of Christ means "the formation and transformation of personal moral identity in keeping with the faith identity of the community" (Birch and Rasmussen 1989:45).

To put it differently, a moral community is one whose goal is the common good of all. Such a community upholds the integrity of life, values the dignity of the human person, includes those who are on the margins or excluded, while not avoiding the reality of structural sin. The moral claim is to respect and enhance the integrity of life *before God.* The main task of a moral community is to nurture the moral capacities of its members, by story telling, by involvement in the work of justice and charity, by upholding the integrity of all life, affirmed by our liturgical practices. In this way the community becomes one of moral deliberation and praxis. "In both Jewish and Christian traditions, faith's

truth is finally a 'performative' one" (Birch and Rasmussen 1989:137). It becomes real when it is embodied. Moral truth and a way of life go hand in hand.

Bruce Birch and Larry Rasmussen in their book *Bible and Ethics in the Christian Life* (1989:47) tell the story of Dom Helder Camara meditating in the middle hours of the night about the attitudes of the rich towards the poor and then writing a poem. This poem speaks to those of us in the church who are not HIV positive and who may be tempted to feel virtuous about our status, perhaps even indifferent to those who are infected.

> I pray incessantly
> for the conversion
> of the prodigal son's brother.
> Ever in my ear
> rings the dread warning
> "this one [the prodigal] has awoken
> from his life of sin.
> When will the other [the brother]
> awaken
> from his virtue?

5. *Life and death*

As I have said, Tamar is lost in the mists of history and we do not know how she lived out her life. Her rape undoubtedly affected her quality of life and her ability to live abundantly. Discovering that one is infected, coping with subsequent opportunistic infections and finally with full blown AIDS, all challenge the quality of life of people living with HIV and AIDS. These are the challenges facing the three women whose stories I have told. How to live productively and hopefully with the knowledge of premature death and then how to face imminent death, raise questions about the relationship between life and death that demand attention in the Body of Christ. What has the Good News say to some one who is infected with HIV or who is dying of AIDS?

I suggest that the place to begin is to affirm that God is a lover of life, so much so, that life continues into eternity.

Certainty about this comes from the promise of the resurrection of the body. Hope is the key to questions about life and death. Not "pie in the sky when you die" kind of hope which is nothing more than the thin skin of religious optimism, but creative, imaginative, expectant and risky hope, maintained only with struggle. Hope is demanding, because we have to live our lives in such a way that that which we hope for, can come about. This kind of hope takes our confessed belief in "the life everlasting" as not only something for one day when I die, but as a confession of how I will live my life this day, in this moment. It is the kind of hope that enabled Dietrich Bonhoeffer when he took leave of a fellow prisoner in Flossenbürg concentration camp and went to his execution to say: "This is the end – for me the beginning of life" (Moltmann 1996:xi).

Life, death and resurrection all belong together – they make up the whole of life. Resurrection cannot be reduced to 'life after death' alone. When John (I Jn. 3:14) writes "We know that we have passed from death into life, because we love one another", he stresses that love is passionate about life, that we must say a hearty "Yes" to life, life which leads to death. What the resurrection of the body means is the subject of theological speculation; resurrection talk, however, remains body talk according to our creeds. Resurrection does not mean a deferred life – something we put off until after we die. In Moltmann's (1996:67) words: "I shall live *wholly* here, and die *wholly*, and rise *wholly* there". Eternal life is all of me, all of everyone, all of creation, all healed, reconciled and completed. Nothing will be lost. Christian faith is shaped by the experience of the dying and the death of Christ and by his resurrection. The process of the resurrection of the dead begins in Christ and continues in the Spirit 'the giver of life' and will be completed in the raising of all the dead. So, I would say to the person dying of AIDS, "Death is not your end. *Every life remains before God forever*". To be raised to eternal life means that nothing has been lost for God: "not the pains of this life, and not in moments of happiness" (Moltmann 1996:71). Thus death both separates and unites. "Eternal life is the

final healing of this life into the completed wholeness for which it is destined " (Moltmann 1996:71).

Unfortunately, there are Christians who believe that AIDS is God's punishment for sin. Susan Sontag in her interesting book *AIDS and its Metaphors* (1989:54), says that "Plagues are invariably regarded as judgments on society....". We are very quick to link any sexually transmitted disease with sin as if there are no innocent victims. Insensitive zealousness has resulted in persons dying of AIDS being told: "Your sin has caused your death". I am cautious, even suspicious of this language of fear. Despite those terrifying mediaeval pictures of judgment tempting women and men to seek comfort and salvation in the arms of the church, people have not stopped sinning. The mere mention of HIV and AIDS raises fear. It seeps into places where we did not know it before: Fear of sexuality, fear of bodily fluids, fear of the communion cup, as Sontag (1989:73) comments "fear of contaminated blood, whether Christ's or your neighbour's." Death can be caused directly by sin. We kill one another. We are destroying our environment. But death is not God's ultimate judgment on us. Admittedly, Christian thinkers like Paul, the old church fathers and Augustine saw death as punishment for 'the wages of sin'. James (1:15) writes that "then, when that desire has conceived, it gives birth to sin, and that sin, when fully grown, gives birth to death". Undeniably death can be caused by sinful acts.

There are other traditions in Christianity that do not see death as a judgment on sin. Schleiermacher and liberal Protestant theology of the nineteenth century disputed the causal connection between sin and physical death (Moltmann 1996: 87-88). Moltmann argues that death may called the 'wages of sin' but that this can only be said of human beings. Angels are dubbed immortal but according to Peter (II Pet. 2:4) they sinned! Animals, birds, fish and the trees do not sin, yet they die. Through human beings death has been brought into nonhuman creation. Death has been with us from the beginning. God's first commandment to human beings was "be fruitful and multiply". We were mortal right from the beginning. From a pastoral point of view, theological speculation about the relationship between sin and death is not particularly helpful for the person dying of AIDS.

The body is implicated in the process of sin. The very context in which we live is affected by sin. Innocence suffers. Everything that is 'born' must die. It is part of our condition. Our responsibility is to live and to die in loving solidarity with that sighing and groaning community of creatures described by Paul (Rom. 8:23), all waiting for "the redemption of our bodies"(Rom. 8:23) (Moltmann 1996:92). We all need redemption. "The death of all the living is neither due to sin nor is it natural. It is a fact that evokes grief and longing for the future world and eternal life" (Moltmann 1996:92). We all await what Letty Russell calls "the mending of creation".[16]

At the centre of our efforts to understand the link between life and death is Christ. For Paul, community with Christ, who is the subject of our hope, extends to the living and the dead. "For to this end Christ died and lived again, that he might be Lord both of the dead and of the living" (Rom. 14:9). Moltmann (1996:105) reads this verse as follows:

> I understand this in the following sense: In dying, Christ became the brother of the dying. In death, he became the brother of the dead. In his resurrection – as the One risen – he embraces the dead and the living, and takes them with him on his way to the consummation of God's kingdom.

As we struggle to understand what it means to live hopefully, we are reminded that life remains unfinished. We have tried to live according to the plan for our lives, but we have failed. We are wounded, incomplete, not yet the persons that God intends us to be. We mourn the death of those we love. We grieve precisely because we have loved. Yet, in grief we try to hold on to hope. There is no quick fix for those who suffer. Life in the midst of suffering and death is a constant struggle, it risks moments of despair and loss of trust and it seeks hope even in the darkest places.

6.   *Eucharist*

So far my re-reading of the Tamar text has raised issues of honest awareness, narrative, embodiment, moral community and issues of life and death. At heart, Tamar's story is one that portrays what can happen when human relationships become corrupted. It is a story of failure and loss of hope as both Tamar's and Amnon's persons are violated, albeit in different ways. Yet, when it is read within the wider of context of the cannon, it is a story of resistance to abuse and to evil power, and an affirmation of the moral code of a people who knew the better way.

By grace, failure does not have the last word in the Christian life. Our hope is in Jesus Christ, the embodiment of our faith, whose life, death and resurrection we celebrate in the Eucharist. Michael Welker (2000:43) reminds us that the Eucharist was instituted "in the night that Jesus Christ was betrayed and handed over to the powers of this world." Its origins do not lie in success or triumph but in the human betrayal of the Son and it is precisely here that we dare to hope. I want to conclude my search for clues with a few thoughts on how the Eucharist links up with the themes which I have already raised and how it offers hope in our present context.

At the outset of this paper I said that the Body of Christ has AIDS. I see a link between the violated body of Tamar, the abused bodies of women and children, the bodies of people living with HIV and AIDS and the crucified and resurrected body of Jesus Christ whom we remember and celebrate in the bread and the wine at the Eucharist. Deep inside the Body of Christ, the AIDS virus lurks and as we remember Christ's sacrifice, we see in his very wounds the woundedness of his sisters and brothers who are infected and dying. Our hope is in Christ who takes the church as his bride, makes it his Body and through this nuptial act sets before us the possibility of relationships in love which are the antithesis of the disordered and morbid expressions of love found in Tamar's story and in the lives of Thembisa, Boniswa and Judy.

The Eucharist is the bodily practice of grace. Nancy Eiesland (1994:112) writes: "Receiving the Eucharist is a body practice of the church. The Eucharist as a central and constitutive practice of the church is a ritual of membership....the Eucharist is a matter of bodily mediation of justice and an incorporation of hope". Because God chose to live with us in the flesh, sacramentality takes physical reality very seriously. We are bodily partakers of the physical elements of bread and wine, Christ's presence in our lives and in our world. The very bodiliness of the celebration of the Eucharist affirms the centrality of the body in the practice of the faith. "The Supper", writes Welker (2000:18), "centers on a complex, sensuous process in which the risen and exalted Christ becomes present. The Supper gives Christians a form in which they can perceive the risen and exalted Christ with all their senses."

The celebration of the Eucharist makes the Reign of God present 'to us' in the form of Christ's body broken 'for us' and Christ's blood shed 'for us'. Christ invites us to the feast, and he is "both the giver of the feast and the gift itself" (Moltmann 1993:250). In other words, the gift of the Reign of God is quite simply present in the person of Christ himself – Christ crucified and risen. Thus the communion meal mediates communion with the crucified one in the presence of the risen one. It becomes a foretaste of the messianic banquet of all human kind. It is the meal at which all are welcome. In Christ's Body, the Eucharist is *the* sacrament of equality. Only self-exclusion can keep one away. At the communion table we are offered the consummate step in forging an ethic of right relationship, across all our differences. "We who are many are one body for we all partake of the one bread". This visible, unifying, bodily practice of relationship with all its potential for healing is ours. For the Eucharist to have meaning in our lives, we need to feel its powerful pull to the radical activity of loving relationships with those who are different. "The Eucharist involves a commitment (*sacramentum*) to sharing with the needy neighbour, for Jesus said, 'The Bread that I shall give is my own flesh; given for the life of the world' (Jn. 6:51)" (Forrester 2000:96).

A covenanted Eucharistic community is a community in relationship with one another and with God. Paul describes us as the Body of Christ, a body which, though it has many members, is one body. "If one member suffers, all suffer together with it; if one member is honoured, all rejoice together with it" (1 Cor. 12:26). It is a body in which the weakest are to be treated with respect for "God has so arranged the body, giving the greater honour to the inferior member, that there may be no dissension within the body, but the members may have the same care for one another" (1 Cor. 12:25). The picture here is one of solidarity in suffering, of mutual support and of a moral community in relationship with one another and with God.

Finally, much has been made of the text in I Cor. 11:27-29, 31-32 about eating the bread and drinking the wine in an unworthy manner, about examining ourselves and about the threat of judgment. Welker (2000:70) comments "...the Supper is no longer a feast of reconciliation but rather an anxiety-producing means of moral gatekeeping. In a sad irony, the feast of unconditional acceptance of human beings by God and among each other was misused for intrahuman moral control!" There is a tension here. Welker points out that in the celebration of the Eucharist, God accepts us unconditionally, while at the same time Paul's concern is that Christians celebrate the meal in accordance with the meal's identity. Rightly so. How we partake of the Meal is deeply significant for how we live as a moral community. "The Eucharist may be understood as nourishment for moral growth and formation", writes Duncan Forrester (2000:95). A community with a moral code and a moral identity partaking in a meal of grace, memory and new life, brings resistance to evil and hope for now and tomorrow for the church with HIV and AIDS.

Tamar's Cry

In conclusion, while conceding at the outset that the Tamar text did not give much apparent cause for hope, I have tried to find clues for resistance and hope that could be useful for church praxis in our present crisis. We live in what Edward Schillebeeckx (1993:4) terms a world that is an "enigmatic mixture of good and evil, of meaning and meaninglessness". In the midst of this bewildering mixture of experiences, there is the human capacity for indignation and moral outrage. Tamar's cry "for such a thing is not done in Israel" allows us to find hope where there is little cause for it, enables us to say "yes" when all else shouts "no" and allows chinks of light to guide our feet. Her cry jars our reality, the reality of those in Shimmer Chinodya's words who are "born at the wrong end of the century". We know what should "*not* be done in Israel". "We know what to do" is a formulation that takes us to the very heart of the scandal that is AIDS; it situates us on the frontier between hope and despair, between action and inertia, between those with the means to 'do something' and those who have little to 'do' but suffer". HIV and AIDS is our *kairos*. It is a time when the ordinary rhythm of life is suspended. Will it be a time of doom or will we find a new unveiling of God's presence and love for us here and now?

Endnotes

1. Quoted from author's *Can we Talk and Other Stories* in Elinor Batezat Sisulu, 'A different kind of holocaust: A personal reflection on HIV and AIDS', *African Gender Institute Newsletter*, University of Cape Town, vol. 7, December 2000.

2. This phrase is borrowed from Wole Soyinka, *Art, Dialogue and Outrage: Essays on Literature and Culture* (New York: Pantheon Books, 1993), 16.

3. Figures quoted here are a combination of estimates published by the United Nations health agencies and the National Department of Health over the last three years.

4. Accessed at www.un.org/news/press/docs/2000.

5. Throughout this paper "Body of Christ" is used as the metaphor for the church. This is done intentionally because the organic nature of this metaphor is important for the argument that when one member suffers all suffer together; if one member is honoured, all rejoice together" (1 Cor. 12:26). Thus the church with AIDS, is the church universal.

6. In passing, a comment on my personal experience of bible reading. Long before I was aware of the technicalities of different kinds of reading, I was in fact familiar with a nascent form of interpretation used by women when studying the bible in groups. For well over thirty years I have belonged to women's bible study groups. We read the biblical stories through women's eyes, seeking meaning for our lives, understanding of our faith and affirmation for our experiences. Often the texts were and are difficult, even off-putting to women. After studies in hermeneutics my approach to such contentious texts in scripture took the route of a *sachkritiek* and I simply rejected them. This I no longer find satisfactory. My present approach is to try and deal with the whole of scripture with its fundamental contradictions, to mull over them, often with irritation and anger, to ascertain how I can live with such texts fruitfully.

7. In 1999 I conducted research for a workshop on homiletics and found that of the 84 people interviewed (which included clergy and lay people) only one had heard a sermon on this text.

8. 16. According to Trible, *Texts of Terror,* 47, the repetition in this passage emphasizes the hatred focused on Tamar. *"Then-hated-her* Amnon   *a-hatred* great indeed *(me'od)*.Truly *(kî)* great(er) *the-hatred* which *he-hated-her* than-the-desire which he-desired-her".

9. Motsei (1993:5) states that contrary to conventional wisdom, research has shown that "the perpetrators of violence against women include men who hold respectable jobs and positions in society.... These include lawyers, doctors, psychologists, psychiatrists, priests and business executives." Furthermore, People Opposing Women Abuse (POWA) found in a study of inquest records that every six days at least one women is killed by her partner and that more than half of all women murdered are killed by a partner or a male friend (*The Star,* 21 November 1995).

10. As a sample, see Anne Mager, 'Sexuality, fertility and male power', *Agenda* 28 (1996) 12-24; Promise Mthembu, 'A positive view', *Agenda* 39 (1998) 26-30. At its core the problem is not simply that rape occurs or that women and children experience violence and fear in the arena of sexuality. Ours is a society that is redolent with patriarchal attitudes and practices. The problem is not just that a man raped his half-sister (incest), though this is serious enough. The problem is not just that rape, incest and violence against

women is all too common. Years of counselling and collecting anecdotal evidence has shown me that, in my context, the problem is that many perpetrators they do not think they have committed rape and do not recognise the difference between ordinary heterosexual activity and sexual violence. The social construction of heterosexual activity is largely based on patterns of dominance and submission in which men are expected to be dominant and women are expected to be submissive.

11. Harvard economist Richard Parker commented in 1996 that "we have begun to understand the perverse consequences caused by specific models of economic development (most often imposed from above) that have in fact functioned to produce and reproduce structures of economic dependence and processes of social disintegration"; see Richard G Parker, 'Empowerment, community mobilization, and social change in the face of HIV and AIDS', paper presented at the XI International Conference on AIDS, Vancouver, July 1996, 4,11.

12. See Whiteside and Sunter (2000:3) for the four key elements used to bolster the belief that HIV does not cause AIDS. Today the majority of the world's leading virologists believe that the HIV hypothesis is correct.

13. Sick without resources these women often die. The story of Nosipho Xhape who died in a strange shack where she tried to find shelter, is not uncommon. This woman left her two children in the Eastern Cape to find work in the city. She could only survive by linking up with a man who would look after her. When it became apparent that she had full blown AIDS, he turned her out one night. She found shelter in a toilet until a neighbour gave her a blanket and water and she moved to a broken down shack. Fifteen hours later she was dead. See *Cape Times*, 12 February, 2000.

14. Taken from the Nicene-Constantinopolitan Creed 381, while the Apostles' Creed speaks of "one, holy, catholic church."

15. I am grateful to Bernard Lategan for pointing out that narrative has the further hermeneutical function of sense-making, an understanding he attributes to the work of Jörn Rüsen's concept of *Sinnbildung*.

16. This term is used by Letty Russell in many of her works to denote the eschatological implications of the Reign of God.

Bibliography

Adams, H. and Marshall, M. (1998). Off Target Messages – Poverty, Risk and Sexual Rights, *Agenda*, 39.

Bal, M., van Dijk Hemmes, F. and van Ginneken, G. (1984). *En Sara in haar Tent Lachte: Patriarchaat en Verzet in Bijbelverhalen.* Utrecht: HES Uitgevers.

Brady, B. V. (1998). *The Moral Bond of Community: Justice and Discourse in Christian Morality.* Washington: Georgetown University Press.

Baylies, C. and Bujra, J.(2000). *Aids, Sexuality and Gender in Africa: The Struggle Continue.* London: Routledge.

Bennett, J. (2000). Gender-based Violence in South Africa, in *Africa Gender Institute Newsletter.* University of Cape Town, vol. 6 (May).

Birch, B. B. and Rasmussen, L. L. (1989). *Bible and Ethics in the Christian Life.* Minneapolis: Augsburg Press.

Dube, M. (2003). "Culture, Gender and HIV/AIDS: Understanding and Acting on the Issues", in Dube, M. Ed. *HIV/AIDS and the Curriculum: Methods of Integrating HIV/AIDS in Theological Programmes,* 84-100. Geneva: WCC Publications.

Dube, M. Ed. (2003). *HIV/AIDS and the Curriculum: Methods of Integrating HIV/AIDS in Theological Programmes.* Geneva: WCC Publications.

Eiesland, N. (1994). *The Disabled God: Toward a Liberatory Theology of Disability.* Nashville: Abingdon.

Forrester, D. B. (2000). *Truthful Action: Explorations in Practical Theology.* Edinburgh: T. & T. Clark.

Human Rights Watch/Africa, (2001). *Scared at School: Sexual Violence against Girls in South African Schools.* New York: Human Rights Watch.

Human Rights Watch/Africa, (1995). *Report on Violence against Women in South Africa.* New York: Human Rights Watch.

Jewkes, R. Vundule, C. et al (2001). Relationships, Dynamics and Teenage Pregnancy in South Africa, in *Social Science and Medicine,* 52.

Keenan, J. F. (ed.) (2000). *Catholic Ethicists on HIV/AIDS Prevention.* New York: Continuum.

Kelly, K. (2000). Conclusion: A Moral Theologian faces the New Millennium in a Time of AIDS, in Keenan, J. F., *Catholic Ethicists.*

Khathide, A. G. (2003). Teaching and Talking about our Sexuality: A Means of Combating HIV/AIDS in M. Dube. Ed. *HIV/AIDS and the Curriculum.*

LaFleur, W. R. (1998). Body, in Taylor, M. C. (ed.), *Critical Terms.*

Lampman, C. (ed.) 1999. *God and the Victim: Theological Reflections on Evil, Victimization, Justice and Forgiveness.* Grand Rapids: Eerdmans.

Lear, D. (1995). Sexual Communication in the Age of AIDS: The Construction of Risk and Trust Among Young Adults, in *Social Science and Medicine* 41, 9.

Mama, A. (2000). Transformation Thwarted: Gender-based Violence in Africa's New Democracies, in *Africa Gender Institute Newsletter.* University of Cape Town, vol. 6 (May).

Marais, H. (2000). *To the Edge: AIDS Review 2000.* Pretoria: Pretoria University, Centre for the Study of AIDS.

Moltmann, J. (1993). *The Church in the Power of the Spirit: A Contribution to Messianic Ecclesiology,* tr. Kohl, M. Minneapolis: Fortress Press.

Moltmann, J. (1996). *The Coming of God: Christian Eschatology,* tr. Kohl, M. Minneapolis: Fortress Press.

Motsei, M. (1993). Detection of Woman Battering in Health Care Settings: The Case of Alexandra Health Clinic, in *Women's Health Project,* 33 (January).

Okure, T. (1995). Reading from This place: Some Problems and Prospects, 52-68, in Segovia, F. F. and Tolbert, M. A. (eds.), *Reading from This Place.* Minneapolis: Fortress Press.

Orubuloye, I., Caldwell, J. and Cardwell, P. (1993). African Women's Control over their Sexuality in an Era of 'AIDS, in *Social Science and Medicine,* 37, 7.

Pendry, B. (1998). The Links between Gender Violence and HIV/AIDS, in *Agenda,* 39.

Poling, J. N. (1991). *The Abuse of Power: A Theological Problem.* Nashville: Abingdon.

Russell, L. M. (ed.) (1990). *The Church with AIDS: Renewal in the Midst of Crisis.* Louisville: Westminster/John Knox Press.

Segovia, F. F. and Tolbert, M. A. (eds.) (1995). *Reading from This Place: Social Location and Biblical Interpretation in Global Perspective*, vol. 2. Minneapolis: Fortress Press.

Seidel, G. (1998). Making an Informed Choice: Discourses and Practices Surrounding Breastfeeding and AIDS, in *Agenda*, 39.

Schillebeeckx, E. (1993). *The Church with a Human Face*. New York: Crossroad.

Schreiter, R. (1990). Marks of the Church in the Times of Transformation, in Russell, L. M. (ed.), *The Church with AIDS*.

Sontag, S. (1989). *Aids and its Metaphors*. New York: Farrar, Strauss and Giroux.

Suchocki, M. (1990). Holiness and a Renewed Church, in Russell, L. M. (ed.), *The Church with AIDS*.

Tallis, V. (1998). AIDS is a Crisis for Women, in *Agenda*, 39.

Taylor, M. C. (ed.) (1998). *Critical Terms for Religious Studies*. Chicago: University of Chicago Press.

Trengove Jones, T. (2001). *Who Cares? AIDS Review 2001*. Pretoria, Pretoria University, Centre for the Study of AIDS.

Trible, P. (1984). *Texts of Terror: Literary-Feminist Readings of Biblical Narratives* Philadelphia: Fortress Press.

Volf, M. (1999). Original Crime, Primal Care, in Lampman, C. (ed.), *God and the Victim*.

Welker, M. (2000). *What Happens in Holy Communion?* tr. Hoffmeyer, J. F. Grand Rapids: Eerdmans.

Whiteside, A. and Sunter, C. (2000). *AIDS: The Challenge for South Africa*. Cape Town: Human and Rousseau.

Williams, R. (1998). On Making Moral Decisions. Unpublished address to Lambeth Plenary Session of the Anglican Communion, Canterbury, England.

Chapter Two

"Barak *God and Die!"* *Women, HIV and a Theology of Suffering*[1]

Sarojini Nadar, University of KwaZulu-Natal

The stench of death has penetrated our nostrils, we smell you everywhere. Your body covered with sores goad us. Pieces of your wormy flesh cling to our own. We have become infected by you, our brother Job. You have infected us, our families and our people. Your eyes searching for justice have filled us with courage, tenderness and hope.... They say that you should suffer in silence and stop defending your innocence. They say that God has punished you and that you should repent. And you, brother Job, in spite of everything you haven't given up .... It's they who should keep silent because you're the one who suffers injustice and experiences its consequences in your flesh and blood (Tamez 1986:50).

Introduction

Theological debates surrounding HIV/AIDS have become, and in a sense have always been, extremely polarised. In the most simplistic terms there are those who believe that HIV/AIDS is a punishment from God and those who do not. Each group acts according to its belief. For example, Nancy Carter, recently quoted in one of her sermons a statistic that only 8% of Americans would be willing to contribute toward AIDS relief work in Africa[2]. 70% of the same group said that they were willing or that they had contributed to funds raised to help victims of the September 11 attacks. What is the difference between the two causes? The first and most obvious is that the September 11 attacks occurred in America, and HIV/AIDS as considered by most of the West seems to be 'Africa's baby'[3]. I suspect, though, that the reason for the refusal of help goes beyond patriotism, since in her sermon, Carter goes on to talk about her American friend Debbie, who died of AIDS, and her parents who refused any person living with AIDS to attend the funeral, so that Carter had to hold a separate memorial service. Undoubtedly the reason for the parents' behaviour and for those Americans who said that they would not contribute funds for HIV/AIDS causes, is that they have subscribed to the most commonly circulated assumption that HIV/AIDS is a punishment from God. Hence, people who are victims of this deadly disease deserve the punishment.

This polarised view of the issue is present in Africa as well. It is articulated, most clearly, in a recent issue of a theological journal in South Africa.

> In most cases AIDS is the result of denying God and disobeying His commandments. It is the outcome of apostasy. It is not primarily a health problem, but a heart problem. For the human heart which frees itself from God also casts off all restraints. It seeks to gratify the self and enter into sin (Scarborough 2001:6).

Banda and Moyo (2001:50) cite similar statements received from church leadership in Malawi, when posed with the question of how to deal with HIV/AIDS. So, it seems that at the heart of the theological debate concerning HIV/AIDS, the world over, is the argument that HIV/AIDS is a punishment from God. This viewpoint is also not restricted to our own century or culture of thought. It can be traced back to Ancient Near Eastern and oriental traditions. Maier and Schroer (1998:178) show that in oriental thought there is a clear connection between a person's actions and his or her well-being. In other words an obedient, God-fearing person prospers, while the godless and those who do not obey are punished.

Given the very close similarities between Ancient Near Eastern and biblical traditions it is not surprising to find a similar strand of thought in the Old Testament. J. D. Crossan, in a recent paper presented at the University of Natal, highlighted this strand of thought found in Deuteronomy 28. The chapter cites blessings for obedient behaviour by the Israelites and curses for disobedient behaviour. An interesting observation noted by Crossan is that the curses outnumber the blessings by about forty-eight verses!

If the Bible, and not just the Bible, but common theological thought over the centuries espouses the view that God curses those who are 'wicked' and blesses those who are 'good', then it would seem that Christians who believe that HIV/AIDS is a punishment from God are justified in their belief. African biblical scholars and theologians cannot and should not be satisfied with this theology, since if this is the only theological voice that speaks in the midst of immense suffering in the HIV/AIDS era, then the future looks bleak. If, however, we listen carefully enough we can discern an alternative voice within the Bible, one that critiques the dominant ideology of retribution and reward. Scholars have already attempted to listen to this voice in relation to HIV/AIDS[4]. Others have done so in different contexts. J. D. Crossan, for example, critiques the theology of blessings and curses found in Deuteronomy 28, referred to above. Although the context of his own argument is not directly related to the HIV/AIDS issue, it strikes profound chords with the way in which we should be thinking about HIV/AIDS in the African context. He shows that the Israelites, whom the chapter is addressing, were in a 'no-win' situation. Israel was placed at the centre of imperial conquest right in the way of the axes of conquest that ran north, south, east and west. Crossan maintains that this theology of retribution and reward in the context of this passage is a 'ghastly' one for the simple reason that:

Since periodical drought and infertility or permanent war and conquest were inevitable in that particular land, deuteronomic believers would have to conclude that they were inveterate communal sinners under almost permanent corporate punishment by their God.... In summary, then, deuteronomic theology was false in its promised blessings and threatened curses but lethal in its personal results and communal effects (Crossan 2002:5).

Crossan's argument holds immense value for the debate surrounding HIV/AIDS in Africa, since deuteronomic Israel and Africa seem to be in a similar predicament. In other words, the related question that we should be asking is, how can HIV/AIDS be a punishment from God when as Njoroge notes: 'Africa has been the most affected continent because it was already vulnerable as a result of abject poverty. The HIV/AIDS virus came to a people already knocked down by an unending spiral of poverty, disease and violence.'

Asking the question means facing up to the challenge that we as biblical scholars and theologians in Africa face. It is the challenge that urges us to find those alternative voices in the Bible: voices that are different to what Walter Brueggemann (1992:22) calls the 'common theology'. This theology is one that affirms the 'legitimated order' of deed and consequence. Brueggemann (1992:25) argues, however, that the common theology trajectory is not the only trajectory that can be found in Old Testament theology. He names this other trajectory the 'embrace of pain' trajectory. This is a trajectory of theological thought that is borne out of the concrete painful experiences of people, not necessarily as opposed to, but in juxtaposition to the 'common theology'. In other words, the two are kept in tension with each other. The book of Job is a classic example of Old Testament theology that keeps these two trajectories in tension with each other. In this paper I seek to tease out this tension in the book of Job, hopefully to emerge with a re-reading of the book that can be used as a resource to those infected and affected by HIV/AIDS. Before I actually begin to do such a reading I want to establish the legitimacy of such a reading first, for those of us who are most infected and affected by the disease.

Points of Identification: Reading Job as a Woman

The book of Job has aptly been called 'wisdom in revolt' (Perdue 1991). This is because the book most obviously, questions the traditional tenets of wisdom that 'good' deeds are rewarded and 'evil' deeds are punished. It therefore provides through very long and intricate poetry a critique of innocent suffering. It does not, as Gustafson (1992:179) citing Terrien notes, answer the question of 'why do the righteous suffer?' Rather,

> while it powerfully portrays the effects of suffering, it also 'through the medium of suffering....shows how the self is discovered in relation to society, nature and the ultimate. It contains a sharp critique of the traditional formulations of the nature of God.

In this paper, I will examine the nature of this critique, for I believe that embedded therein are the resources and the alternative voices that speak to the context of immense suffering in the HIV/AIDS era. Before I begin, however, to examine the nature of this critique and how it is worked out in the narrative, I want to examine to what extent women (particularly women in Africa) can identify with the critique. This is a vital question given that my aim in re-reading the book of Job is to seek out a source of biblical hope for those infected and affected by HIV/AIDS. It has been shown that women are the most infected, affected, and the most vulnerable to the disease[5]. It is imperative, therefore, that a reading of Job that attempts to grapple with the apparent convoluted and often obscure theological debate surrounding HIV/AIDS should take into account whether women can identify with such a reading. From a superficial look at the book one is tempted to say no.

The book seems to be about and for males. All the conversations and the important theological debate seem to take place between men. Job's wife, the only woman who is given a voice, has never got good press in traditional readings of the book. Her characterisations have ranged from foolish woman to nagging wife even to 'agent of Satan'. If we are able to free ourselves from the shackles of past interpretations that might seem to colour our picture of Job's wife I think that we could come up with an alternative interpretation of her[6]. In fact, I would suggest that Job's wife is the key to the way in which we read the book, and her intervention is what glues the structure of the book together. Given that it is almost a general consensus that the book of Job is divided into prose and poetry, it is interesting that Job's wife appears in the prose section[7]. The prose section we are told, is a 'popular narrative which was used by the author of the book as a framework for the discussion of the problem of suffering which begins in chapter 3 (Wittenberg 1994:62). The impression that we get, therefore, is that the real theological deliberation and reflections take place in the poetry section. Hence Job's wife is considered peripheral to the main story.

However, I submit that Job's wife is integral to the way in which the narrative is worked out, because it is her words that most poignantly captures the ensuing theological discussions, which centre primarily and almost exclusively around the dualistic notions of issues of blessing and cursing, rewards and punishment. Job's wife is introduced to us in the prologue with the statement: 'Do you still persist in your integrity? Why don't you *barak* God and die?' The word *barak* is ambiguous in the text since within the text itself it is taken to mean both 'bless' and 'curse'. Many scholars have taken note of the ambiguity in this term, and most have attempted to resolve it in either one or the other way, sometimes ending up with both positive and negative interpretations. I would rather keep the ambiguity of the word, since I believe that the very ambiguity of the word is what encapsulates God's response to Job and his friends in the end. God highlights God's ambiguous nature, in God's choice to appear in a storm. Bechtel (1995:237) shows that the storm can be either destructive in its violent nature or renewing in that it gives life through rain. The question that Job's wife raises is integral to the central question that the narrative as a whole raises. Do our actions and the way in which we speak about God decide the way in which we are either rewarded or punished? The ambiguity of the word *barak* somehow points us to an answer to this question. Hence, we could read the word in either way, but Job's response to his wife seems to have defined the way in which subsequent readers have read the text. Whatever we may take her statement to mean, and however Job has interpreted her statement, the fact is that it is she who sets the tone for the engaging debate cushioned in intricate poetry that follows. The issue, however, does not just stop at God-talk but the way in which our worldviews are determined by our gendered outlooks. Job's wife offers an alternative to the traditional patriarchal thinking of God. As West (1991:116) notes, 'in a narrative so clearly dominated by males and reflecting male interests her very presence offers a vantage point from which to deconstruct male hegemony.'

Her words have been taken to mean an abandonment of Job (Wittenberg 1994:65). Job's response seems to indicate that she does not understand the way in which we should respond to God in times of suffering ('Shall we accept good from God and not trouble?' – 2:10). The next words we hear from Job after the encounter with his wife are those of his wife! Newsom (1992:140) notes: 'Though he does not curse God, he curses the day of his birth. Though he does not die, he speaks longingly of death.... his wife's troubling questions have become his own.' What we can conclude, therefore, is that Job's wife is much more theologically astute than Job and his friends. Even God indirectly acknowledges this at the end. By acknowledging that Job's friends have not spoken well, but rather that Job has spoken rightly, (even though Job has debated with God in very strong terms concerning his suffering) God indirectly vindicates Job's wife, because Job does what his wife hints at – he begins the process of questioning his suffering in terms of his belief system.

By accepting that women are able to grapple theologically with the issue of suffering, by understanding that Job's wife's economic, household and religious functions would have made her more 'critically aware of their perilous situation than Job' (West 1991:111), women have an in-road into this text, that would otherwise seem to be for and about male suffering only. The question whether we as women are touched by Job's suffering, as women, can be partially answered through such an interpretation of the character of Job's wife as provided above.

Points of Identification: Reading Job from the Perspective of the Poor

Job is undoubtedly a patriarchal male – a very rich patriarchal male. Although HIV/AIDS has not been discriminating in that both the rich and the poor have been infected, it is the poor that suffer most from this deadly disease. President Thabo Mbeki has been criticised for not granting pregnant HIV/AIDS women and rape victims access to anti-retroviral drugs. I think that the criticism against him regarding his refusal is fully justified. Unfortunately, the scope of the broader argument that he is making has been subsumed by the drugs issue. In other words, he draws our attention to a very important issue concerning the disease, and that is that the disease has a direct relationship with wider economic, gender and political contexts. The argument that AIDS did not come to the 'Jobs' of Africa would seem justified, since those most infected are the poorest of the poor. In the same way that we asked whether women can identify with this text we have to ask whether the poor can identify with such a text. After all it seems that Job's tragedy is felt most acutely because he was a respected wealthy member of society. How often do we hear the cliché: 'S/he had so much going for him/her.' What about those who are most severely hit by the disease who have 'nothing going for them?' It seems that such persons might experience difficulty in identifying with the plight of Job. However, to say this is to miss the point that Job actually lost all his material wealth and support structures before he was struck with this terrible illness. In fact, Job's questioning of God only begins after he is struck with extreme physical illness. His response when his material wealth is stripped away from him is very simplistic: 'Naked I came from my mother's womb, and naked I shall depart. The Lord gave and the Lord has taken away; may the name of the Lord be praised' (1:21). His physical suffering, which, as Wittenberg (1994:61) points out, ultimately leads to psychological and social suffering, is what prompts his very strong questioning of God's justice. Questioning of God's justice then becomes central to the rest of the chapters in which Job engages in a deep theological debate with his friends and with God concerning this very issue – how can God be just when God allows poor people to suffer? It is only because Job's suffering is experienced as a poor person that he is able to articulate the kinds of arguments that he does. In chapter 24 he laments the fact that those who cause the suffering of people, those who oppress and exploit are not punished. He sees the injustice of it all from the perspective of the poor, not as a rich farmer. He is only able to do this because he himself has become poor; he himself has experienced the pain and suffering that the poor undergo.

Now that we have established that there are points at which those affected and infected by HIV/AIDS can identify with the text of Job, we can turn our attention to the actual debates between Job, his friends, and God, in our search for the alternative voice within the text. Unfortunately time and space do not allow me to dwell on the individual speeches made by each character. Following Newsom (1992:141) I want to focus on Job's friends' sources of authority for their arguments. I then want to focus on Job's responses to them and finally God's response to all of them.

Sources of Authority

We are told in 1:11 that Job's friends came to him to 'comfort and sympathise with him'. By the end of the book it is very clear both through the words of God and in our own reading of the text that they have done everything but that. Because they cannot understand why such a wealthy and prosperous man like Job should suffer, they figure according to traditional wisdom principles that he must have sinned. After sitting with him for seven days, and watching him suffer excruciatingly, after hearing him even curse the day he was born, the friends still find it appropriate to convince Job that his suffering must be his own fault. The bulk of the poetic sections of the book are spent on the friends' attempts to convince Job of this point. Newsom (1992:141) identifies in these speeches sources of authority upon which these friends base their arguments. In what follows I outline each of the categories in detail for I think that it is the most facile way to deal with the bulky amount of text that we have in relation to the speeches made by Job's friends.

1. *Common sense*

Newsom identifies the first source of authority as *common sense*. Eliphaz says to Job in 4:7, 'Consider now: Who, being innocent, has ever perished? Where were the upright ever destroyed?' This sort of common sense argument should make sense in an ideal world, but it did not make sense to Job in his world and it certainly does not make sense in our own continent ravaged not just by HIV/AIDS but also by the devastating effects of colonialism, apartheid, genocides, and the most recent of our woes, globalisation. We see the innocent perish and we certainly see the upright destroyed. We see people that robbed other people of their lands, their homes, their children and their dignities, those that performed illegal medical experiments on them, we see them live in comfort while those that they have stolen from, those that they have experimented with, suffer from the consequences of the oppressors' actions. Job sees this in his own time too. In chapter 24 he recognises that those who have seized flocks that are not theirs and those who have robbed the widow and the orphan are 'blessed' with longevity and security. Common sense does not seem to work here.

2. *Observation*

The second source of authority noted by Newsom is *observance*. It is Eliphaz again who draws on this source of authority: 'As I have observed, those who plough evil, and those who sow trouble reap it' (4:8). The perspective from which he has made this observation is important for our analysis. Eliphaz, who is a friend of Job's, obviously has to be a wealthy man himself. One would be right in thinking that he was probably a wealthy farmer too. From his perspective, an example of 'those who sow trouble' would probably be those poor peasants who do not pay their debt. These people would then reap their 'just' punishment by having their children seized from them for not paying their debt. From the perspective of a wealthy farmer, such as Eliphaz, this is the kind of justice by which the world is ruled. He is not able to identify with the plight of the poor, and he is able to make the kind of judgmental remarks which he makes because the perspective from which he 'observes' prevents him from having any other insight into this issue. I would think that Job, being a wealthy farmer, would have 'observed' from a similar perspective. Chapter 24, however, portrays Job as lamenting the cause of the innocent poor, who are never allowed to reap the benefits of their hard work:

> The fatherless child is snatched from the breast; the infant of the poor is seized for a debt.
> Lacking clothes, they go about naked; they carry the sheaves but they still go hungry.
> They crush olives among the terraces, they tread the winepresses yet they still suffer thirst.
> The groans of the dying rise from the city, and the souls of the wounded cry out for help. But God charges no one with wrongdoing (24:9-12).

The question is: what causes Job to have a different perspective from his friend? I would argue that it is only because he himself is now in a situation of poverty that he is able to think through these issues of unjust suffering more clearly. As Gutierrez (1987:16) notes: Job 'realizes that the issue here is not simply the suffering of one individual.

The real issue, he sees, is the suffering and injustice that marks the lives of the poor.' In other words, it is only because he himself suffers unjustly, that he is able to see things from the perspective of the poor. Were he not, I suspect that his conversation would have taken the form of conversations that we hear around the *braai* [8] in affluent circles in South Africa. The conversations that centre around 'common sense observations' such as 'African people are most infected by HIV/AIDS because African people are by nature more promiscuous.' Common sense observations!

Unfortunately, Job's transformation is ambiguous. Although Job shows this solidarity with the oppressed he again slips into his role as wealthy patriarch in chapters 29 and 30 where he fondly remembers the times in which he commanded respect from the poor. He betrays his contempt for them with the words:

> But now they mock me, men younger than I, whose fathers I would have disdained to put with my sheep dogs.
> Of what use was the strength of their hands to me, since their vigour had gone from them?
> Haggard from want and hunger, they roamed the parched land in desolate wastelands at night....
> A base and nameless brood, they were driven out of the land.
> And now their sons mock me in song (30:1-9).

It is clear from Job's ambivalent statements regarding the plight of the poor that he still does not understand the complexities of unjust suffering. He does not see the realities behind the reason for their suffering. As Newsom (1992:142) notes:

> The moral world of ancient patriarchy was an essentially paternalistic and hierarchical one. It placed high value on alleviating the distress of the poor and the weak, but for the most part it could not conceive of the fundamental changes in the organization of society that would prevent the powerlessness and the destitution that so often struck the widow and the orphan.

Job, at this point does not understand the nature of unjust suffering fully, neither does Job's friends. God's response sheds some light on the issue but we are still left with questions that only we as individuals can answer at the end of the book.

3. Theology

The third source of authority identified by Newsom is *theology and transcendent authority of revelation*. Elihu, the last friend who comes to visit Job draws most strongly on this theological source of authority in chapter 34:

> So, listen to me, you men of understanding. Far be it from God to do evil, from the Almighty to do wrong.
> He repays a man for what he has done; he brings upon him what his conduct deserves.
> It is unthinkable that God would do wrong, that the Almighty would pervert justice (34:10-12).

Eliphaz draws on this transcendent source of authority in chapter 4:

> A spirit glided past my face, and the hair on my body stood on end.
> It stopped, but I could not tell what it was. A form stood before my eyes, and I heard a hushed voice:
> Can a mortal be more righteous than God can? Can a man be more pure than his Maker? (34:15-17)

Both Elihu and Eliphaz seem to speak great theological truths. One draws on well-known theological thought, while the other draws on actual revelation with respect to these thoughts. How is it possible to dispute these thoughts? Wittenberg (1994:64) notes that this doctrine is handy for explaining the suffering of others, but for Job who actually experiences the suffering such explanations are incongruent. He goes on to argue that 'these statements trap him in the logic of a system, without offering him any real help in his own distress. Instead this theology becomes a theology of repression hiding its cruelty against the suffering of others in the pious garb of theological language purporting to defend God' (Wittenberg 1994:64).

Job has to find another way of speaking of his suffering. He has to find a way of disentangling himself from the trap of theological language. The only way that he can do this is to insist on his own experience as a valid and legitimate source of God-talk[9]. He cannot talk in theological abstraction when his suffering is a reality. When confronting the theological arguments of his friends he moves beyond his own suffering to the suffering of others as well. He sees that those who cause the suffering live on. If God does not pervert justice then why is it all the same? Why does God 'destroy both the blameless and the wicked'? (9:22). Job homes in on the realities of the unjust suffering of people without getting entangled in the theological language. He can speak only from his own reality and the reality of those who suffer. Soelle (1975:115) argues that in other biblical experiences, such as the exodus, it is God who is the answer to oppression. She asserts though that 'once the question is radically raised, no answer can be given in the context of an understanding of God that combines justice and omnipotence.' Job's friends ask him to find peace with God, who in this case does not seem to be the answer to oppression. ('Submit to God and be at peace with him'. 22:21). Job cannot be at peace with this God and at the same time accept his suffering. He has to question and wrestle with God. Ultimately abstract theological thinking, which talks *about* God such as those offered by Job's friends become useless to Job. He ultimately learns how to talk *to* God (Gutierrez 1987:64). In doing this he is able to secure a response from God.

God's Response: The Voice from the Storm

When Job eventually begins addressing God, he challenges God to appear, either to charge him with wrongdoing or to vindicate him. God eventually answers Job in a voice from the storm or the whirlwind (38-42:6). Perdue (1991:197) cautions scholars against taking 'the risky path of attempting to find the meaning of the book in the content of the divine speeches.' I believe that my search for resources in the book of Job that can help those infected and affected with HIV/AIDS, can ultimately be completed only through an examination of the divine speeches. I therefore take the risk that Perdue warns scholars against and in the following paragraphs attempt to explore the meaning contained in the divine speeches.

Granted, there is no general consensus regarding the meaning of the divine speeches[10]. Some scholars argue that 'God's zoo full of animals is irrelevant to Job's question,' (Bechtel 1995:222). In fact most scholars would agree that God does not answer Job's questions directly for even though Job's eventual encounter with God is borne out of 'complaint, bewilderment, and confrontation' (Gutierrez 1987:55), God does little to address those issues. Instead, as Van Wolde (1995:209) notes, 'God chooses the arena of creation rather than the Hall of justice' to address Job's troubling and complex questions. God answers Job with equally complex statements that seem to have little to do with the questions posed. However, if we examine the text closely enough it is possible to find that every aspect of God's appearance is important for the way in which we interpret the divine speeches.

As indicated earlier, Bechtel (1995:237) demonstrates that even God's appearance in a storm is significant. Hence, God's oppositional role is played out in the very appearance of God in the storm. She also relates this kind of understanding of divinity to the Goddess tradition, in which Goddesses very often are oppositional in their roles, sometimes even as one person. Newsom (1992:143), although not arguing for the Goddess tradition, also argues that: 'Job had envisioned God in his own image, as the divine patriarch.... The radicalness of the book of Job lies in this: the rejection of Job's model of God as inadequate. The God who meets Job in chapters 38-41 is not the great patriarch Job had anticipated.' This kind of re-reading of the way in which God is perceived is indeed significant for our own reading of the book of Job, in the HIV/AIDS era. The reason that theologians and others fail to see the impossibility of HIV/AIDS being a punishment from God is because the vision they have of God is that of a great patriarch – one who sits in judgement of his clan, when they have erred in their ways. Transforming the way in which we see God is the first step toward transforming the way in which we see God in our suffering.

So, the very form of God's appearance to Job is significant for the way in which we theologise about suffering. The second factor is the content of God's speeches. As asserted before scholars are quick to point out that God does not answer Job's questions. The point, however, is not that God has not chosen to answer Job, it is that God has chosen to answer Job in a way that is radically different from the way in which Job expects. Job's and his friends' categories of speaking of God have been inadequate. 'Job's deuteronomic theology obscures the divine principles upon which creation is based, principles which Job does not understand' (Bechtel 1995:238). God does not show Job directly what his theology should be transformed to. Rather God points Job toward a different way of thinking by asking Job questions: 'Who is it that darkens my counsel with words without knowledge? Brace yourself like a man and I will question you and you shall answer me' (38:2-3). The question is meant to guide Job toward a new way of thinking. God does not in true patriarchal fashion enforce laws on the way in which God is supposed to be understood in the midst of suffering. Instead God points Job to issues other than rudimentary justice, retribution and reward notions. God points him to the miracle of nature, both the arbitrariness and the control that exist in nature.

The question remains. If God does not give Job an answer, but only leads him away from his theological thinking, then where is God leading Job through the divine speeches? God leads Job to a point where Job can say:

> 'You asked, "Who is this that obscures my counsel without knowledge?" Surely, I spoke of things I did not understand, things too wonderful for me to know.... Therefore I despise myself and repent in dust and ashes' (42:3-6).

What are the things that Job did not understand, and the things that were too wonderful for him to know? Is this God's simple answer to the problem of suffering – that God is in control of everything and therefore God can choose to do as God likes? Are we meant to leave the text of Job with an impression of God as an arbitrary, capricious tyrant[11]? I do not believe so. In fact I believe that God does not provide any significant answer as to how we should talk about God in times of suffering. What God shows both Job and his friends is how we *should not* talk about God in times of suffering. Job's friends were stuck in dualistic categories of punishment and reward. Job himself was stuck in these dualistic categories of punishment and reward. It is for this reason that he begs God constantly to show him where he had gone wrong, so that he could repent and not be 'punished' anymore. His ambivalence slips simultaneous protests of innocence. So, even though Job was trapped by his theological insights, his own experience was taking him to a new level of understanding, especially in his questioning with regard to the poor. Unfortunately he gets trapped in the dualistic understanding of God constantly. What he eventually realises is that God is not confined to the categories in which we want to box God. Rather God is much more complex than that. The fact that Job begins to realise this is what prompts God to pronounce that Job's friends have not spoken well of God. It is Job that has. Job has caught a glimpse of the non-dualistic God, and that should be the beginning of the way in which the suffering should begin to talk about God.

Conclusion

As we have seen from the foregoing analysis, the book of Job does not offer us a solution to the problem of suffering. Neither Job, nor his friends, nor even God give us the answer to the question of suffering. What the book of Job does is to tell us how *not to* talk about God in times of suffering. This in itself provides a way in which to counter inadequate pastoral care, corrupt theological interpretations and unjustified fear with regard to HIV/AIDS. I do not think that the book of Job provides a holistic answer to the problem of suffering. It provides an alternative voice to a theological trajectory that is so entrenched in the biblical texts that it has become the hallmark of the way in which we theologise today. The alternative views presented from an African feminist re-reading of the text of Job has hopefully provided a new starting point from which those infected and affected by HIV/AIDS can begin to talk of God in the midst of their suffering.

Endnotes

1. A version of this paper was published in Old Testament Essays 16/2.

2. Taken from AIDSWATCH AFRICA.

3. I use this term only to highlight the way in which the West seems to think of AIDS. We should take Katongole's (2001:149) concern that this disease is labelled in this way very seriously. He argues that given Africa's 'endless woes', 'AIDS seems to be the last evidence that Afro-pessimists needed to write off the continent.'

4. See eg, Johanna Stiebert (2001:174-185) who shows through an investigation of disease and illness in the Hebrew Bible, that the Hebrew Bible should not be used as an example that HIV/AIDS is a result of divine retribution: 'as a severe punishment for serious wrongdoing on a grand scale.'

5. See Masenya (2001:187) for reasons why black South African women are particularly susceptible to the disease.

6. See also West (1991:110-112) who, using Meyers' 'behind the text' reading, provides compelling arguments for Job's wife's response to him.

7. The prose section is made up of the prologue (chaps 1 and 2) and the epilogue (chap 42:7-17).

8. barbecue.

9. Articulating the realities and legitimacy of our experiences as women, over and against abstract theological doctrine and dogma, is something that womanists and feminists have been struggling with for decades.

10. See Perdue (1991:197-198) for a summary of some of the scholarly views regarding the divine speeches.

11. Williams (1992:208-231) makes the strongest argument for this view. He argues that the theology that God espouses is inadequate. 'This glimpse of an adequate theology, a theology of the God of victims that would not base itself on sacrifice and scapegoating but on divine-human community of justice and love, is not carried forward in the theophany.' Gutierrez (1987:102) puts forward a different argument. He sees the answer in Job. 'Job shows us a way with his vigorous protest, his discovery of concrete commitment to the poor and all who suffer unjustly, his facing up to God, and his acknowledgement of the gratuitousness that characterizes God's plan for human history.' Gutierrez's argument is borne out of concrete suffering which he witnesses in Latin America on a daily basis. For those of us who witness the suffering of millions of people on our continent dying of AIDS, Williams' arguments concerning God seems to be an academic luxury we cannot afford.

Bibliography

Banda D. M. & Moyo F. L. (2001). The role of the Church in combating HIV/AIDS in Malawi: Challenges and prospects. *Journal for Constructive Theology* 7, 45-62.

Bechtel, L. M. (1995). A feminist approach to Job, in Brenner 1995: 222-251.

Brenner, A. (ed). (1995). *A feminist companion to Wisdom Literature.* Sheffield: Sheffield Academic Press.

Brueggemann, W. (1992). A shape for old theology, II: Embrace of pain, in Miller, P.D. (ed), *Old Testament theology: Essays on structure, theme, and text*, 22-44. Minneapolis: Fortress.

Carter, Nancy 2001. The dawn has come. Sermon taken from AIDSWATCH AFRICA (teologie@yahoo.com).

Crossan, J. D. (2002). The bodily resurrection of Jesus in its Jewish context. Unpublished paper presented at the University of Natal, 23 April 2002.

Gustafson, J. M. (1992). A response to the book of Job, in Perdue, L G & Gilpin, W C (eds), *The VOICE from the whirlwind: Interpreting the book of Job.* Nashville: Abingdon.

Gutierrez, G. (1987). *On Job: God-talk and the suffering of the innocent.* 4th publ 1991. Maryknoll, NY: Orbis Books.

Katongole, E. M. (2001). Christian ethics and AIDS in Africa today: Exploring the limits of a culture of suspicion and despair. *Missionalia* 29, 144-160.

Maier, C. & Schroer, S. (1998). What about Job? Questioning the book of 'the righteous sufferer', in Brenner, A & Fontaine, C (eds), *Wisdom and Psalms – a feminist companion to the Bible,* 175-204. Sheffield: Sheffield Academic Press.

Masenya, M. J. (2001). Between unjust suffering and the 'silent' God: Job and HIV/AIDS sufferers in South Africa. *Missionalia* 29, 186-199.

Newsom, C. A. (1992). Job, in Newsom, C A & Ringe, S H (eds), *Women's Bible Commentary: Expanded edition with Apocrypha,* 138-144. Louisville, Kentucky: Westminster John Knox Press.

Perdue, L. G. (1991). *Wisdom in revolt: Metaphorical theology in the book of Job.* Sheffield: Almond Press.

Scarborough, J. D. (2001). HIV/AIDS: The response of the church. *Journal for Constructive Theology* 7, 45-62.

Soelle, D. (1975). *Suffering,* tr by Everett R Kalin. Philadelphia: Fortress.

Stiebert, J. (2001). Does the Hebrew Bible have anything to tell us about HIV/AIDS?' *Missionalia* 29, 174-185.

Tamez, E. (1986). A letter to Job, in Pobee, J & Von-Wartenburg-Potter, B (eds), *New eyes for reading: Biblical and theological reflections by women from the third world,* 50-52. Geneva: WCC.

West, G. O. (1991). Hearing Job's wife: Towards a feminist reading of Job. *OTE* 4/1, 107-131.

Williams, J. G. (1992). Job and the God of victims, in Perdue, L G & Gilpin, W C (eds), *The VOICE from the whirlwind: Interpreting the book of Job.* Nashville: Abingdon.

Wittenberg, G. H. (1994). Counselling AIDS patients: Job as a paradigm. *Journal of Theology for Southern Africa* 88, 61-68.

Van Wolde, E. (1995). The development of Job – Mrs. Job as catalyst, in Brenner 1995: 201-224.

Chapter Three

Women's Sexuality and Stigma in Genesis and the Prophets

Johanna Stiebert, University of Tennessee

Reflections from Southern Africa in the Context of the HIV/AIDS Pandemic

Originally, the Greek word 'stigma' referred to a physical sign, or brand-mark, such as a cut or burn, that was intended to expose something defective about its bearer. Nowadays, however, 'stigma' most often conveys a quality perceived as shameful rather than the bodily evidence of it. Erving Goffman distinguishes three types of stigma: first, various physical deformities; secondly, blemishes of character (such as rigid beliefs, promiscuity, or addiction); and thirdly, tribal stigma (pertaining to race, nation or religion and transmitted through lineage). All result from labeling and constitute 'a special kind of relationship between attribute and stereotype' (Goffman 1963:4). As Goffman explains, a person's perception of having a stigma incorporates an awareness of societal standards in conjunction with negative self-evaluation:

> the standards he [sic] has incorporated from the wider society equip him to be intimately alive to what others see as his failing, inevitably causing him, if only for moments, to agree that he does indeed fall short of what he really ought to be. Shame becomes a central possibility, arising from the individual's perception of one of his own attributes as being a defiling thing to possess (Goffman 1963: 7).

The stigma of being either HIV+ or suffering from AIDS is considerably more profound than the stigma attending many other illnesses or diseases. The reason for this appears to be neither its infectiousness,[1] nor its deadliness[2] per se: influenza, or malaria, or cancer does not confer comparable shame and stigma. Instead, it seems to be the dominant mode of infection – namely, through sexual contact – that has exacerbated the negative perception of sufferers most. Discrimination thus results from perceptions about the infected person's moral fiber and behavior. Consequently, the second type of stigma, pertaining to blemishes of character, is at issue here. In sub-Saharan Africa, where prevalence is highest, HIV is, for the most part, passed on through heterosexual contact. In this region more women than men are infected.[3] Many of them are suffering not only the effects of a fragile immune system but also fear, shame and stigma. Negative perceptions about women's sexuality[4] are often at the heart of this emotional suffering.

This paper will examine the depictions of women's sexuality in Genesis and the Prophets. As the Hebrew Bible (or Old Testament) is canonical for both the Jewish and Christian communities, it continues to have a profound impact. An examination of this literature is, therefore, pertinent and important. I have chosen to focus on excerpts from Genesis and the Prophets in particular to expose the existence of differing perceptions regarding female sexuality: there exists both a relatively positive, or neutral (Genesis) and a decidedly more negative, even gyno-sadistic (selected prophetic texts), perception. In discussing the tendency of some biblical texts to demonize and stigmatize women's sexuality, I will draw attention to the potential dangers this poses for the fight against HIV/AIDS.

Let me stress at the outset that HIV+ status is by no means confined to sexually active, or promiscuous, women and men. Many of the afflicted are children or survivors of sexual abuse. It is my firm belief that the HIV/AIDS pandemic cannot be made bearable for sufferers and their loved ones, let alone controlled or contained, unless we break down the stigma attending the virus. Only then and by talking openly about sex and sexuality can the first steps towards reducing denial and acknowledging our collective vulnerability be achieved (Rao Gupta 2000: 4). The Hebrew Bible contains *both* texts that hold scope for some hope and optimism and texts that could contribute to exacerbating the situation in contemporary sub-Saharan Africa. Given this degree of internal diversity alongside the pressures exerted by the pandemic, I advocate that readers make the responsible choice of promoting the former and recognizing the harmful potential of the latter.

Female Desire in Genesis

Female desire is first mentioned in Genesis 3:16 where the repercussions of eating of the fruit from the tree of knowledge of good and evil are spelled out. Here the woman is told that her pains in childbearing will be multiplied and that her desire or longing (Hebrew *tᵉšûqâ*) will be for her man, who will rule over her. While, admittedly, desire is mentioned alongside physical pain and subjugation and could, therefore, be construed as a weakness and punishment, it is interesting to note that the woman's desire is actually mandated by YHWH (I am using a transliteration of the *tetragrammaton*, the four letters of the divine name conventionally translated 'the Lord'). As Susan Brayford illustrates, this divine consent is particularly remarkable when we compare the Hebrew text with the masked translation of the Septuagint. This early Greek translation renders Hebrew *tᵉšûqâ* using the word *apostroph* (from *apostrophe*, meaning 'turning away, averting'). Brayford explains that this rendering eliminates the dimension of female sexual pleasure and thereby deprives the woman of 'some compensatory conjugal desire' (Brayford 1999: 169). In the Hebrew text, however, this is not the case, suggesting perhaps that a pejorative regard for women's sexuality was a later (regrettable) development.

Furthermore, as Brayford has already implied, like so much else in the story of Genesis 2-3,[5] desire is ambiguous and it is far from clear whether this emotion is perceived in an unequivocally negative way. The word appears only twice more in the Hebrew Bible: at Genesis 4:7 and Song of Songs 7:11. The first instance occurs in the story of Cain and Abel, where God tells Cain, 'If you do what is good, will you not be accepted? But if you do not do what is good, sin will crouch at the open door and for you will be its desire but you must rule over it.' As in the earlier passage, ideas of good versus not good (evil/sin) and of ruling over (from the Hebrew *mašal*) are in the proximity of the noun meaning 'desire'. The word *tᵉšûqâ* appears to refer to a strong emotion, perhaps an emotion which makes one vulnerable to another person's capacity to control or rule over one. Whether *tᵉšûqâ* is in itself negative is, however, uncertain.

The usage of the word in the Song of Songs does not serve to elucidate its meaning significantly. The verse, spoken by the female lover, states, 'I am my lover's and for me is his desire.' As this verse is in the context of a love song and as much of the book as a whole is devoted to praising the love and desirability of the beloved, it is likely that the word has here both a sexual and a positive denotation.[6]

Although the depiction of women's sexuality is very much within the parameters of the stereotype of motherhood,[7] it does not, also in other parts of Genesis, have the edge of disapproval and perversity that we will soon encounter in the Prophets. Sarah, overhearing a prediction that she will bear a son in her old age, laughs to herself, saying, 'after I am worn out, will I still have delight when my husband is old?' (Genesis 18:12). The Hebrew word for 'delight' here is *'ednâ*. The word is unique within the Hebrew Bible but the context clearly indicates sexual pleasure. As Brayford points out,

> Why not enjoy herself with some (nonprocreative) intercourse, then, since Abraham would be sure to do 'what was necessary' to beget his promised son? Sarah's laughing thoughts imply her divinely ordained desire, not only for her husband, but also for the pleasure that she might be able to experience (1999: 169).

The idea that sexual activity is construed as pleasurable (though possibly in the context of procuring procreation)[8] is also implied in Genesis 26:8. Here Abimelech, king of the Philistines, happens to see Isaac caressing Rebekah. (The word for 'to caress' is from the Hebrew semantic root *sachaq* and refers to enjoyment.) The action Abimelech witnessed was one that persuaded him that Rebekah was not Isaac's sister (as Isaac had claimed in order to protect himself from anyone who might desire Rebekah for her beauty) but his wife. It is, therefore, safe to assume that it entailed something of both a pleasurable and sexual nature. Again, therefore, we have evidence for sexual pleasure (though we cannot be certain if the pleasure is Isaac's, or Rebekah's, or mutual) and again it is recounted in a manner that is not disapproving.

Most often women's sexuality in Genesis is linked with procreation. Barrenness is depicted as very lamentable and stories of initially infertile women who go on to give birth to a son, or sons, form a veritable topos. Sarah's infertility transpires in conflict with her maidservant Hagar (Genesis 16), a conflict which continues even after she gives birth to Isaac (Genesis 21:1-21); Rebekah, initially barren, gives birth to twin boys after Isaac prays on her behalf (Genesis 25:21-26); Rachel announces that she will die unless she conceives (Genesis 30:1) and later gives birth to Joseph and Benjamin; Tamar, widowed twice with no children, embarks on a daring plan and conceives twin boys by Judah (Genesis 38).

Tamar's story of seduction and conception and the story of Joseph and Potiphar's wife in the ensuing chapter are the last stories of women's sexuality in Genesis. Judah (Tamar's father-in-law) announces that Tamar is more righteous than he and that her actions (of disguising herself as a prostitute and conceiving sons by him) have exposed his failure to give her to his son Shelah to be impregnated. Tamar is favorably remembered by tradition (Ruth 4:12) – in spite of the fact that her union with Judah directly violates the Torah's incest laws (Leviticus 18:15; 20:12). Potiphar's wife, on the other hand, is despised. Her demands for sexual union with Joseph are motivated by her attraction to his good looks (Genesis 39:6), meet with his resistance and transpire in her false accusations of attempted rape and, consequently, Joseph's imprisonment.[9]

Athalya Brenner is correct, I believe, in drawing a distinction between the 'positive' and 'negative' temptress-type of the Hebrew Bible. Tamar, she argues, being motivated by the desire to produce male offspring and successful in manipulating her chosen male victim belongs to the positive category (as does Ruth). Potiphar's wife, on the other hand, who is *not only* foreign (as both Tamar and Ruth are) *but also* married (and therefore ready to commit adultery) and motivated by lust *(pace* McKay, note 9) is one of the negative temptresses (1985: 106-114). It is quite possible, however, that what is primarily contemptible about Potiphar's wife is not her sexual desire per se but, instead, her attempted adultery and her false accusation.

The overall picture that emerges from Genesis, therefore, is that female sexuality is not necessarily condemned or associated with stigma. YHWH, in fact, mandates sexual desire. Both women's enjoyment of sexual intercourse and their desire for children are (to some extent at least) taken for granted. The idea of women's sexuality being depraved, excessive or evil is not prominent.

Dangerous Metaphors: Women's Sexuality and the Prophets

In the Prophets there are a number of passages in which female sexuality is depicted as rampant and depraved. Particularly striking among these passages are the following: Hosea 1:2-3:3, Jeremiah 2:20-25, Ezekiel 16:1-63 and 23:2-49. The Hosea passage draws a parallel between Hosea's adulterous wife Gomer, and unfaithful Israel. The woman is here depicted as pursuing lovers and conceiving her children in disgrace. Before any reconciliation with her husband is possible, she is rebuked, publicly stripped naked, deprived of drink and enjoyment, walled in, bought like a slave and ordered to be faithful. In Jeremiah, meanwhile, Israel is compared to a prostitute offering her services on every hill and under every spreading tree. Her promiscuity is likened to that of an unrestrained animal on heat. Most detailed and sustained, however, are Ezekiel 16 and 23. These chapters will receive particularly focused attention in the discussion to follow.

While all of these prophetic depictions of depraved female sexuality and the necessity for violent punishment are couched in metaphor, they could nevertheless be said to have very negative and damaging implications for actual women. The feminist biblical scholar Naomi Graetz thus argues that 'it is no longer possible to argue that a metaphor is less for being a metaphor' (1995: 135), and David Halperin that such metaphors have 'effected the subjection and humiliation of the female half of our species' (1993: 5). It indeed appears to be the case that Hosea, Jeremiah and Ezekiel reflect a societal ethos that evaluated female sexuality in decidedly pejorative terms. Furthermore, as these texts are part of the canon and, therefore, authoritative, they can and possibly have been used to scorn women's sexuality and continence.

It is important to draw attention to the note of caution and alarm struck by some biblical interpreters responding to these disturbing prophetic metaphors. Graetz, for instance, explains that in using female sexuality as a symbol for evil, a woman reader is forced to identify against herself and accept both blame and brutal punishment. She highlights how the imagery of Hosea 1-3 is not dissimilar to real-life domestic violence and stresses the threatening implications of this connection:

> Israel has to suffer in order to be entitled to [a] new betrothal. 'She' has to be battered into submission in order to kiss and make up at the end.... The premise is that a woman has no other choice but to remain in such a marriage. True, God is very generous to Israel.... But despite the potential for a new model of a relationship between God and Israel, it is not a model of reciprocity. It is based on suffering and the assumption that Israel will submit to God's will. Hosea, however, rejoices in this transformation and in the 'ordeal [which] has fit the woman for a new, enhanced relationship with God'.

> The reader who is caught up in this joyous new
> betrothal and renewed covenant overlooks the fact that
> this joyous reconciliation between God and Israel follows
> the exact pattern that battered wives know so well. Israel
> is physically punished, abused and then seduced into
> remaining in the covenant by tender words and caresses
> (Graetz 1995: 141).

The Jeremiah passage adds the twist of animalizing
female sexuality. The image of the lascivious prostitute is
followed by comparisons with a she-camel and donkey on
heat. According to Brenner this vivid metaphor will only
have the desired effect of arousing disgust and shame in
the audience if 'the listeners recognize the validity of the
description for female sexual behaviour in general' (Brenner
1995: 263). The audience, therefore, is likely to have been
a misogynist one. As Brenner elaborates,

> Does this new development express fear of the female
> and misogyny? If we readers feel that the textual voice
> disapproves of women as wild and (un)natural animals;
> that the target audience is drawn into sharing this
> disapproval; that the pornographic fantasy feeds on the
> view that female sexuality is uncontrollable – then, yes,
> misogyny underscores this dehumanized, animalized
> depiction. This is not 'just a metaphor' (1995: 264).

Notable about Ezekiel 16 and 23 is not only, how
sustained, pejorative and vulgar these woman-metaphors
are but also that the virulent rhetoric occasionally steps
out of the figurative realm to address actual women (16:38;
23:44-45, 48; perhaps also 23:10). While the image of
Jerusalem as a defiled and shameful woman is intended to
refer to all the citizens (men and women), it is easy to lose
sight of this inclusiveness. As Katheryn Pfisterer Darr points
out, 23:48, for instance – 'thus I will put an end to lewdness
in the land, *so that all women may take warning and not
commit lewdness as you have done'* (emphasis added) –
admonishes *women* but not men to refrain from illicit sexual
behavior (Darr 1992: 115).

In chapters 16 and 23 Jerusalem is given a detailed
biography and depicted as polluted from her youth. While

Hosea is able to appeal to an ideal past when the relationship between Israel and her God was pure and joyful (Hosea 2:15), Ezekiel depicts Jerusalem's entire history as marked by defilement. The woman/city begins her life in the land of the Canaanites and is of Amorite and Hittite parentage (Ezekiel 16:3): she is, therefore, descended from races that feature in some biblical literature (and possibly in the public consciousness) as traditional opponents of Israel (cf. Exodus 33:2; Deuteronomy 7:1). Jerusalem is, furthermore, described as unclean (Ezekiel 16:4), neglected (Ezekiel 16:5) and as defiling herself in blood (Ezekiel 16:6). Blood reappears as pejorative signifier of pollution at 16:9 (where YHWH washes the blood from the matured Jerusalem's body) and of blood-guilt at 16:36 (where she is accused of child-sacrifice). The word for blood (*damayik*) in 16:9 is in the plural and may refer to birth blood, or menstrual blood, or both: there is no mention of the birth blood being cleansed off. Despite her inauspicious beginning she grows up under YHWH's protection richly blessed. While Ezekiel deletes the idea of a honeymoon stage of initial fidelity, YHWH *is* proud of his wife (Ezekiel 16:14). She, however, neither responds (cf. Hosea 2:17), nor follows (cf. Jeremiah 2:2). Instead, she is first passive and then actively and excessively rebellious, repaying YHWH's gifts with lewd conduct (Ezekiel 16:15), and child sacrifice. Throughout the uncontrollably perverse nature of the woman/city is stressed.

Ironically, Jerusalem's obscene behavior offends even the Philistine daughters (Ezekiel 16:27). Presumably, the Philistines were considered proverbially uncouth. In much of the biblical literature they are depicted as traditional enemies and God's tool for chastisement (e.g. Judges 3:2-4; 10:6-8). Following this, her offensiveness is spelled out in yet more appalling detail. She is insatiably promiscuous and brazenly public with it (16:28-31). Worse than a prostitute, furthermore (who was, presumably, an ostracized but tolerated woman whose sexual activity violated no man's right), Jerusalem is accused of adultery (16:32), an offence depicted in biblical literature as unequivocally intolerable and punishable by death (Leviticus 20:10). Highlighting the unnaturalness of her conduct, she does not act lustfully in return for payment but actually gives payment to her lovers (Ezekiel 16:34). Jerusalem's perversity and unnaturalness are stressed also in chapter 23, where transgression is signified in terms of sexual depravity, particularly in the active pursuit of foreign lovers (Ezekiel 23:5, 12).

While punishment in Ezekiel is described in virulent and violent terms, it is also, given Jerusalem's shameful conduct, presented as somehow appropriate and proportionate. Still drawing on the woman/city metaphor, which served to illustrate transgression, YHWH's punishment entails public stripping (16:37), destruction of property (16:39; 23:46-47), murder of offspring (23:47), stoning (16:40; 23:47) and dismemberment (16:40; 23:47). In light of the preceding catalogue of the city's sinning, juxtaposed with YHWH's extravagant care and the statement that her treatment is deserved due to breach of covenant (16:59), this brutality is, by implication, reasonable and in order. Ezekiel thus presents the imminent destruction of Jerusalem not as impulsive act but as fitting consequence on account of human culpability. As the punishment anticipated is extreme, so the sin is depicted as suitably gruesome.

The punishment of Jerusalem described in Ezekiel is extremely brutal but the disturbing nature of this does not receive acknowledgement in the biblical text. Perhaps because the divine sanctioning of and participation in such brutality is so troubling, some feminist commentators have sprung to the defense of the woman/city. Majella Franzmann, in no unstinting terms, calls the portrayal of YHWH as vicious warrior-rapist a scandal and argues that such a representation supports men in their victimization of women by the authority of the metaphor (Franzmann 1995: 17-19). Darr, too, expresses her uneasiness at the woman/city's degradation, public humiliation, battery and murder constituting a means towards healing a broken relationship and has sympathy for her woman student who rejected chapters 16 and 23 (Darr 1992: 115). Fokkelien van Dijk-Hemmes, meanwhile, designates Ezekiel 23:3 an example of pornographic writing and attempts to liberate the women of the text. In the NIV this verse reads, '[Samaria and Jerusalem] became prostitutes in Egypt, engaging in prostitution from their youth. In that land their breasts were fondled and their virgin bosoms caressed.' Van Dijk-Hemmes points out that this event is one not of activity but of receptivity, which has for her particular implications:

> As an F [Female/Feminine] reader I have some difficulties in naming such a being-acted-upon situation as 'playing the harlot', so I suggest…[i]t would have been more adequate to describe the events during the sisters' youth in the following manner: 'They were sexually molested in Egypt, in their youth they were sexually abused'…. This way, justice would have been done to the fate of these metaphorical women, and the audience would not have been seduced into viewing women or girls as responsible for and even guilty of their own violation. In short, there would have been no question of 'blaming the victim' (van Dijk-Hemmes 1995: 250-251).

She accuses the text, furthermore, of not only misnaming but also distorting female experience. The image of Oholibah/Jerusalem's desire for stallion-like males with animal-like members, she argues, 'Instead of reflecting female desire…betrays male obsession', the alleged intention being 'to stress that [women's] sexuality is and ought to be an object of male possession and control' (van Dijk-Hemmes 1995: 253).

The prophetic metaphors discussed above can be exploited for condemning women's sexuality. By saying that these feminized metaphors have an affinity with women's conduct, in other words, by claiming that women are *actually* prone to excessive sexual incontinence, it could be argued that they are culpable and, consequently, that violent punishment – including the ravages of HIV/AIDS – is justified.

The abusive, distinctly masculine depiction of God alongside the image of the brutalized woman also holds another very dangerous implication in the HIV/AIDS era. This is because there is a documented correlation between male violence against women and women's vulnerability to HIV. Research shows that women who have been sexually abused are more likely to engage in unprotected sex, to have multiple partners and to exchange sex for money or drugs. Also, women who fear physical violence or abandonment from their male partners are significantly less likely to negotiate condom use, or discuss their partner's faithfulness, or to leave the relationship (Rao Gupta 2000: 3). YHWH of Ezekiel in particular, therefore, is setting men a bad example, an example that if followed can be deadly for both women and men living in an environment where HIV is prevalent. There is good reason for drawing attention to the toxic potential of the selected prophetic passages.

Women's Sexuality and the Hebrew Bible in the Era of HIV/AIDS

Robert Carroll points out that the images of YHWH in the Prophets

> frequently reflect a blood-thirsty figure, wading through blood, blasting everything in sight and threatening further violence to generations and generations of people and their children's children (e.g., Jeremiah 2:9). The representation of the deity is generally that of a berserker god (1999: 114).

As we have seen, the prophetic depiction of YHWH is certainly often detrimental to women and to perceptions about their sexuality. While Carroll concedes that there are also benign images of YHWH in the Prophets, he maintains that as a reader in the late twentieth century

> ...a century remarkable for its sustained practices of violence, deportations and destructiveness – the images of violence and horror stick more in the mind than all the friendlier images of a non-rampaging YHWH (115).

Carroll's comments remain valid for readers in the twenty-first century also and the images of horror in the wake of the HIV/AIDS pandemic – of emaciated sufferers, overcrowded hospital wards, of Nkosi Johnston's premature death at the age of twelve, of the thousands of orphans – can be added to his list.

As active readers we do, however, have choices. We do not have to submit to the damaging possibilities of the woman metaphors of some prophetic books – instead, we can highlight and resist them and promote, instead, biblical texts which do not vilify women's sexuality. Women's sexuality is not itself negative and it is not the cause of either HIV/AIDS or its spread. Not women but HIV/AIDS is the enemy. By losing sight of this point, progress in stemming the spread of this terrible virus is hampered. Women should not deny or be ashamed of their sexuality or of the desire to have children: for those for whom the Bible is canonical, they are affirmed by such biblical texts as portions of Genesis and the Song of Songs. Emphasis instead should be placed on practicing sex or having children as safely as possible.

It is encouraging to see that recent publications of the popular press of South Africa celebrate women who are living with HIV. The December 2001 issue of *True Love,* a popular women's magazine, for example, contains no fewer than three articles focused on HIV. The women who should inspire us are the four women profiled in 'Staying Positive with HIV'[10] and Jabulile Ngwenya, infected with HIV by her own father who sexually molested her, who is now working in AIDS education in the community of Mafikeng.[11] Allowing dangerous texts of the Bible to demonize women's sexuality can facilitate the stigmatization of people afflicted with HIV and AIDS and thereby silence these courageous women. Of course the presence and prevalence of HIV/AIDS demands adjustments in behavior and strategies for containment. What is required is responsible sexual behavior – as succinctly expressed in the ABC campaign (Abstain-Be Faithful-Condomize) – in conjunction with a three-component plan comprising 1) intensified efforts to reduce vertical HIV transmission from mother to child, 2) the provision of HIV medication and 3) a widespread and intensive education campaign on how to avoid HIV. For this to work we need these women's courage alongside the life-giving energy of Eve, the initiative of Tamar and the ability of Sarah to find joy even amid adversity.

Endnotes

1. HIV (the Human Immunodeficiency Virus), which according to the majority of scientists leads to AIDS (the Acquired Immunodeficiency Syndrome), is a relatively weak virus. Its reproduction number – that is, the number of other people an infected person is likely to infect – is around five. By comparison, the reproduction number for malaria is one hundred. For a more detailed discussion, see Whiteside and Sunter (2000: 1-11).

2. It is a fact that many diseases, including some cancers, kill more rapidly than AIDS. Also, where there is access to antiretroviral treatment, the life expectancy of people with HIV is increased considerably. In the developed world, therefore, advances in medical treatment have resulted in a dramatic decline in the mortality from HIV. Yet AIDS is, of course, a disease claiming many lives. 95% of people with HIV live in the developing world and 70% of the world's infections are clustered in sub-Saharan Africa, an area with just 10% of the global population. In the past decade AIDS has claimed an estimated twelve million lives in this region and a fifteen-year-old in Zambia today has a 60% chance of dying from AIDS. Only a small number of children born HIV+ in the developing world survive beyond five years of age. Around half of all people who acquire the virus become infected before they turn twenty-five and typically die within ten years. See Whiteside and Sunter (2000: 29-46).

3. The dominant modes of infection in sub-Saharan Africa are first, through unprotected heterosexual sex and second, through transmission from an infected mother to her child. Other modes of transmission (through unprotected homosexual sex, intravenous drug use with contaminated needles and use or transmission of infected blood or blood products) are not nearly as prevalent. Fifteen studies conducted in rural and urban areas in nine African countries indicate that between twelve and thirteen women are infected for every ten men. At the end of 1999, UNAIDS estimated that 12.2 million women and 10.1 million men aged 15-49 were living with HIV in sub-Saharan Africa. The discrepancy is not due to women being more promiscuous. Rather, male-to-female transmission through unprotected vaginal sex is higher (1-2 per 1000 exposures) than female-to-male unprotected vaginal sex (0.33-1 per 1000 exposures). See Whiteside and Sunter (2000: 10-20 and 45).

4. As explained by Geeta Rao Gupta, sexuality is subsumed within the concept of gender. Gender refers to the social and cultural construction of males and females and determines the behavior and roles deemed appropriate for each. Sexuality, more particularly, refers to the social construction of the biological sexual drive. A person's sexuality is defined by whom one has sex with, how, why, under which circumstances and with what outcomes. As Rao Gupta elaborates, 'It is more than sexual behavior; it is a multidimensional concept. Explicit and implicit rules imposed by society, as defined by one's gender, age, economic status, ethnicity and other factors, influence an individual's sexuality' (2000: 1-2).

5. There is considerable debate as to whether this story, traditionally called 'The Fall', is not also about a rise in stature (cf. Genesis 3:22) and whether the woman's action of eating from the tree and giving of its fruit also to the man with her is an event that inaugurates *only* disaster, or *also* autonomy and liberation. The curse of pain in childbearing is attended by the blessing of life-giving. The complexities and ambiguities of this seemingly simple story are expounded in Phyllis Trible's detailed analysis 'A Love Story Gone Awry', in *God and the rhetoric of sexuality* (1992: 73-143). Elsewhere I have discussed the double-edged depiction of the emotion of shame, which is also central to this story (cf. Genesis 2:25, 3:7). Shame, as depicted in the Hebrew Bible, constitutes both a *positive* restraint on one's behavior (i.e. to have proper shame and a sense of decency) and a *lack* of appropriate restraint (i.e. to be shameful and act in a manner that invites disgrace) (see Stiebert 2002: 167-68).

6. On the basis of the Song of Songs a strong case can be made for the existence of a positive and affirming regard for women's sexuality. Sensual delight and pleasure-giving and receiving between a man and woman are central to this concatenation of love poems. Throughout, the female voice is dominant. The woman can take initiative and is not shy to speak erotically to her lover. She is nowhere demonized for such conduct – except, possibly, by the watchmen who emerge, however, as ruffians (5:7). I have resisted focusing my discussion on the Song of Songs because it is such an anomaly within the Hebrew Bible. Still, the fact that it is present in the canon at all points to the probability that there is a long-standing tradition of interpreting women's sexuality in more ways than one. Alongside the toxic depictions of the prophetic metaphors, therefore, there exist also texts that redeem and celebrate women's sexuality.

7. As Ilona Rashkow points out, 'biblical motherhood is construed as the ultimate destiny of essential womanhood. Narrative accounts amplify and clarify the importance of (male) offspring to a woman. "Give me children or I shall die," cries Rachel to Jacob (Gen 30:1).... And although women appear in many roles in Hebrew Scriptures, it is a very rare positive image of a woman who is not identified as the mother of a son, reinforcing the position that the best thing that can happen to a young woman (the passive is significant here) is to have lots of (male) children' (Rashkow 2000: 66). In the context of the HIV/AIDS pandemic, foregrounding motherhood as a feminine ideal can make women more vulnerable to infection. This is because, under pressure to conceive, women might avoid using barrier methods when having penetrative sex (Rao Gupta 2000: 3).

8. The idea that Abraham has sexual relations with Sarah (though it be by divine decree) even *after* she is past childbearing age implies the existence of the notion of sex for pleasure rather than procreation. Admittedly, however, there is little to go on.

9. Heather McKay interprets this story as related to that of Tamar in that both depict women who 'employ increasingly complex stratagems to achieve children sired by one of the biblical patriarchs' (McKay 1999: 218). McKay proposes that Potiphar was a eunuch (also Rashkow 2000: 35) who might, if things had developed differently, have turned a blind eye to Joseph's sexual activity with and impregnation of his wife. While I am not completely persuaded by McKay's proposal, she does argue persuasively that the text indeed allows for such a reading.

10. Busi Mkhwanazi, Musa Njoko, Priscilla Mashifane and Feroza Mohamad are profiled and celebrated for their remarkable resilience and optimism *(True Love,* December 2001, 97-98).

11. Jabulile Ngwenya is one of six finalists in the 'Revlon's Absolutely Fabulous' competition. Her achievements are summarized in 'Women Who Won't Stay Down' *(True Love,* December 2001, 130-135).

Bibliography

Brayford, S. A. (1999). To Shame or Not to Shame: Sexuality in the Mediterranean Diaspora, in *Semeia,* 87: 163-76.

Brenner, A. (1985). *The Israelite woman: Social role and literary type in biblical narrative*. Sheffield: JSOT Press.

Brenner, A. (1995). On Prophetic Propaganda and the Politics of 'Love': The Case of Jeremiah, in *A feminist companion to the Latter Prophets*. Ed. A. Brenner. Sheffield: Sheffield Academic Press, 256-74.

Carroll, R. P. (1999). YHWH's Sour Grapes: Images of Food and Drink in the Prophetic Discourses of the Hebrew Bible, in *Semeia*, 86: 113-31.

Darr, K. P. (1992). Ezekiel's Justification of God: Teaching Troubling Texts, in *Journal for the Study of the Old Testament*, 55: 97-117.

van Dijk-Hemmes, F. (1995). The Metaphorization of Woman in Prophetic Speech: An Analysis of Ezekiel 23, in *A feminist companion to the Latter Prophets*. Ed. A. Brenner. Sheffield: Sheffield Academic Press, 244-55.

Franzmann, M. (1995). The City as Woman: The Case of Babylon in Isaiah 47, in *Australian Biblical Review*, 43: 1-19.

Goffman, E. (1963). *Stigma: Notes on the management of spoiled identity*. Englewood Cliffs, NJ: Prentice Hall.

Graetz, N. (1995). God is to Israel as Husband is to Wife: The Metaphoric Battering of Hosea's Wife, in *A feminist companion to the Latter Prophets*. Ed. A. Brenner. Sheffield: Sheffield Academic Press, 126-45.

Halperin, D. J. (1993). *Seeking Ezekiel: Text and psychology*. University Park, PA: Pennsylvania State University Press.

McKay, H. A. (1999). Confronting Redundancy As Middle Manager and Wife: The Feisty Woman of Genesis 39, in *Semeia*, 87: 215-31.

Rao Gupta, G. (2000). Gender, Sexuality, and HIV/AIDS: The What, the Why, and the How. Plenary Address, Thirteenth International AIDS Conference in Durban, South Africa. Published in a pamphlet by the International Center for Research on Women, 1-8.

Rashkow, Ilona. (2000). *Taboo or not taboo: Sexuality and the family in the Hebrew Bible*. Minneapolis: Fortress Press.

Stiebert, J. (2002). *The construction of shame in the Hebrew Bible: The prophetic contribution*. Sheffield: Sheffield Academic Press.

Trible, P. (1992). *God and the rhetoric of sexuality*. London: SCM.

Whiteside, A. and Sunter, C. (2000). *AIDS – The challenge for South Africa*. Cape Town: Human & Rousseau.

Chapter Four

Can These Bones Live?
Re-reading Ezekiel 37:1-14 in the HIV/AIDS Context

Dorothy BEA Akoto,
Trinity Theological Seminary

Introduction

The Bible does not make mention of HIV/AIDS, explicitly. However, the issue of HIV/AIDS can be said to be implied by the message of the Bible. It is, therefore, appropriate that a topic such as "HIV/AIDS and the Bible" be chosen for discussion. The topic is appropriate also for the fact that the HIV/AIDS pandemic has become a universal canker and needs to be given attention. The disease has become so devastating that there seems to be no hope for the future as far as HIV/AIDS is concerned. The intention of this paper is to take a critical look at Ezekiel Chapter 37:1-14 as the focus of the topic, "HIV/AIDS and the Bible." Both those infected and those affected by the disease can be likened to the "very many" and "very dry bones" on the "face of the valley." The call to become messengers to be used by God to bring the dead back to life, to instill hope into the hopeless situation into which HIV has plunged us, is pertinent. A situation in which we cannot help ourselves in the face of this deadly annihilator except God comes to our rescue is created. The question for me here is the same as was posed to Ezekiel by Yahweh, "Can these bones live (37:3b)?" Can there be a handle on the HIV/AIDS pandemic? I must say from the onset that a topic of this nature is so hydra-headed that it would be impudent for anyone to claim absolute mastery over it. I would, therefore, attempt to scratch only the surface of it as I invite others who are also concerned to join in the discussion.

According to Peter Poit, the Executive Director of UNAIDS, at a meeting of Ministers of Health of the Organization of African Unity (O.A.U.), on HIV/AIDS in Ouagadougou in 2000,

> HIV behaves in the society in the same way as it behaves in the human body, the virus erodes the very institutions that are supposed to defend the social fabric.... the virus kills teachers, doctors, farmers, fathers and mothers and we know that everyday in Africa, tens of nurses and doctors die of AIDS.... today, there is no single factor that so systematically, undermines the achievements of five decades of investment in human resources, education, health and the welfare of entire nations (2001:1).

This statement, contained in the *Safco AIDS in West and Central Africa*, quarterly bulletin of the UNAIDS of October-December, 2001, reveals the extent of devastation caused by HIV/AIDS. It can be deduced from Poit's words that HIV/AIDS is no respecter of persons. It is indiscriminate in whom it attacks and kills. The effects of this disease are not only economic but also social and spiritual. They are not national but also international. They are not continental but global. The whole fabric of society is affected by it to such an extent that Ezekiel's vision of the valley of dry bones (Ezekiel 37:1-14) becomes a befitting description of the global village in which we live.

Brief Background to Ezekiel

Judah has gone into exile and has lost all hope of ever coming back to life. Earlier in Ezekiel 33:10, the exiles had posed a question to Ezekiel, "How then can we live?" Later, in 37:11, they confess, "Our bones are dried up." Even though their condition at the time was created by their own, their ancestors' and others' deeds, they had become demoralized and dejected. They were dead both physically (several of them having died in the many battles they had fought) and spiritually (their Temple had been destroyed). They needed revival both ways. In the midst of this devastation and loss of hope, the hand of *Yahweh*, God, brings Ezekiel to an ecstatic experience of the situation in which Judah finds herself. The *ruah Yahweh* "Spirit of God," by the command of the prophet, brings the numerous dry bones, scattered on the face of the valley, to join together, be enfleshed and come to life. In a situation such as ours, HIV/AIDS has dried up our bones as were the bones Ezekiel encountered in the valley. Theirs were dried up by the conditions of the Babylonian exile and ours by our own political, social, economic, et cetera conditions. The conditions we experience have broken us apart and we need to be brought back together for our revival.

Ezekiel, a priest and prophet, had lived at a very crucial moment of Israel's history – in the heat of the Babylonian exile of ca 583 BC – before Jerusalem was finally destroyed. All the able-bodied Israelite men had been taken away to Babylon. The Jerusalem Temple had been torn down around 571 BC. The Davidic dynasty had been removed. Both politically and theologically, Judah had been crippled. In the midst of such great tragedy, Ezekiel prophesied – first as a prophet of doom and then as one of restoration. Ezekiel 37, part of which is the basis of this paper, is one of the prophecies of Ezekiel designated "hope, salvation or restoration oracles" (chs 33-39).

Even though, literally speaking, the world is not in exile and devastation as Judah was at the time, the afflictions, abuses, ailments, mental, social, religious and cultural diseases, which continue to gnaw at the fabric of our society, could easily be identified with the situation of the people of Judah. Our many bones have become "very dry", especially, in the face of HIV/AIDS. All and sundry in our world are either infected or affected by the disease and are as good as dead. Ron Russel-Coons, in the chapter on "The Church with AIDS" in Letty Russell's *The Churches with AIDS Renewal in the Midst of Crisis,* states this clearly: "We All

Are Living With AIDS" (1989:33). Yes, we are because if we have not been infected, we are definitely affected by it because our relatives, friends and other community members are infected or affected. As Ezekiel, in the valley of dry bones, no matter where we turn, to borrow the title of Cecil Williams' book, *There is no Hiding Place.* Ezekiel is caused to go round and round the valley as we all are going right now in the midst of the effects of the killer disease, AIDS. We can feel dryness in our own selves as well as all around us. The dryness is political, social, economic, theological and, in fact, in all aspects of our lives. This is so because as John Mbiti puts it, "I am, because we are; and since we are, therefore, I am" (1979:108-109). We are in a community, a universal global village, and dependent on one another. The question to ask again is, "Can these bones live?" If they can, then I submit there is the need for a prophet to be caused by *Yahweh* to cause these bones to come back to life.

The Valley of Dry Bones (Ezekiel 37:1-14)

Before we proceed with the conversation on hand, let us take a brief look at the story of Ezekiel's vision of the valley of dry bones. The hand of *Yahweh* brings Ezekiel by *Yahweh's* spirit into a plain strewn all around with dry human bones. Here Ezekiel is caused to have an overwhelming encounter with the power of death. The story is divided into two main parts. They are a vision (37:1-10) and its interpretation (vv. 11-14). In the first part of the vision, there is a prophetic summons, which causes the "very many" dejected, "dry bones," lying about "on the face of the valley" to join "a bone to its bone." Sinews or flesh come upon them and they form a very large community (vv 1-8). There is also the invitation of the *ruah Yahweh* to come into the bones and cause them to come to life (37:9-10). The second part of this vision is its interpretation, which is given to the prophet by *Yahweh.* It is presented as Israel's own lamentation of her predicament, "Our bones are dried and our hope is perished; we are *nigzarnu,* cut off to ourselves?" (v. 11b). This lament is met with *Yahweh's* hope-full response. This part of the oracle is made very dramatic by the vision of the former part. A final part can be identified, which has undertones of eschatology. This bit is a divergence from the pre-apocalyptic idea of death. The pre-apocalyptic idea held that death was central to Sheol, a place of shadowy half-existence of the dead. In the eschatological idea in Ezekiel, there will be a revival or restoration, in which there will be a future settlement in the land. The belief of the early rabbinical school in the resurrection from the dead is also promoted by Ezekiel's eschatological conclusion. *Yahweh* will be very instrumental in bringing this about and the people will come to "know - *wida'tem* - that *Yahweh* had spoken and had done." *Yahweh* speaking and doing generate newness, knowledge, which produces hope. This can be supported by Walter Brueggemann: "The newness from God is the only serious source of energy. And that energy for which people yearn is precisely what the royal consciousness cannot give" (1978:79). Furthermore, "The risk that must be run is because exiles must always learn that our hope is never generated among us but always given to us. And whenever it is given we are amazed" (ibid.). The initial and final decisions are *Yahweh's*.

HIV/AIDS can also be looked at along similar lines. There is a stage of utter hopelessness. Here both the affected and infected are devastated and have lost all hope, especially in the face of the accompanying stigmatization. There is another stage, which is that of concerned care giving. This takes the form of "comprehensive sex education and compassionate programs that enhance care initiatives through the active but critical support of the intervention programs that governments have drawn to stem the tide of the spread of HIV/AIDS" (Asante 1999:127). These can generate some peace even though the ultimate, which perhaps is the cure has not yet been discovered.

The passage in Ezekiel is supposed to be part of the Qumran texts in English of 4Q Pseudo-Ezekiel^b (4Q 386 4QpsEz^b). This Qumran text seems to start from the second part of verse 4 through 10 of Col. I (=4Q385 2) passage. It begins with *Yahweh's* imperative to Ezekiel, "And he said:

"prophesy over the bones ...] and a large crowd of men 10 [will rise and bless YHWH Sebaoth who caused them to live]" (Martinez 1996:287). The essence of the role the community can play is underlined here. First there is the need for the broken parts to be reunited before the spirit of *Yahweh* can come and enter them to bring about regeneration. As far as HIV/AIDS is concerned, there is the need for the entire global community to come to consensus and make conscious efforts to combat the disease. It is only when this has been done that there can be hope of healing or better revival.

Several expressions used to describe the gravity of the situation in the valley of dry bones produce the effect of absolute hopelessness. This vision occurring in *habbiq'ah* (the valley) or plain, carries the impression of absolute hopelessness. The situation in this valley is one of desolateness. The valley is *melia'h* (full). One would expect grass as the surface covering of the valley but it was covered by *rabboth meod* (very many) and *yibeoth meod* (very dry) *'asamoth* (bones) *sabbib sabbib* (all around). These "very dry" and "very many bones" paint the picture of a very vast parched emptiness. They are very effective in conveying the message of the seriousness of the predicament in which Judah was at the time. The exigency of the situation to which the prophet was to react instantly, is communicated by the use of causative verbs (hipils) and imperatives. Ezekiel says, "he made me to pass," "prophesy to these bones," "and say to them." God causes or issues commands, which Ezekiel had to carry out to bring the bones to life. From the onset, Ezekiel sees the disintegration of the bones as an irreversible phenomenon. The bones were arid. Their numbers were very great. They had died a long time ago. Their coming back to life is very slim. When he is questioned, "Can these bones live again?" he replies, "Lord you know." There is a sense of resignation here. Humanly speaking, it is impossible for the condition of the bones to be reversed. Judah's bleak future was portrayed in the dryness of their bones. The institutions, political power and the nation of Judah were dead (exiled). There was no suggestion as to their coming back to life or having a change in their situation. After all, Ezekiel had been familiar with the idea of Ecclesiastes 12:7, where in death, "dust returns to earth, and the spirit returns to God who gave it." Ezekiel's response reveals the status of the exiles as they see their own predicament. All the false hopes they had held had been shattered by their devastation and Ezekiel is called upon to act to instill hope into their condition. Their despair at their condition was very high but *Yahweh* was able to regenerate, reanimate and resurrect "the whole house of Israel" (v. 11a).

In the face of HIV/AIDS, there is a kind of exigency, a *kairos,* an opportune time that HIV/AIDS must be taken more seriously by following the command of God. We all are desperate. Our hopes of survival are shattered. There is no suggestion of a change in our circumstances. but even as *Yahweh* was able to do for the house of Israel so is he able to do in our situation. There is hardly any life in our bodies supported by our bones. However, God can turn around our situation and cause our dejected bones and demoralized systems to rise and receive new hope even as promised by I Thessalonians 3:16. Here restoration will be by God's own initiative without human participation. There is the impression that humans will be passive recipients of *Yahweh's* absolute benevolence. The image of restoration in this passage from Ezekiel is twofold. It is a resurrection from the dead and restoration from exile. HIV/AIDS also requires a twofold restoration. First there is the need for acceptance of the fact of the disease and then an acceptance of those infected and also those affected (those devastated by the disease). This acceptance on both levels will cause us to merit *Yahweh's* intervention in our situation.

The Hand (yad), Command ([wayy]'omer) and Spirit (ruah) of Yahweh

The indispensability of *Yahweh's* responsibility for the deliverance of Judah is seen in the activity of the hand *yad,* command *[wayy]'omer* and spirit *ruah* of *Yahweh.* The expression of the hand, *yad* and word, *[wayy]'omer Yahweh* had been used in the call of Ezekiel and (1:3 and 3:22,24) and also the spirit, which brings Ezekiel to attend to *Yahweh* in two earlier visions. These uses as well as the ones in 37:1-14 are characteristic for *Yahweh* from the creation. In all these instances, *Yahweh* always takes the initiative. In the passage in chapter 37, *Yahweh's* hand and spirit come on Ezekiel and make him rest in the very full valley of dry bones. The same cause him to pass all *sabib sabib,* round and round among them. Ezekiel's initial expression in this passage, "The hand of the Lord was upon me," is an expression characteristic of Ezekiel and is used to authenticate the extraordinary divine, ecstatic experiences in his life. This expression differs from the characteristic prophetic formula of, "Thus says the Lord" or "The word of *Yahweh* came to me". This suggests the prophet's passivity in the whole experience. *Yahweh's* divine hand was upon him to bring him to the scene of the lifeless bones and *Yahweh's* spirit causes him to pass among them over and over again. The word or command of *Yahweh* then causes the prophet to prophesy to the bones to bring them together before their regeneration. The language employed here of the hand of *Yahweh* and the activity of the *ruah Yahweh* seem to be drawn from the primitive prophetic traditions of the legends or sagas of the Former Prophets (1 Kings 18: 46; II Kings 3:15; I Kings 20:13,28-II Kings 5:8). The bones in this valley, which are dried up signify the people of Judah who have lost their will to survive. However, they are revitalized by the *ruah Yahweh* and are activated through the word of *Yahweh* addressed to the great community of the "whole house of Israel." The work of the hand, word and spirit of *Yahweh* bring to the fore what Jesus had said, "for without me ye can do nothing" (John 15: 5c). If we will be able to combat HIV/AIDS, we need to entrust God with all that we do.

Prophecies in Ezekiel 37:1-14

Three distinct commands are issued to Ezekiel, by *Yahweh*, to prophesy and each accomplishes a specific task. The initial command is to prophesy to the bones. This prophecy causes the bones to be joined together to each other and to be covered by flesh. This scene is very dramatic, if not melodramatic, for as Ezekiel prophesies, there is a great *ra'ash* "shaking" as the bones drew near and bone connected to its bone and flesh came up and spread over them. Even though Ezekiel prophesies here, his prophecy is still passive for he was to tell the bones to hear the word of *Yahweh*. In Ezekiel's own words, "So I prophesied as I was commanded." The picture painted here calls to mind the Psalmist's words, "Unless the Lord builds the house, those who build it labour in vain" (127:1) and the earlier, "Be still and know that I am the Lord" (46:10). Here Ezekiel is only a tool in the hands of *Yahweh*. In the face of the HIV/AIDS pandemic, we can only be tools in the hand of *Yahweh* to heal the devastating conditions in which we all find ourselves. There is the need to become available so that we can be used for healing the woundedness of others. As Henri Nouwen put it, we are

> Called to recognize the suffering of our time in our own heart and make that recognition the starting point of our service. Whether we try to enter into the dislocated world, relate to a convulsive generation, or speak to a dying person, our service will not be perceived as authentic unless it comes from a heart wounded by the suffering about which we speak (1990:xvi).

This statement of Nouwen's was initially directed at the minister and is contained in his book *The Wounded Healer: In Our Own Woundedness, We become A Source of Life for Others*. Ezekiel's experience can be equated to being wounded to be able to give life, which he does. In the face of HIV/AIDS, we too need to experience or put ourselves in the shoes of those infected or affected in order to be able to put life into their dryness, whether physical or spiritual. We too have been called "a chosen generation, a royal priesthood and a holy nation" (1 Peter 2:9) and must avail ourselves in bringing hope into the hopeless situation of HIV/AIDS.

The second of Ezekiel's prophecies follows the same pattern. This time he is to prophesy to the four winds to breathe upon the lifeless bodies to bring them to life and so regenerate them (v. 9). In this verse, another dimension is introduced. Here the spirit of *Yahweh*, after taking Ezekiel to the valley of dry bones (v. 1), is to be caused by Ezekiel's prophecy to animate human life (v. 5). The spirit, *ruah Yahweh*, is further made to revive the rejoined enfleshed bones by bringing the breath of life into them (v. 9). Thus the *ruah Yahweh* is employed on three different levels, of wind, breath and Spirit, to weave the text together. The power of the spoken word and the work of the *ruah Yahweh* go hand in hand to bring about regeneration. First, flesh is formed on the rejoined dry bones (vv. 4-8) and then the bodies are animated (vv. 9-10). This act is reminiscent of the patristic tradition of the formation of 'adam, from the dust of the earth and his being brought to life by *Yahweh* breathing the breath of life into his nostrils (Genesis 2:7). It is clear from this activity that only *Yahweh* can bring about regeneration. With HIV/AIDS destroying the fabric of our society, there is the need to be ready for the *ruah Yahweh* to activate our bodies and our society. There is the physical level, where we must avail ourselves for *Yahweh* to use us to instill hope, and then the spiritual level to be activated, not only once, but also continually by the *ruah Yahweh* to sustain the hope. To succeed in these, Setri Nyomi (the current General Secretary of the World Alliance of Reformed Churches (WARC) has this counsel to give:

> If we want our land healed and abundant life realized, then we have to repent. We have to repent where there is apathy in the church. We have to repent for having exclusive structures often worse than the structures in the secular society ..... We have to repent as individuals, as churches, as denominations, as national councils, as a continent-wide conference of churches, as leaders and members (1994:43).

This was part of his address on "Abundant Life in Jesus" at the All Africa Conference of Churches (AACC) Sixth General Assembly, under the Theme: "Vision and Hope." Even though this counsel encompasses the churches more than anything else does, it is apt for our situation in the midst of our devastation by HIV/AIDS. There is the need for repentance. Ezekiel does not know if the bones could live but in his humility – submitting to the command of *Yahweh*, he causes the bones to come to life. In our own repentance, we will be better placed to fight the HIV/AIDS pandemic and be sure of victory.

The final prophecy of Ezekiel's is in response to the lamentation of Israel regarding her devastation. It is also a prophecy of restoration to their land. Judah sees herself as a graveyard of very dry bones and *Yahweh* was going to reactivate them and bring about regeneration in their lives. In this vision, the imagery of dry bones shifts to *qibroth* "graves," which will be opened and the people "will be brought out of them." The sense of passivity is still strong here. This is endorsed by *Yahweh's* declaration, "And I shall put my spirit in you and you shall live. And I will put you in your own land. And you shall know that I, *Yahweh*, have spoken and have done it (vv. 12-14)." This expression is a rehashing of an earlier part of this prophecy (vv. 5-6), where the dry bones are rejoined, enfleshed and animated. The prophet Joel had earlier declared that the spirit of the Lord will be poured on all flesh and miracles will happen (2:28-32). Judah is seen as unable to create her own future, politically, theologically or socially. God must act in the situation. God was going to move and this movement was imminent and all nations were going to know Israel's God as Lord. A declaration that had been made earlier in the Former Prophetic material of 1 Kings 18:39b that "*Yahweh* he is Lord. *Yahweh* he is Lord" is reiterated here in Ezekiel 37:14.

Universality of Ezekiel's Message

The vision in Ezekiel 37: 1-14 takes on a universal character by speaking to a universal human experience. The message here was meant for the Jews in exile but it could be appropriated by later generations and in situations that are not quite similar. For this paper it is the situation of HIV/AIDS. This epidemic is a universal one and as such must be the concern of all and sundry. In the opening chapters of Ezekiel, one sees a typical ecstatic having bizarre inexplicable visions and declaring doom in the hopeless situation of the Jews. However, from chapters 33 to 39, Ezekiel is transformed into an instrument for bearing the message of *Yahweh's* unconditional forgiveness and restoration. In our AIDS infested situation, which held no hope at all, until quite recently, we are being called to advocate for, support and get involved in programs and activities that would help curb the devastation if not produce a cure. Walter Brueggemann's call is pertinent. For him,

> The task of prophetic ministry is to nurture, nourish and evoke a consciousness and perception alternative to the consciousness and perception of the dominant culture around us ... not primarily with addressing specific public crises but with addressing, in season and out of season, the dominant crisis that is enduring the resilient, of having our alternative vocation co-opted and domesticated.... The alternative consciousness to be nurtured serves to energize persons and communities by its promise of another time and situation toward which the community of faith may move ... lives in fervent anticipation of the newness that God has promised and will surely give.

There is the need to criticize and dismantle the dominant consciousness. The several myths that have surrounded HIV/AIDS, the socio-cultural, ethical challenges they pose and the laser faire attitude towards it, in society, must give way to a systematic awakening and conscious effort to fight the disease. All and sundry are invited to this task, which I may compare with part of the great commission of Jesus, "Go and teach all nations (Matthew 28:19a)." The prophet

Hosea also carries the message that "For lack of knowledge my people perish" (6:4). These are urgent calls for us to wake up, break away from the status quo and begin to educate our communities in the bid to combat HIV/AIDS. There is the need to appropriate the content of Jesus' own ministry on this earth. In Luke 4: 18-19 Jesus declares, "The Spirit of the Lord is upon me, because he has anointed me to bring good news to the poor. He has sent me to proclaim release to the captives and recovery of sight to the blind, to let the oppressed go free, and to proclaim the year of the Lord' favour." This short portfolio calls on us to strive at meeting the economic, sociological, physiological, political and theological needs of persons. We are being called upon, in the devastating face of HIV/AIDS, to become prophet–advocates for the downtrodden and abused. The call is for us to recognize that we deal with real people in particular locations, with their collective sense of history [herstory] and tradition. As such, even as Christ's ministry was not limited to any particular class, race, sex or condition, we too must endeavour to satisfy holistically all needs of God's people in whatever predicament. HIV/AIDS is no exception. Ezekiel's prophecy was indiscriminate and the effects of it, so. As such there is the need to be indiscriminate as the Bible admonishes in dealing with HIV/AIDS, which itself is indiscriminate in its action.

Conclusion

As I close the discussion on "HIV/AIDS and the Bible," I still want to lift up the question posed to Ezekiel, by *Yahweh*, "Can these bones live?" I will reply as Ezekiel did, "Lord, You know" but with reservation. A complete change of attitude, a mental reshuffle and a complete departure from the "dominant culture" are needed to handle the menace of HIV/AIDS. The creation of "an alternative consciousness" that moves the community toward faith in God and God's promise that will surely come to pass is needed. This must be coupled with an absolute dependence on the power of the hand, word and Spirit of *Yahweh* as displayed in Ezekiel chapter 37:1-14. These will be great resources in our fight against HIV/AIDS as far as the Bible is concerned. Above all, there is the need to embrace wholly all the members of our global village irrespective of status to be able to bring life and regeneration to the lifeless, hopeless situation created by the HIV/AIDS pandemic. Accepting every member would mean the humility of allowing us to be wounded by feeling what others feel, in order to heal them.

Bibliography

Asante, Emmanuel. (1999). *Stewardship Essays on Ethics of Stewardship*. Wilas Press.

Bosch, David J. (1992). *Transforming Mission: Paradigm Shifts in Theology of Mission*. Maryknoll, New York: Orbis Books.

Brown, Robert McAfee. (1987). *Kairos: Three Prophetic Challenges to the Church*. Grand Rapids, Michigan: Eerdmans.

Brueggemann, Walter. (1978). *Prophetic Imagination*. Minneapolis, U.S.A.: Fortress Press.

Buama, Livingstone K. (1993). *Christian Understanding of Human Existence*. Accra, Ghana: Compugraphics.

Costas, Orlando E. (1982). *Christ Outside the Gate: Mission Beyond Christendom*. Maryknoll, New York: Orbis Books.

Cunningham, Sarah. (1992). *We Belong Together: Churches In Solidarity with Women*. New York: Friendship Press.

WCC. (1997). *Facing AIDS: The Challenge, the Churches Response*. A WCC Study Document. Geneva: WCC.

Hollies, Linda H. (1992). *Inner Healing for Broken Vessels: Seven Steps to a Woman's Way of Healing*. Nashville: Upper Room Books.

World Bank. (2000). *Intensifying Action Against HIV/AIDS in Africa: Responding to a Development Crisis*. Africa Region. The World Bank.

Kendirim, Protus O. and Mercy A Oduyoye eds. (1998). *Women, Culture and Theological Education*. Enugu, Nigeria: SNAAP Press Ltd.

Martinez, Florentino Garcia. (1996). *The Dead Sea Scrolls Translated The Qumran Texts in English*. Leiden: E.J. Brill.

Mbiti, John S. (1979). *African Religions and Philosophy.* Nairobi: Heinemann.

Mutambirwa, Jane. (1994). "Indigenous Religion and Culture" *in Claiming the Promise: African Churches Speak.* Margaret S. Larom ed. New York: Friendship Press.

Nyomi, Setri. (1994). "Abundant Life in Christ: Vision and Hope" in *Claiming the Promise: African Churches Speak.* Margaret S. Larom ed. New York: Friendship Press.

Nouwen, Henri J.M. (1972). *The Wounded Healer: In Our Own Woundedness, We Can Become A Source of Life for Others.* New York: Image Books Doubleday.

Oduyoye, Mercy A. (1995). *Daughters of Anowa: African Women and Patriarchy.* Maryknoll, New York: Orbis Books.

Russell, Letty M. Ed. (1990). *The Churches With AIDS: Renewal in the Midst of Crisis.* Louisville: John Knox Press.

Stendal, Kristen. (1966). *The Bible and the Role of Women.* Philadelphia: Fortress Press.

Talbert, Ethelou. (1976). "Take Time" in *Images: Women in Transition.* Compiled by Janice Grana. Nashville, Tennessee.

Villarosa, Linda. Ed. (1994). *A National Black Women's Health Project Book: Body and Soul. The Black Women's Guide to Physical and Emotional Well-Being.* San Francisco: Harper Collins.

William, Cecil with Rebecca Laird. (1992). *No Hiding Place: Empowerment and Recovery for our Troubled Communities.* San Francisco: Harper Collins.

Part II

New Testament,
HIV/AIDS and Gender

Chapter Five

Talitha Cum! *A Postcolonial Feminist & HIV/AIDS Reading of Mark 5:21-43*

Musa W. Dube, Scripps College

Introduction: How Not to Stay Dead

Talitha Cum! The Markan writer explains that the phrase means, "Little girl, get up!" The story tells us that Jairus' twelve-year-old daughter was at the point of death. Her father comes to Jesus saying, "Please, come and put hands on her so that she may be made well and live" (v. 23). Jesus starts walking with Jairus to heal the sickly child. He could have, perhaps, arrived in time, save that a woman who had been bleeding for twelve years, one whose resources had been depleted by her search for healing, is determined to get her healing. She touches his garment silently from behind. Not only does she get healed, she gets Jesus to stop and listen to her tale of twelve years in search for healing. Meanwhile the little daughter dies. Jesus goes to Jairus' home, takes hold of her hand and says, "*Talitha Cum!*" And, as the story tells us, "immediately the girl got up and began to walk about!"

How would such a story read from the multiple levels of postcolonial, feminist and HIV/AIDS perspectives? There are, no doubt, many ways of reading any text. But more importantly each of the above-mentioned paradigms is a diverse field of methods and theories. Mine can only be a combination of some small aspect of each of the above paradigms. My exposition will be done first through providing a background of a narrative reading of the plot and setting of the story. While the analysis of characters will also come through in this section, it will largely be covered in all the other sections also. The narrative reading will therefore be brought to interact with the methodological narratives of postcolonial, feminist and HIV/AIDS frameworks. Yet the use of the postcolonial here denotes that my reading is both on and through the surface – that is, while I read narratively, I also assume a concrete history of the Roman Empire (Dube 2000:127-128). The paper, shall be asking the following questions, which largely serve as sub headings and shall be treated in their given order:

> ➢ 1st how does the setting and plot of the story read under a narrative lens?

> ➢ 2nd how does the story of Mark 5:21-43 read under a postcolonial lens?

> ➢ 3rd how does the story of Mark 5:21-43 read under a feminist perspective?

> ➢ 4th how does the story read in the HIV/AIDS epidemic?

While each framework is seemingly treated separately, this needs to be seen as a communication strategy, for they in fact intersect at many levels and on many issues. That is, the postcolonial, feminist and HIV/AIDS struggles share many assumptions, questions, concerns and categories of reading the text and reading the world for liberation. For example, the issues of gender, class, race, ethnicity, international relationships and other categories of analysis cut across the postcolonial, feminist and HIV/AIDS paradigms.

Before we look at the above individually, it is in order to explain why this particular combination is appealing or important for me. First, I could very well say, one of my major assumptions of *reading the text is that it is about reading the world, not only to understand it, but also to change it.* I should underline, to change it for the better. This methodological combination right now enables me to address some key issues of concern. The postcolonial allows me to probe our international relations of the past and present as well as to read for liberating international relations in our today's world, a factor that is essential for the HIV/AIDS era. The feminist perspective is central to any search for understanding oppression and the search for liberation for it deals with gender, a category of analysis that concerns and affects the construction of males and females, or just about all people regardless of their identity. Lastly, an HIV/AIDS reading. This epidemic was discovered in the past twenty-two years and has become a global crisis, which has now claimed at least 22m lives and infected about 40m within this short space of time (UNAIDS 2002:8-22). It has not only devastated the infected but has affected us all. It is therefore an undeniable imperative that all members of the earth community should wrestle with its reality. Asking what and how can the New Testament interpretation help us to understand and to deal with HIV/AIDS is a must. I have thus found myself struggling with the following questions "what is the contribution of New Testament studies towards healing the world in the HIV/AIDS era? How can the New Testament scholarship contribute towards HIV/AIDS prevention, quality care, access to affordable treatment, the breaking of stigma as well as to address social evils that fuel the epidemic? How does HIV/AIDS challenge us to extend our reading paradigms?" On these questions, I have described myself as more of a 'nomadic scholar', one who is inconstant move and search than a settled practitioner (Dube 2002a: 65-66).

My interest in undertaking this methodological framework is also informed by my social location, which exposes me to a sharpened awareness of international relations of the past and present; the identity of being a woman and all the joys and burdens that come with it; and the reality of living in the HIV/AIDS active zones. With these introductory remarks I begin by doing a brief narrative reading of the setting and plot of Mark 5:21-45, a story that has come to be affectionally known as the story of *Talitha Cum* among African women theologians.

Talitha Cum! *A Narrative Reading of the Plot and Setting of Mark 5:21-43*

A narrative analysis asks the question "how does the story mean?" (Malbon 1992: 24). In and through this question, the reader pays attention to the narrative rhetorical devices of conveying meaning such as plot, setting, characters, narrator, narratee, implied reader, repetition, juxtaposition, symbolism and irony. How these narratives devices are constructed is designed to persuade the reader to take certain perspectives and to distance themselves from other perspectives. In short, a narrative is not neutral; neither does it expect its reader to be neutral. If you are treated to a story, then you are also expected to respond to its worldview. The setting defines the place and the time where the narrative takes place, while plot defines the structural arrangement upon which the events or acts of the characters are arranged to give a particular effect.

Emergency journeys

The opening setting of the story is by the lake. Jesus has just landed in a new place, using a boat. He is surrounded by crowds. But then the story takes us on a journey from the open public space, by the lake, where Jesus is thronged by crowds, to a private space, Jairus' house, where Jesus restricts entry into the place where the sick, dying and dead child was laid. Here he calls, *"Talitha cum!"* and the child rises and begins to walk about. She must have walked out of her room or the place where she was laid, for crowds saw her and they were 'overcome by amazement' (v. 42).

Yet it is the time setting that punctuates this story, determining its tension, its pace and its climax. In a word, this time setting could be named as "an urgent and critical moment." It is Jairus, the synagogue ruler, who defines this time setting for us. He comes in desperation and pleads repeatedly: "My little daughter is at the point of death." He pleads with Jesus "to come and lay your hands on her, so that she may be made well and live." This is how urgent it is – it is a matter of life and death. The main difference lies with the arrival of Jesus in time to lay hands on her and give her the chance to live before death snatches her.

Jesus must have fully grasped the urgency of the time in Jairus' words and action. Without any word or question, he began to journey with Jairus towards the dying child. Basically, Jesus has received an emergency call. In our own modern days we may choose to hear the cry of and flashing lights of an ambulance as it slides past busy traffic and as every driver is obliged to make way for lifesavers, to give life a chance. Every second and minute count here. The reader who is invited to travel with Jesus and Jairus is aware of this emergency journey. This urgency adds to the pace of the story, for the reader is aware of the necessity for the plot to be fast forwarded towards Jairus' house – to save a life which is at the point of death.

But as the saying goes in such moments, "all that can go wrong, will go wrong," the urgent time is arrested. The plot is diverted. A woman comes from behind. It is not entirely wrong to see her behind the scenes' approach as a planned sabotage, for she had a plan. She is a woman who has been bleeding for twelve years, and she has sought out many doctors, who seemingly took her money, but did not deliver healing to her anaemic body. This woman will and does slow down the fast forward pace of the story. She interrupts the linear plot, by inserting her story into the story of Jairus and his dying daughter. In so doing, she does the unimaginable – she slows down and even stops Jesus from his emergency call.

While it is not entirely out of the way to see her as a hijacker, it is quiet possible that she may in fact have wished to respect this emergency call on Jesus. Indeed, the story says she had heard about Jesus (v. 27). But if she was among the crowds, she may have heard the plea of Jairus. It could be that she was also close enough to see the response of Jesus to the plea of Jairus; namely, that Jesus responded positively, by walking with Jairus right away towards saving a dying daughter from death. This woman, who had been searching for healing for twelve years, must have been struck by this sudden appearance of a sign of hope embodied by Jesus' response. That is, Jesus, a man who was only a few meters away from her, is going to heal a girl who is at the point of death. Surely, such a man can heal her too from her long and impoverishing ailment. She fully acknowledged the urgency in the walk of Jesus, Jairus and the accompanying crowds as they journeyed towards the dying daughter. But she could not let this moment pass. She could have decided, therefore, to try her luck silently and from behind the scene. This could have very well been her way of respecting the emergency journey of Jesus and Jairus.

With that, the bleeding woman began to push her way through towards Jesus. The story tells us that she said, "If I but touch his clothes, I will be made well" (v. 28). She touches and she is healed. But, if the woman had expected that her act would go unnoticed, she is out of luck. Even more seriously, Jairus and his daughter were now in a worse situation. Jesus is immediately aware that power had gone out of him. He stops; he turns and asks, "Who touched my clothes?" (v. 30). This question rightfully startled his disciples, given the crowd that is surrounding him, but perhaps given the emergency situation. They respond, "You see the crowd pressing on you; how can you say, 'who touched my clothes?'" (v. 33). Basically, they are saying, it is a ridiculous question. If the woman had expected the answer of the disciples to convince him, it did not. She was again out of luck. Jesus continued to search. As the narrator tells us, "he looked all around to see who has done it!" (v. 32). The woman realized that she could no longer hide from behind scenes. Much like Jairus, "she came in fear and trembling, fell down before him and told him, the whole truth" (v. 33).

The problem is that the 'whole truth was, most probably, a twelve year long story of her search for her healing. While Jesus is listening to her, we can feel the impatience of Jairus. Time is not on their side. His daughter is at the point of death. They really did not have time to listen to such a long tale. Jairus' worst fears are confirmed. Messengers from his house arrive and they say to him, "Your daughter is dead. Why bother the teacher anymore?" (v. 35). The girl is now outside the tick of time. She is late. The urgency that had so far propelled the plot forward, the journey towards Jairus' house, has been brought to a full stop. It was too late. They had lost all time. Hence they underline, 'Why bother the teacher?" (v. 35). The readers and the listeners expect the emergency journey to cease, for there is nothing as final as death.

Journeys of faith

But no, the journey forward continues. Jesus turns to Jairus and says, "Do not fear, only believe" (v. 36). They continue walking towards Jairus' house. At this point of the story, the time setting of urgency is shown to be limited. It has become clear that it is not the defining factor in the progress of the story. The reader/listener is rudely recalled to retrace her/his steps and forced to realize that much is not hanging on time, rather on faith. It was Jairus' faith that moved Jesus to travel with him to save his sick daughter. It was the woman's faith that made Jesus to stop and insist on asking, "Who touched me?" Indeed, in acknowledgement of her move, Jesus said, "Daughter, your faith has made you well; go in peace and be healed of your disease" (v. 34). And so at this time, precisely when the story has lost all time to save the dying girl, Jesus reminds and encourages Jairus to maintain the energy of faith. The story does not give us any hint on how Jairus responded. But it is clear; they walked together to his house. And so they arrive. They find the house in commotion, with loud mourners and wailers. This setting underlines that the daughter is dead. Yet Jesus poses a question to them: "Why do you make commotion and weep? The child is not dead, but sleeping?" (v. 39). His words could not have been further from reality. The mourning crowds, however, underline that the child is indeed dead, by laughing at Jesus. Death, they insist, cannot be equated to temporary sleep – it is final! The mourners are acting on real time while Jesus is operating on faith.

Jesus enters where the dead child is and takes her hand and says, "*Talitha cum,*" and immediately the girl got up and began to walk about (vv. 41-42). Much, if not all, is meant to highlight the character of Jesus. Thus the narrative presented him as swamped by a crowd, denoting his fame. The story has shown us both Jairus and the bleeding woman demonstrate incredible faith in the healing powers of Jesus. Jairus believes that Jesus can save a child who is about to die; while the bleeding woman believes that he can heal a twelve year old incurable disease. He can heal a disease that many doctors could not handle. The woman's expectations are fulfilled, but Jairus gets higher than what he had bargained for. That is, while he believed that Jesus could save his child from dying, Jesus actually returns her from death. The plot that began running on the time line of urgency came to run solely on faith. Why this shift? What is its function and meaning?

In his book, *The Art of Biblical Narrative*, Robert Alter argues that such changes are in fact pregnant with meaning and should not be glossed over (1981). In this story, the change is in fact an important narrative device in the characterization of Jesus. The reader notes that from the point where the child is declared dead, no other person speaks again, save for Jesus. On this axis of faith, where time is no more, Jairus remains silent, the mourners laugh, and then, I quote, "they were overcome with amazement" (v. 42), when they saw the dead girl walking about. The shift, therefore, moves the reader from the realm of human space of possibilities, where you rush to beat time, to an exceptional space of faith, where not only time is no more, but where the humanly impossible becomes possible. In this space the dead rise. Death is nothing but sleep to Jesus. For all its powerfulness – death does not have the final word. Jesus does. In this way, the characterization of Jesus moves from powerful to amazing, from human to divine. Here the plot comes to its height, featuring Jesus as the main actor and it naturally follows that everyone, the mourners, the readers and the listeners, are overcome by amazement (v. 42). They are called to move from living with the human possibilities to the realm of faith, where the impossible are possible.

From a theological point of view, and for postcolonial, feminist and HIV/AIDS concerns, it is this dwelling between death and life; this challenge to hear the call to arise from death; the invitation to walk in hope in the face stark hopelessness and this amazing act of actually rising from death that my paper seeks to explore. Given that postcolonial, feminist and HIV/AIDS are, after all, paradigms that are concerned with counteracting various forms of death dealing forces in relationships, how does this story interact with each of the above paradigms?

Talitha Cum! *A Postcolonial Story of Rising from the Dead*

But how would this story interact with the postcolonial framework? How can we read this story as a postcolonial narrative of resistance, collaboration and search for justice, the search for life against death dealing forces? They are, of course many different ways of doing postcolonial analysis (Sugirtharajah 1998; Dube 2000; Donaldson 1996; Segovia 2000). In this paper, my postcolonial assumption includes, first, acknowledgement of the historical reality of various forms of imperialism and colonialism through different times and places of the world as a phenomenon that characterizes our ancient and current world. Second, and coming to the text, the realization that the Markan narrative was written by a colonized group. It is therefore a postcolonial narrative, and thus it contains within it, seeds of resistance, which we must recapture. And, of course, the Markan narrative will also embrace collaboration, given the strength of the Roman Empire at that time and the patriarchal culture of its origin. My other assumption is that as readers we participate, intentionally or not, in reading for, against or in collaboration with, the empire as it appears in the story. We are not neutral readers. Lastly, that the ideological kernel in such narratives can and do work to endorse particular relationships of domination and oppression between the powerful and less dominating nations in today's world, hence the need for us to read not only as resisting feminist readers, but also as decolonizing feminist readers (Dube 1997).

Some of the questions that I sometimes put to the text to hold a postcolonial dialogue are as follows:

➢ Does this text have a clear stance against the political, cultural, and economic imperialism of its time?

➢ How are the readers reading the text – as colonizers, the colonized or collaborators?

➢ Does this text encourage travel to distant and inhabited lands? If so how does it justify itself?

➢ Which side of the text am I journeying as a reader? (Dube & Staley 2002e:8-9).

➢ Does this text use gender representations to construct relationships of subordination and domination? If so which side am I reading from – the colonized, the colonizer or the collaborator? If I read as a decolonizing reader, does this translate into a depatriarchalizing act or vice versa?

➢ How does imperialism affect women and men? (See Dube 2002a: 57).

To start with the historical context of Mark, scholarship agrees that Mark was written within the geographical boundaries of the Roman Empire (Powell 1998:40-50). The exact place remains inconclusive, but most debates oscillate between Rome (Follower of Paul) or Jerusalem (follower of Peter, the young man who ran naked). The time of Markan authorship is closely linked with the Jewish Roman war of AD 66-70, which destroyed the temple and Jerusalem. The debates also remain inconclusive on whether Mark was a gentile or Jewish Christian. Yet scholarship is generally agreed that Mark as a writer was not polished, he writes most as a less educated person, of low class. Possibly, his audience is also of low class (I Cor. 1:26-28). He is not, therefore, amongst the ruling class of the Roman Empire. Rather, the author and his community of believers live under the dominating power of the Roman Empire, which explicitly demonstrated its rule of suppression and domination through the Jewish Roman war of AD 66-70. Definitely, the Markan community included both gentiles and also Jews, people who were wounded by the violence of the Empire that brought to demise their central symbol of worship and through its demanding taxes. The advice that Mark gives in chapter 13 indicates an apocalyptic tone, which is a tone of resistance.

In Mark 5, where our passage is located, what comes through? Does the author present a narrative of the colonizer, that is, one who embraces the ideology of international domination and suppression? Does the author present a narrative of the colonized and collaborators? It is helpful here for us to take the literary context of the whole chapter into consideration. Prior to reading the story of the *dying* little girl and the bleeding woman, we begin with Jesus and his encounter with the demoniac of Gerasene, a gentile territory. The man comes from the tombs and begs Jesus to leave him alone. Jesus asks him, "What is your name?" And he answers, "My name is Legion, for we are many." Jesus casts out the spirit of Legion into a herd of swine grazing by and the spirit drives them into the ocean. Jesus is forced to leave the country of the Gerasenes. The subversive political tones of this story are evident. Legion was a term used for "a unit of the Roman army" (Dewey 1994: 481). "A full strength legion consisted of 6000 infantry, 120 cavalry and associated auxiliaries. The term legion might also be used for a battalion of 2,048" (Perkins 1995:584). The man is presented, therefore, as entered and possessed by the Roman imperial powers, that manifests themselves as demonic. "The demons have stripped this man of every shred of humanity" to the point where he was hurting himself (1995:538). What the story says, therefore, is that to be colonized is equal to being entered by evil spirits of the Legion and to be relegated to live among the dead – by the tombs. His physical address, as Tinyiko Maluleke (2002:554) points out, is at the grave yard. The narrative, therefore, highlights that being colonized is equal to being entered and possessed by the evil spirits of death. One co-habits with the dead. One's humanity is reduced to less than human as characterized by this man.

But even more importantly, the story presents Jesus as a liberator. The encounter of Jesus with the dominating powers of the empire makes them tremble, makes them feel threatened by a higher power. The Legion spirit recognizes the power of Jesus and begs to be accommodated somewhere, amongst the swine. Jesus effortlessly casts out the spirit of legion, the spirit of Rome, the evil spirit that has brought people to co-habit with death. Jesus therefore is presented as a powerful healer and political liberator. Jesus represents the dawn of God's kingdom. The Roman spirit of colonialism trembles in front of him. As Pheme Perkins points out, "An astonishing visual image results: As soon as Jesus steps into the Gentile territory, a legion prostrates itself. God's kingly power has subdued imperial domination" (1995:584). For Dewey, "drowning demons in the lake is a political allusion to the destruction of the Roman army of occupation" (1994:481).

But his acts of liberation are so amazing in the gentile country, the people ask Jesus to leave. How should we interpret their request? It underlines for us that once people are colonized they sometimes become collaborators and prefer to remain under their colonizer. In any case, this is how Jesus comes to land by the lake, where Jairus found him, with a large crowd that followed him.

In this story of the bleeding woman and the dying girl the first hint that the political agenda underlines the narrative is the use of gender to speak of imperial subordination and the search for liberation. This is best captured by the reference to the number twelve that is linked to both the bleeding woman and the dying/dead daughter. The woman has been sick for twelve years, and the girl is twelve years old. The number twelve is closely linked to the nation of Israel, going back to the twelve sons of Jacob, who were to constitute the twelve tribes of Yahweh or Israel. This Jesus, who has been fearlessly resisting the empire in a gentile land, is brought face to face with the bleeding woman in his own homeland – a woman who has been seeking healing endlessly. He is brought face to face with the twelve year old dying daughter, whose father believes she will live if Jesus comes and lays hands on her.

If we are agreed that this figure of twelve that sandwiches the stories is a statement about the national situation of Israel, then we have come face to face with use of gender to articulate relationships of subordination and resistance. We would have to see and read Israel, where it speaks of the bleeding woman and where it speaks of a dying girl child. The statement made here is that Israel is a desperate bleeding woman, one who has lost all her funds in search for healing. Israel is a young girl who is at a point of death. The situation of Israel is thus pretty much of one desperately in search for healing and for life. Her exploitative doctors have exploited her to her very depth. Bleeding has made her, much like the Gerasene demoniac, unclean. Similarly the young girl, much like the demonic who lived by the tombs, was closer to death than life. In general, "we find that in Mark five each episode is more radical political and religious depth" (Dewey 1994: 480).

The good news, however, is that such a story of imperial oppression need not continue. Jesus is the healer, the liberator. I would not hesitate that within the literary context of Mark five and the historical context of Markan writing, this story is definitely a story of resistance. It is the story of the colonized, the chained, the bleeding, the unclean (because they have been entered by a foreign and evil power) and the dying. The narrative insists the empire has not and will not have the last word. Hope for liberation is embodied in Jesus' acts of casting out legion, healing the sick and bringing the dying back to life. Hope for liberation lies in the oppressed pushing and pressing for power. It lies in the dead rising to life. The text insists the power of the empire cannot stand in front of Jesus the liberator. Mark writes then as a colonized subject who occupies a resisting stance against the empire. Indeed, it has been noted that, "Mark's story was first told among 'unofficial people' who delighted in that it said nothing good about officialdom – Roman, Jewish or apostolic faith" (Thurston 1998:66-67).

The question that we need to ponder here is why the colonized Israelite nation is pictured as a woman? Would such an ideological stance empower women or endorse their position of powerlessness? Elsewhere, I have argued that

that narrative of colonial dominance and resistance tend to use the woman's body to articulate their agenda of domination, but that whenever such metaphors are used the subordination of women is also embraced (Dube 2000:117). First, one may say it is gratifying, perhaps, that this perspective of using women to symbolize oppression is to some extent counteracted by the presentation of the Gerasene Demoniac. But one may well say, he represents the empire, while the bleeding woman and the dying girl represents the subjugated, the colonized. To some extend the Markan narrative, therefore, highlights that imperialism is oppressive to both men and women in the colonized zones. The colonized people come to co-exist with ill health and to walk too closely to death. However, the gender ideology encapsulated in the story inadvertently subscribes to the subordination of women, as many postcolonial national activists have tended to do – that is argue for 'first things first,' which means that the struggle for liberation from imperialism was/is given priority over the feminist struggle for gender empowerment. The fact that a colonized nation is identified as a sick woman, who needs healing, underlines that the narrative rises from a patriarchal society, where land is equated to women's bodies. It also indicates that while colonization is not tolerated, patriarchy is largely accommodated. This, I believe, underlines the need for a feminist analysis of the story that seeks to scrutinize gender construction encapsulated by this story as well as search for the signs of hope, the touch point that allows us to escape the deadly disease of gender and colonial/globalization/international oppression.

Talitha Cum! *A Feminist Story of Rising from Death*

When we do a narrative gender analysis of a story, we ask how men and women are characterized and why. We examine if they are named and what their social roles are. We examine what they say and what they do not say and if they are major or minor characters. We ask how this characterization reflects gender ideology. Turning to the setting and plot of the narrative, we examine where women and men are found, when and how this is related to gender construction. Feminist readings also make efforts to re-read the story for gender empowerment of men and women. I now turn to Mark 5:21-43 and apply some of these questions to the text to examine the gender constructions and the possibilities of a feminist re-interpretation. I begin by identifying all the women who appear and give them a gender-feminist analysis from narrative point of view.

There are three women who are singled out in the story: the bleeding woman, the dying child and her mother. Possibly, there were other women amongst the crowd and the mourners (Dewey 1994:481) in Jairus' house. If we scrutinize these women, we find that they are not named. Two of them are named after their ailments, while the other one is identified as the mother of the child, and by extension the wife of Jairus. None of them holds a public social role. Both the daughter and the mother are found in the gendered space of the home. The best social power that these two may enjoy is that of being identified with the synagogue ruler, Jairus.

The bleeding woman, on the other hand, is found in the public space, in the midst of a thick crowd, where she ought not to be, given her status of bleeding. As Bonnie Thurston notes, the bleeding "woman is marginalized on four counts: she is female, without a male relative to be her advocate, without financial resources and she is subject to blood taboo" (1998:71). She breaks the rule of ritual cleanness, perhaps because of her desperation, her poverty and the fact that her illness means that she could not marry.

Turning to what these women do and say, we note that the mother and the daughter never said a word. Jairus speaks for them and Jesus speaks to the dead girl. In terms of her deeds, the mother is best imagined as a nurse, one who was taking care of a dying child, but she never speaks a word. The daughter's action – in fact, if we could relegate this to action – she is dying and she in fact successfully dies. She also hears the voice of Jesus, wakes up and starts walking around. But she never speaks.

Turning to the bleeding woman, she acts, by deciding to come behind Jesus, to touch his garment in order to get well. She certainly did not ask for permission, but hoped that she would escape unnoticed. She took it upon herself to get healed, thereby subverting cultural barriers that did not allow her to come out in the open and interact with people given her health status, for she was unclean. When Jesus begins to search for the person who touched him, she comes forward, although in fear and trembling, and tells her story. These acts characterize her.

If we have a close look at what she says, we find that her words are recorded as internal, thoughts. First the narrator tells us that she reached for Jesus for she said, "If I but touch his clothes, I will be made well." But these are words that are never verbalized openly. The second opportunity for her to speak openly was when she comes forward to tell her story. But here again the narrator reports to us that she told Jesus the 'whole truth.' What that truth entailed, remains unspoken to us. At the end, the bleeding woman is largely silenced. She is not allowed to speak out in direct speech by the author of the narrative. Perhaps, we could say even her act of reaching out for healing from behind was squarely within the gendered frameworks of keeping a low profile and silence.

Turning to the men in the narrative, we have Jesus, Jairus, Peter, James, John, and those who are in the crowds, messengers and some among the mourners. Notable here is that those men who are singled out are named. Second, if we look at their social status, we find that Jesus is a famous healer who is thronged by crowds. He is surely prophetic, for he knows when he has been touched to draw power from him. Jairus is a synagogue leader, while Peter, James and John hold the social status of being the disciples of a famous teacher – those who are privileged to have the secrets of the kingdom, Mark 4. And by virtue of being disciples of such a teacher, one day they will be as good as him, or even better!

Turning to what the men in the story say and do, it is proper to start with Jairus. He comes to Jesus and falls at his feet and speaks to him and asks for the healing of his daughter. The direct words of Jairus are reported. Jairus speaks openly. But it is when we compare what Jairus says and does with the bleeding woman that the gender disparities become evident. First, we acknowledge that they were both in need of healing from Jesus. But we note the differences in their approach. While Jairus comes out openly, goes straight on to Jesus, and verbally articulates his need, the bleeding woman does the opposite. She secretly comes from behind, does not say a word to Jesus, and rather prefers silently to get her healing without being noticed. It is only when she is thoroughly searched out, and perhaps fearing to be caught, that she comes out in fear and trembling to identify herself.

Turning to Jesus, he seems to do a lot, which has prompted such a crowd to follow him. The sample of his deeds is highlighted for us in two healing miracles that he performs. In fact he even has power over death. Jesus speaks. He feels free to say someone has touched him, even when most people thought the question was quiet ridiculous. He feels free to tell Jairus that he should not fear when his daughter is declared dead. He feels free to look at wailing and weeping mourners and say an amazing thing: "Why do you make a commotion. The child is not dead but sleeping." He is free to say to a dead girl, "*Talitha Cum.*" In all the four occasions in which Jesus speaks, his words closely correspond with the plot and the setting: they depict him as well above the normal human being. He has divine character or, to go with that Markan characterization, amazing power.

Turning to his disciples, we see that they travel with him. The very fact that they are his disciples means that they have the privilege to learn from him and to gain his skills (Mark 4:34). Hence when they reached Jairus' house they had the privilege to come with Jesus where the dead girl was sleeping. We see the disciples are free to articulate themselves. When Jesus begins, saying, "Who touched my clothes?" they freely say it is a ridiculous question given the crowd that is pressing around Jesus.

Clearly, a gender analysis indicates sharply gendered females and males in the story. If the women characters are saved, it is not without the gender confines. Can this story be used for gender empowerment, beyond exposing apparent gender inequalities? On the latter, many feminists' interpretations of this text speak for themselves. Teresa Okure holds that "the woman had one great assert, namely, her determination to be cured and to take her rightful place in the society. It was this determination which led her to brave the crowd and find her way to touching Jesus" (1992: 227-8). J. Dewey holds that she "claims healing and takes it for herself, without permission from anyone, violating taboos by being in public" (1994:481). Bonnie Thurston commends her for breaking "both social custom and ... blood taboo" (1998:71). For Pheme Perkins "the woman is a hero of persistence and faith" (1995:590). For Mary Ann Tolbert, "her healing occurs completely at her own initiative" (1992:268). Moreover, for many feminists her independent move is further endorsed by the response of Jesus. Okure holds that Jesus "brought her forward, made her a public figure, called her daughter, and sent away in peace" (1992:229). Thurston notes that Jesus "speaks to the woman in a public place" and "calls her 'daughter', including her as a kinswoman" (1998: 71). Dewey takes it a step further, holding that "her action may have helped the Markan Jesus to free himself from the patriarchal assumptions and male privilege of ancient culture" (1994:482).

It is important for the feminist interpretations to interrogate themselves concerning both the patriarchal and colonial ideologies embedded in this story. First, the story identifies the land with women. The question to ask is will the healing of Israelites from Roman Imperial oppression become the healing of gender relations among the Israelites? History suggests not. Second, what is problematic, however, is that most feminist interpretations focus on gender issues and empowerment to the exclusion of oppressive international relations that are addressed by this story. Women of the world are, however, sickened by both colonial and patriarchal system. And women will remain oppressed as long as feminists address patriarchy to the exclusion of imperialism/colonialism/globalization, or the prevailing unjust international relations. A postcolonial feminist approach is, therefore, imperative.

Talitha Cum! *A Story of African Women Rising From Death*

It is undeniable that this story has been central to the theology of African women to a point where, perhaps, if there is name that can be given to African women's theology, then it could be named the *Talitha Cum* theologies – referring both to the rise of the bleeding woman to health and the dead girl's rise to life. Mercy Oduyoye, who is rightfully the mother as African women's theology, has named her women's center after this story, *talitha cum*. Indeed, three books of African woman theologians have repeatedly been named after the story of Mark 5:21-43. The first one to be published in 1992 was called *The Will to Arise: Women, Tradition and The Church in Africa*. The second one, which consisted of conference proceedings, published in 1990, is named *Talitha Cum*. The latest to be published in 2001 also honors the bleeding woman again, taking on the title of *Talitha Cum! Theologies of African Women*. Perhaps too many African women have frequently walked too close to death – the death of living under various colonizing powers, of living under various patriarchal powers, of living under poverty, disease, war. Perhaps. Perhaps not. Perhaps it is also the stubborn hope that rises in hopelessness, the reaching out, the touching, the rising from colonial and patriarchal diseases and death, the rising against various forces of death that remain the highlights of this story for many African women theologians.

I have to confess to having paid many and long visits to the bleeding woman and the rising daughter of Mark 5:21-43. I have held many long talks and walks with the bleeding woman. I have tried to listen carefully to her unspoken story. I have found myself fascinated by her untold story of bleeding for twelve years. I have been fascinated by the nameless doctors who subjected her lot of suffering, took her money and left her in a worse health condition than when they first met her. I have tried to retell her story as the story of Africa and African people and their various encounters with many different colonizing powers (Dube 2001a:50-60). I can remember how the *talitha cum* story accompanied me to Oslo for the Diakonia International Day,[1] and to Johannesburg for the World Student Christian Fellowship (WSCF) women's meeting.[2] I have traveled with the bleeding woman and the dying and the rising daughter, trying to make their stories my stories and the story of the Africa and African women, struggling against various forms of colonial and patriarchal oppression, as well as finding the courage to rise.

However, at times I have found myself quite irked by the fact that both the bleeding woman and the dying daughter are at the end of the day presented as weak women, who are saved by men. This has brought me, not only to underline the initiative of the bleeding woman, but to also do some retelling, where Jesus even losses his power of calling *"talitha cum."* The power to call the dead/dying back to life is sometimes transferred to a woman figure (Dube 2001b:5). Of late, the idea of confronting an incurable disease that totally exhausts all individuals' and family funds while patients get worse – one that travels through various other social epidemics; one that earns the sick intensified stigma – and then the idea of hope that arises out of what is seemingly a hopeless situation, have once more prompted a few revisits to this story in the light of HIV/AIDS (Dube 2001c), which brings me to the last part of my paper, the reading of Mark 5:21-43 from a postcolonial feminist HIV/AIDS perspective.

Talitha Cum! *An HIV/AIDS Story of Rising from Death to Life*

Twenty-two years into the HIV/AIDS epidemic, it is now known that it is an epidemic within other social epidemics of poverty, gender inequality, violence, international injustice, discrimination on the basis of age, race, ethnicity and sexual orientation (UNDP 2000:26-37). Any individual, community or group of people who are denied their human rights become more vulnerable to infection, to lack of quality care and to lack of access to available drugs. It has become more acknowledged that HIV/AIDS is not simply about individual morality. Rather it is also about social injustice, which denies people the right to have access to information, and when they have access, it denies them the right to make choices and take decisions that protect them or enables them to live longer. HIV/AIDS is also about international injustice. It is about globalization, which increasingly makes social welfare services such as health and education privatized, commercialized and unaffordable; and globalization, which creates job insecurity and separation of families as people go searching for jobs. Globalization also intensifies the feminization of poverty and gender relations, for patriarchal traditions and religions feel threatened (Garba & Garba 2000:24-27). "Globalization as an anti-social force worsens poverty, escalates mobility, encourages the trafficking of women and girls and sex work, thereby creating fertile grounds for the spread of HIV/AIDS" (Dube 2002b: 536). HIV/AIDS is also about unjust international relations that have reduced some countries' economic viability to non-existence; it is about refusal to allow countries in the Two-Thirds World the copyright permission to produce affordable drugs for managing HIV/AIDS opportunistic infections. HIV/AIDS is about unequal gender relations that render many women unable to insist on safer sex, to abstain or to be protected by faithfulness. It is also about the powerlessness of children, who are subjected, by some, to sexual abuse, stigma and labor exploitation, when orphaned. It is also about stigma, the discrimination of the infected and their families. HIV/AIDS is also about racism that underpins many of these decisions. HIV/AIDS is about civil wars that promote the use of rape against women and which render social welfare services inoperative. In sum, the mating ground for HIV/AIDS is in the social evils that are allowed to breed in our backyards. But it is good to remind ourselves that HIV/AIDS is a preventable and manageable epidemic if we address the

social evils that sponsor it. A postcolonial feminist HIV/
AIDS reading of Mark 5: 21-43, therefore, seeks to examine
the meeting points of international relations, gender
inequalities and HIV/AIDS struggles in order to tell a new
narrative of rising from death.

Reading the Mark 5:21-43 Story with the Story of HIV/AIDS

When one reads the story of Mark 5:21-43 together with
the story of HIV/AIDS, one finds many similarities. One
finds the equation of international injustice/colonialism to
a disease that sickens the oppressed. This is because those
who are under economic and political oppressions are not
able to run effective health services and economies. They
are not able to use their resources for the well being of
their citizen. One also finds patients/nations that have been
sick for a long time – patients/nations that have spent all
they had searching for healing, but instead of getting better
they got worse. The readers find patients/nations that are
highly stigmatized and regarded as unclean by other nations
due to their ill-health. One also finds qualified physicians,
who have attended the sick, received their money but could
not heal them – instead they made them worse.

The reader is struck by the sick and dying young people/
nations. Desperate parents/social leaders, who are trying
to find healing for their children/nation characterize this
story. Nations are weeping aloud for their dying children.
The reader finds the sick and poor women/nations and
children, who have no right to speak. The reader is struck
by women care-givers, who are sitting at home, silently
watching over their sick children and waiting for help to
come until their children die. If the number twelve
represents international/colonial-subjugated nation, then
postcolonial feminist readers, like me, are struck but their
own history of colonialism, neo-colonialism and
globalization, which has brought them to co-habit with
disease and death. The story sounds too familiar.

But perhaps what is important is the difference that Jesus brings. As a liberator Jesus brings healing. He casts Legion out of a possessed and demonized and diseased man into the swine. Burdened exploited and sick nations can touch Jesus. While international exploitation has brought people to live too close to death: to live in sickness and stigmatization, Jesus brings one into a new family, where the exploited and oppressed are welcomed as daughters, rather than being stigmatized and excluded for their bleeding condition. The difference that Jesus brings to a situation of desperation has to do with the fact that he brings hope in hopelessness by his willingness to be in solidarity with the suffering in their search for healing. That is, while the bleeding woman had searched for twelve years without any healing, she is suddenly healed and restored to the community/liberation as a daughter. Hope is restored as Jesus says to a fearful parent, "Do not fear, only believe." Indeed, hope is restored when Jesus makes those who mourn to laugh. Jesus, therefore, makes a big difference by defying the death dealing forces of both colonial and patriarchal oppression that attacks the physical, spiritual and social body. He calls a dead little girl to life and she rises and starts walking about! This is liberation – liberation that breaks the bonds of patriarchal and colonizing international relations.

The challenge here is: how can New Testament readers and Christians stand in the narratives of postcolonial, feminist and HIV/AIDS search for justice and healing the world? How can they walk and empathize with those who are invaded by HIV/AIDS and pronounce hope and life in the midst of despair and death? How can their relationship with Jesus, as individuals and communities, as academicians and churches, become a point of breaking the bonds of death (colonial, patriarchal and HIV/AIDS exploitation and oppression) and bring healing? While I have no particular formula to give, what I definitely know is that this is a fitting duty for all of us who live in the HIV/AIDS era and who read for healing and liberation. That is, it should be a central part of our learning, living, researching, writing and teaching as the academy (Dube 2002d: 121-133) and also as communities of faith (Dube 2002b: 535-549) to bring hope, healing, liberation and life to a world that is often overshadowed by death. If a reader does not necessarily live in the HIV/AIDS hot zones one must still ask how patriarchy and the unjust international relations of their particular countries and regions contribute to the ill health of those nations and individuals who are sick in other countries and nations. One must ask how the economic and political policies of their country have led to bleeding and death of many nations, who need the healing touch of justice. But even more importantly, one must struggle with how they can take the challenging role of calling, *"talitha cum!"* to the dying and the dead in the age of HIV/AIDS epidemic.

Endnotes

1.   See Musa W. Dube, "Twenty-two Years of Bleeding," the last chapter in this volume.

2.   See *Talitha Cum!* Calling the Girl Child and Women to Life in the HIV/AIDS & Globalization Era," a paper that was first presented in to the WSCF women's pre-assembly meeting, in Johannesburg, February, 12-13, 2002 and which has appeared in Isabel Phiri et. al, *African Women, HIV/AIDS and Faith Communities.* Pietermaritzburg: Cluster Publications, 2003.

Bibliography

Alter, Robert. (1981). *The Art of Biblical Narrative.* San Francisco: Harper Collins.

Garba, Abdul-Ganiyu & Kassey P. Garba. (1999). "Trade Liberalization, Gender Equality and Adjustment Policies in Sub-Saharan Africa," pp.7-40. In Yassine Fall ed. *Africa: Gender, Globalization and Resistance.* New York: AAWord.

Dewey, Joana. (1994). "The Gospel of Mark," pp.470-509. In Elisabeth Schüssler Fiorenza ed. *Searching the Scriptures Volume 2: A Feminist Commentary.* New York: Crossroad.

Donaldson, Laura. Ed. (1996). *Semeia 75: Postcolonialism and Scriptural Reading.* Atlanta: SBL.

Dube, M.W. Ed. (2003). *HIV/AIDS and the Curriculum: Methods of Mainstreaming HIV/AIDS in Theological Programmes.* Geneva: WCC.

_____ (2000). *Postcolonial Feminist Interpretation of the Bible.* St Louis: Chalice Press.

_____ (1997). "Towards a Postcolonial Feminist Interpretations of the Bible." *Semeia* 78, 11-23.

_____ (2001a). "Fifty Years Of Bleeding: A Storytelling Feminist Reading of Mark 5:24-43," pp. 50-62. In Musa W. Dube ed. *Other Ways of Reading: African Women and The Bible.* Atlanta: SBL.

_____ (2001b). "Introduction: Little Girl Get Up," pp. 3-24. In Nyambura Njoroge & Musa W. Dube, eds. *Talitha Cum: Theologies of African Women.* Pietermaritzburg: Cluster Publications.

_____ (2002a). Re-reading the Bible: Biblical Hermeneutics and Social Justice, pp. 57-68. In Emmanual Katangole ed. *African Theology Today: Volume 1* Scraton: The University of Scraton Press.

_____ (2002b). "Theological Challenges: Proclaiming the Fullness of Life in the HIV/AIDS & Global Economic Era." *International Review of Mission* 91, 535-49.

_____ (2002c). "Villagizing, Globalizing, and Biblical Studies," pp. 41-64. In Justin Ukpong, Musa Dube *et al. Reading the Bible in the Global Village.* Atlanta: SBL.

_____ (2002d). "Healing Where There is No Healing: Reading the Miracles of Healing in an AIDS Context," pp. 121-133. In Gary Phillips & Nicole W. Duran eds. *Reading Communities Reading Scripture: Essays in Honor of Daniel Patte.* Harrisburg: Trinity Press International.

Dube, M. W. and J. Staley. (2002e). "Descending From and Ascending into Heaven: A Postcolonial Analysis of Travel, Space and Power in John," pp. 1-10. In Musa W. Dube & Jeffrey Staley eds. *John and Postcolonialism: Travel, Space and Power.* Sheffield: Sheffield Academic Press.

Malbon, Elizabeth Suthers. (1992). "Narrative Criticism: How does the Story Mean?" pp. 23-49. In Janice Capel Anderson & Stephen Moore eds. *Mark and Method: New Approaches in Biblical Studies.* Minneapolis: Fortress Press.

Maluleke, T.S. (2002). "Bible Study: The Graveyard Man, The Escaped Convict and The Girl-Child: A Mission of Awakening, An Awakening of Mission." *International Review of Mission* 91:550-57.

Oduyoye, M.A. Ed. (1997). *Talitha Cum!* Ibadan: Daystar Press.

Oduyoye, M.A. & Musimbi Kanyoro. Eds. (1992). *The Will to Arise: Women, Tradition and the Church in Africa.* Maryknoll: Orbis.

Okure, Teresa. (1992). "The Will to Arise: Reflections on Luke 8:40-56," pp. 221-230. In Mercy Oduyoye and Musimbi Kanyoro eds. *The Will to Arise: Women, Tradition and the African Church.* New York: Orbis.

Perkins, Pheme. (1995). "Mark," pp.507-734. In *The New Interpreters Bible.* Nashville: Abingdon.

Powell, Mark Allan. (1998). *The Gospels: Fortress Introduction.* Minneapolis: Fortress Press.

Segovia, Fernando. (2000). Decolonizing *Biblical Studies: A View from the Margins.* Maryknoll: Orbis.

Stoller, Paul. (1995). *Embodying Colonial Memories: Spirit Possession, Power and the Hauka in West Africa.* New York: Routledge.

Sugirtharajah, R. S. Ed. (1998). *The Postcolonial Bible.* Sheffield: Sheffield Academic Press.

Thairu, K. (2003). *The African and the AIDS Holocaust: A Historical and Medical Perspective.* Nairobi: Phoenix Publishers.

Thurston, Bonnie. (1998). *The Women in the New Testament: Questions and Commentary.* New York: Crossroad.

Tolbert, Mary Ann. (1992). "Mark," in *The Women's Bible Commentary.* Knoxville: Westminster Press.

UNAIDS. (2002). Report *on the Global HIV/AIDS Epidemic.* Geneva: UNAIDS, 2002.

UNDP. (2000). *Botswana Human Development Report 2000: Towards and AIDS-Free Generation.* Gaborone: UNDP & Botswana Government.

Chapter Six

John 9: Deconstructing the HIV/AIDS Stigma

Malebogo Kgalemang, University of Botswana

> It is now common knowledge that in HIV/AIDS, it is not
> the condition itself that hurt most (because many other
> diseases and conditions lead to serious suffering and
> death), but the stigma and the possibility of rejection
> and discrimination; misunderstanding and loss of trust
> that HIV positive people have to deal with.[1]
>
> *(Rev. Canon Gideon Byamugisha)*

Introduction

HIV/AIDS is a disease that really took most of us by surprise
and shock. The first time I heard about the disease was
about 14 years ago over the local radio station. I was still
very young, maybe, about 12 years old. I never really took
seriously the broadcast about the disease, its spread, its
effects, its affects and its dangers. It sounded so distant. It
was alien and foreign, for it had been discovered somewhere
far in the West. It was not a disease that I could care much
about, let alone understand what it was about. Of course, I
knew about sex, about lovemaking, dating, boyfriends and
girlfriends, because by then I was at my adolescence stage
and I grew up reading Mills and Boons, Comics which talked
about love, sex, and heterosexual relationships. Before long
somebody I knew died of the disease. He had been studying
abroad. When he came back home, he just worked for a
short while and later died because of the disease. Somehow,

I was made to believe that it is a disease that comes from the West. I was wrong; for it began to affect everybody even people who had never set a foot in an aeroplane, or who had gone overseas to study. My own construction about HIV/AIDS as something foreign, alien and distant and from western countries had been proved false.

But HIV/AIDS did not just come alone; it brought with it a package labeled STIGMA. Stigma has been part and parcel of HIV/AIDS and an epidemic too, which unfortunately hinders both prevention and care. We need to ask ourselves; why are people living with HIV/AIDS stigmatized? Why do we think about members of stigmatized groups the way we do? What functions does stigmatization in general and beliefs about the stigmatized or the HIV/AIDS in particular or the larger social unit play? How does stigma have an impact on the people who have already been marginalized? Is stigma a natural phenomenon? God created or is it a product of human thought? What does stigmatization entail? What role does it play in the society? And, do we have any biblical concepts on the issue of stigma and disease? What does the bible say to us concerning stigma and disease?

While this essay seeks to explore some of the above questions, it also seeks to deconstruct the ideology of stigma. Deconstruction is a method or a strategy of reading that seeks to "decenter, un-structure, de-construct, de-stabilize and un-settle, better undoing and decomposing" (2000:55) that which has been constructed to be central and normal. When we deconstruct, we identify points of failure in a system, points at which the system is able to feign coherence only by excluding and forgetting that which it cannot assimilate, that which is "other" to it (*Postmodern Bible* 1995:122). Deconstruction as a method of criticism makes explicit what is hidden, repressed, or denied in any ordinary reading and it confuses and undercuts the binarism of non-stigmatized and stigmatized; it will also help to show how stigma is a strategy for constructing and regulating power relations and to show how in stigma who has been given the authority to speak and to dictate. Thus it poses a serious challenge to constructions of stigma. Using deconstruction, I seek to identify points of failure in the system and construction of stigma, I seek to dismantle the structure of stigma and show how it was put together in the first place. Deconstruction in relation to exegesis opens up a perspective that can provide a new dimension to existing insight. I shall ask what does the construction of stigma leave out? What does it repress? The essay shall seek to expose and deconstruct stigma by following the outline below:

1. Defining Concepts of Stigma
2. Defining HIV/AIDS Stigma
3. Highlighting the Gendered Face of HIV/AIDS Stigma
4. Discussing the Impact of Stigma of HIV/AIDS on the Infected and Affected People
5. Highlighting how John 9 deconstructs the stigma that associates illness/ill-health with sin/curses from God

Definition and Concepts of Stigma

Under the above sub-heading, definitions and concepts about stigma will be thoroughly discussed with reference to the following questions. Why are people living with HIV/AIDS stigmatized? Why do people think about members of stigmatized groups the way they do? What functions does stigmatization in general and beliefs about the stigmatized or the HIV/AIDS in particular, have for the individual or the larger social unit.

In the opening of his book entitled *Stigma*, Erving Goffman states that the Greeks used the term stigma to refer to "bodily signs designed to expose something unusual and bad about the moral status of the signifier. These signs were cut or burnt onto the body and hence advertised that the bearer was a slave, a criminal, or a traitor – a blemished person, ritually polluted, or to be avoided, especially in public places" (1964:11). In agreement with Goffman, Robert M. Page says that stigma dates back to the Greek word for "tattoo-mark," which was a brand made with a hot iron and impressed on people to show that they were devoted to the services of the temple or, on the opposite spectrum of behavior, that they were criminals or runaway slaves (1984:2). These marks were used somehow to expose infamy or disgrace of people who had sinned against society and God. The marks were bodily signs that called attention to some moral failing on the part of the person bearing them and often involved a sense of moral disapproval, denigration and avoidance. Today stigma is more associated with the "opposite spectrum of behavior" (1984:2) that is those who are stigmatized are people who supposedly have sinned or have not met the expectation of societal norms and values. Thus stigma connotes a moral taint, it calls attention to some moral failing on the person bearing them.

Tracy Luchetta defines "Stigma as a mark or brand of shame that has been elaborated by social scientists to refer to the social label conferred upon individuals or groups by virtue of their possession of a characteristic indicative of a deviant condition" (1999:17). People who are stigmatized are usually considered deviant or shameful, and as a result are shunned, discredited, rejected or penalized. Stigma is "a powerful and discrediting social label that radically changes the way the individual view themselves and are viewed as persons" (1999:17). S/he will be reduced in our minds from a whole person to a taunted, tainted, discounted one and the discrediting effect is very extensive, sometimes it is a failing on the person who will be stigmatized.

On the other hand, Lerita Coleman gives a social scientific definition of stigma and views it, "as a representative view of life; a set of personal and social constructs; as a set of social relations and social relationships; a form of social reality. Stigma has been a difficult concept to conceptualize because it reflects a property, a process, a form of social categorization, and an effective state" (1986:211). Therefore, it is a concept imbued with cultural meaning. It is not a property of the individual but it is related to social, cultural, and historical phenomena that reflect the individuals' experience of stigma (Becker and Arnold 1986). The cultural meaning ascribed to an attribute/behavior will define how it will be perceived in many societies. In simple terms, stigma is a construction, a system, something that has been assembled. As a construction, stigma works by exclusion. It excludes the deviant, the stigmatized, from those that are viewed as normal, living a good moral life. Therefore, stigma has been constructed around normality and abnormality. Since pairing of normal/abnormal, un-stigmatized/stigmatized are not natural but are social perspectives and constructions, they have been built on binary oppositions. Binary Oppositions are pairs and opposites, that is, they relate and exist in relation to one another. One cannot exist without the other. That is un-stigmatized/stigmatized, normal/abnormal cannot exist without one another. In such a pair, the first term is always assumed to be superior to the second one and has been forcibly elevated over the other, and such an opposition is founded upon suppression; therefore, the relationship between normality and abnormality is one of subordination rather than equality (Stephen Moore 1992:85). They are tied together in a perpetual inferior/superior relationship. Stephen Moore makes reference to Jacques Derrida who says that "all such oppositions are founded on suppression; therefore, the relationship between the two elements is one of subordination rather than equality" (1992:84). Thus the binary couplet shows that such pairs reflect a relationship of power, or marginalization, superiority and one of subordination and placing the so-called "normal" person at the center whereas the "abnormal" one is at the periphery. The social control aspects of stigma are pervasive and powerful in the sense that they empower the stigmatizer and strip the stigmatized of power. The stigmatized person is constructed as possessing a behavior that does not meet the required status of that particular society; in other words, society defines what it is normal and what is abnormal. Thus stigma is "essentially a relational construct; a stigmatized person must be marked or labeled as deviating from a social standard or norm and the label must be socially constructed as negatively valued" (Luchetta 1999:20). Therefore it is a social stigma, a construction, a creation of society, a reflection of culture itself and not a property of individuals. And this means that the cultural meaning of HIV/AIDS is attributed to the cultural definition of certain behavior and effects in society. As Goffman, who began studying stigma long before social scientists did, insists that the "normal" and the "stigmatized" are not persons but perspectives. There is nothing inherent in the attributes of any persons that qualify them for stigmatization (1964:4). The "normal" believe that the person with a stigma is not fully human. On this assumption, the "normal" exercises varieties of discrimination, which effectively, if often unthinkingly, reduce the stigmatized person's life chances, survival and coping mechanism. And society therefore constructs a stigma theory, an ideology to explain the stigmatized inferiority and account for the danger s/he represents. Sometimes this consists of an animosity based on other differences, such as those of a social class (1964:15). Thus stigma is a construction, a system and like all other systems, it is in fact a system of exclusions.

Stigma also connotes a power relationship. It allows some individuals to feel superior to others. Superiority and inferiority, however, are two sides of the same coin. In order for one person to feel superior, there must be another person who is perceived to be or who actually feels inferior. Stigmatized people are often needed in order for many non-stigmatized people to feel good about themselves. There are issues of power that are reflected in such binary relationships. Since stigma also indicates that those who possess power, the dominant group, can determine which human differences are desired and undesired, it largely reflects the value judgments of a dominant group. But again it can reflect the value judgments of a group that feels inferior. Thus the stigmatized individual is stripped of social power s/he possesses and is left powerless. The problem with power is that it is both pervasive and invasive; therefore stigma becomes a powerful and pernicious social tool. In the social construction of stigma, the normal has been invested with the authority to speak and the deviant has been deprived of it. In a nutshell, stigma largely reflects the value judgments of a dominant group. Thus the French philosopher, Michel Foucault (cited in *The Postmodern Bible*) argues that, "the "deviant", the *nonstigmatised* in all its diverse guises (the insane, infirm, criminal, perverse, *HIV/*

AIDS positive) the stigmatized, is created and exists specifically so that the "norm", (rationally, healthy, moral, normal) can be defined. This naming of the "other" is what enables the manufacture of identity and that naming is always violent and discriminating (1995:143). Thus stigma is a manifestation of power and oppression, because it is an important mechanism by which a society exerts negative influence.

Stigma again is a special case in the specification of difference; that is, it is very much in the foreground of our attention and is negatively evaluated. According to Ainlay and Crosby, difference refers to "variation between or within types" (1986:7). If something varies from something, it means that the thing departures from a former or normal condition or action or even from a standard type. Human difference within stigma involves abomination of the body and the person bearing the abomination. It is a response to the dilemma of difference. It is a consequence of social comparison. It stems from differences and it involves concepts that negatively value differences. Difference according to Lerita M. Coleman "represents a continuum of undesired differences that depend upon many factors" (1986:217). These differences can be something that we have not chosen: race, gender, shape of the nose or head, or even a disease that we suddenly find ourselves diagnosed with. HIV/AIDS is an undesired difference. It is stigmatized because it varies from or it deviates from the normal or expected normal behavior of a human body, because it is linked to sexuality, immorality and death. Most of the time there will be differences that will be highlighted; others will be suppressed. Whether or not we notice differences may depend, in large part, upon what definitional qualities we may bring into focus and what others we force into the background. But with HIV/AIDS, it is a different case because once somebody we know becomes HIV/AIDS +, we begin to see that s/he is a different person, we begin to act in abnormal way, we do not even know what to say to him or her. I remember when I was told that a close friend was HIV/AIDS+. I did not know how to respond. I was dumbfounded. The first thought that came to my mind was this person is going to die (by then the government had not yet introduced the Anti-Retroviral Drugs). I was haunted by the thought that he was going to die and at the same put in a dilemma of what words to say to him. Would they be words of comfort, of sympathy, of pity and of compassion? I struggled with overwhelming disbelief, refusal to accept, and frustration, anger and bitterness. When I finally went to visit him, I still didn't know what to say. I tried to search for words but it was impossible. I knew that he was different and I could even see that indeed he was different because now he had an incurable disease. But this difference also largely had something to do with how the rest of the people and I related to him: he was now silently marked as "bearing a deadly disease if not death itself" (Theodore De Bruyn 1999:16).

As humans, we tend to focus on the differences and we actively create stigmas and we forget that any attribute is potentially stigmatizable. There are differences within and amongst us that serve as the basis for stigmas. As human beings we use differences to exile or avoid others. This affects the nature and quality of our interaction with other people, for HIV/AIDS sufferers, because the person with HIV/AIDS possesses a negatively evaluated difference. His or her condition certainly prompts the avoidance, revulsion and disgust and fear of death associated with AIDS. Thus the process of difference involves a process by which we catalogue differences. It raises the same issues of volition, morality and blame that are embedded in social systems. As human beings, we hold, share, and perpetuate these negative evaluations. The processing of these human differences (since So and So is HIV positive, she is different from me) involves both privately held and socially shared relevant structures.

The other problem with stigma is that it is not descriptive but rather prescriptive. Prescription according to Paulo Freire is "the basic elements of the relationship between the oppressor and oppressed" (1976:19). In the context of stigma, it is one of the elements of the relationship between the stigmatized and the stigmatiser. He continues to argue "every prescription represents the imposition of one individual's choice upon another, transforming the consciousness of the person prescribed to into one that conforms with the prescriber's consciousness. Thus, the behavior of the oppressed is a prescribed behavior, following as it does the guidelines of the oppressor" (1970:29). This is because it dictates to people how the world ought and ought not to be, it sets the principles by which the world ought to be looked at, it lays down rules on how we are to look at the affected, whether we will support or not support them. Stigma is a product of the human need to bestow meaning upon experience; it provides individuals with an ordered sense of the world around them, and attests to the feature of human experience. But such conceptions raise questions. Does society have to create such oppressing structures, does society need to put some at the periphery, at the margins and look down upon them, does it need to work by exclusions so as to make sense of the world? The moment it begins to create such excuses and constructions, it creates an ideology of difference. Therefore the behavior of the stigmatized after s/he has been stigmatized is not really a descriptive behavior nor is it inherent in him/her but it is prescriptive behavior. It has been imposed upon him /her and it will determine how s/he deals with the illness.

Therefore, HIV/AIDS can be said to be "color, religion, age, and gender, social class-blind" (Lulama 2002:116) it affects all of us. Below, I shall investigate some of the social constructions that have served as the foundation of HIV/AIDS stigma.

HIV/AIDS Stigma

The process of stigma is inextricably bound up with the concept of morality and an explanation of human social tragedy. This is due to the fact that religious organizations have labeled HIV/AIDS positive people guilty of promiscuity or sexual immorality. In his essay entitled "AIDS: Some Theological Reflections," Anthony Lovegrove opens the essay by quoting the beginning of the vivid, strong powerful, harsh and stern sermon of Father Paneloux in Camus' novel, *The Plague.*

> If today the plague is in your midst that is because the hour has struck for taking thought. The just man need have no fear, but the evildoer has good cause to tremble. For the flail of God and the world is His thrashing-floor, and implacably. He will thresh out his harvest until the wheat is separated from the chaff (1996:139).

Whenever, there is disaster, be it a terrorist attack, a train crash, or an epidemic disease or any communal tragedy there will inevitably be someone around who voices out such sentiments. HIV/AIDS has not been an exception. Religious institutions have viewed it as God's punishment of our world. But it is amazing how, for example, we have not seen God's hand on those who die of cancer, the women who die of breast cancer. We have tended to believe that the person who has HIV/AIDS has committed some immoral act and that the stigma is punishment for this moral transgression. The view that HIV/AIDS is a punishment from God is often done with judgments and preconceived ideas, and such religious or moral beliefs lead some people to conclude that having HIV/AIDS is the result of a moral fault, such as promiscuous or "deviant sex," that deserves punishment. In research done by two University of Botswana lecturers, Burton Mguni and Molebatsi, evidence from focus groups shows that some people in the religious communities understood AIDS as punishment meted against humanity by God. To some church people, the numerous deaths are a sign of the coming of the Kingdom of God – *"ke motlha wa bofelo"*, meaning that "these are the last days" (1999:12). They liken the HIV/AIDS epidemic to the deluge that wiped out all species except those who were lucky to find space in Noah's ark. Moreover, the spread of HIV/AIDS is viewed as resulting from lack of reference to God. As one church leader put it, *"ga gona poifo Modimo,"* translated as, "there is no fear of God" (Molebatsi and Mguni 1999:12). This is one perspective that has led to the construction of stigma, the stigmatized individual is perceived as guilty in some way for having caused or maintained their "marked" condition, even when no evidence for their culpability is readily apparent and available. Thus this shows that some churches view HIV/AIDS as merely a matter of and for personal ethics and tends to give a willful denial or a stigmatization of the HIV/AIDS epidemic (Maluleke 2002:60-65). When evidence of personal responsibility is lacking, observers tend to rely on stereotypical beliefs to make such attributions. The group accorded greater stigma is held "personally responsible for its condition because it has engaged in behaviours labeled deviant by the culture, such as same sex sexual conduct and illegal drug abuse" (Luchetta 1999:8). This reveals the church's tendency to exclude others, through our interpretation of the scriptures and the theology of sin has all combined to promote the stigmatization, exclusion and prevention efforts and suffering of people living with HIV/AIDS. This has undermines the effectiveness of care, education and prevention efforts and has inflicted additional suffering on those already affected the HIV. Responding and giving an overview of the approach of many faith based organizations, Dr. Catherine Sozi makes a point that the "for most of us, our faith or religious beliefs play a major role in our sense of our personal identity, our thought processes, our moral judgments and out of perception of disease" (2001).

In Francistown, a city in Botswana, Kenneth Fugewane, a cheerful, elderly volunteer counsellor, sits in an empty USA funded clinic that offers fast, pinprick blood tests, pondering how to break through the silence. The city suffers one of the world's highest infection rates, but people deny the disease because HIV is linked with sex. "We don't reveal anything," he says. "But people are so stigmatized even if they walk in the door." "If a man comes here, people will say he is running around," says Fungwane, though he acknowledges that men never do come. "If a woman comes, people will say she is loose. If anyone says they are HIV, they are despised" (Time Magazine, 2001:40). David Ngele is another HIV+ person who has been stigmatized because of his status. He is the first person to go public about his status in Botswana. He says he faced hostility wherever he went after going public about his status. In his own words, he says, "some said I should be killed, others said I should be quarantined and then many stopped being my friends." His eldest child had problems getting into a school and he lost his job as a driver because "they didn't want me to use their vehicle." This social stigma associated with HIV/AIDS may prevent PLWAs from living a free and self-fulfilling life and thus such acts violate his rights as a human being and as a citizen of the country.

Such stigmatizing attitudes do not help at all. In fact, they create and isolate a group among us who supposedly are different and worse than the rest simply because they have become HIV and are seen entering centers for testing HIV. They also encourage people to deny and hide the real extent of the problem, simply so that they themselves can avoid the blame and its consequences. They fail to address the reasons why change may be, or may have been, difficult for some of us. They can also sustain a false sense of security among people who actually risk or may soon risk HIV itself in their daily life. Although openness about HIV/AIDS calls for responsibility from the affected to help prevent the disease, it can only do so in a society where infection itself can be recognized and openly discussed without discrimination and punishment, and in which each person takes responsibility for knowing and acting on an accurate understanding of their own risk.

Gendered Face of HIV/AIDS

The construction of gender has been and is still one of the ways that have enhanced the spread of HIV/AIDS. Gender has been defined as the "social construction of the biological sex" (Anderson 1992:103). Geeta Rao Gupta supports this definition by describing gender as "a culture-specific construct" (2001:1, cited by Musa Dube). This means that different societies describe what it means to be either female or male, they define the social and expected responsibilities and roles of the different gender groups. Gender defines what it means to be either male or female. And within every society, there are "significant differences in what women and men can do or cannot do in one culture as compared to another. But it is fairly consistent across cultures" (Dube 2001:115). The different roles assigned to each gender might differ slightly within societies. Gender is not "synonymous with sex" (Gupta 2001) nor is gender natural, nor is it divine but it has to do with the social relationships of women and men" (Dube 2001:115). The different assigned roles, expectations and inequalities between females and males have made gender become a "major driving force behind the spread of AIDS" (UNAIDS 2000:21). In most societies women have no voice and they are prone to contracting the virus, firstly because of their biological make-up and secondly because of the fact that they are powerless. They cannot stand for themselves and insist on fidelity from their partners nor can they insist that their partners should use condoms when having sex or even refuse sex when its demanded from them.

Poverty and unemployment too has led to the spread and effect of HIV/AIDS among women. The story of Thandiwe, a woman from Zimbabwe, will illustrate the point. She is a sex worker and according to her she has never wanted to be a sex worker. She was working illegally in a restaurant in Johannesburg where she met a man from Zimbabwe. They got married and had two daughters. One day the husband was gunned down and she had to take him back home for burial. Her parents then sent her to her in-laws to be "cleansed". This is a common practice and it gives a dead husband's brother the right, even the duty, to sleep with the widow. She then went for an HIV test and tested negative. But then her parents-in-law wanted to keep her children and decided to marry her off to an old uncle. She fled. Now she did not have a job nor any means of economic survival and support, she knew that going back to her parents' place would not be the answer, they would send her back to her in-laws. She then met a friend who introduced her to sex work. She says that she does not want her children to suffer and she has not even told her family what she does but says she does shifts. She is aware of HIV/AIDS but says she doesn't have a choice at the moment because of unemployment. She has resorted to using two condoms per client and sometimes three. If a guy refuses she refuses too, but then some of the guys hit her if she insists on a condom. She desires to stop but she sees it as impossible. She is ashamed and has even stopped going to church. She says she asks herself everyday, "when will this business stop?' and she hopes to get a job (*Time* 12 Feb 2001:42). The story reveals the plight of a woman who does not want to be a sex worker. Her parents-in-law are marginalizing and oppressing her when they wanted to use her to serve their own interest in wanting to marry her off. She is a powerless woman who has no right over her body. Her "career" makes her vulnerable to infection, although she uses two or three condoms. This reveals two irrevocably linked issues about women. Firstly that, as long as women are neither educated nor trained for greater economic opportunity, their position will be one of economic disadvantage and underdevelopment. And the second is that, even if women were to have economic autonomy and stability, which most of the time they do not have, the nature and level of gender oppression and sexism as acted out in family relations and through social norms is such that women are not able to ask men to wear condoms without the consequences.

Though women are prone to the infection of HIV/AIDS, men seem to be aware of the disease but do not want to take action. For instance, in the study of HIV/AIDS in Africa by *Time Magazine*, the writer tells about a trucker driver who has been doing his driving for twelve years. He is a married man with three children. He is always on the road for many months around Southern Africa and when he is on the road he always stops for a "quickie" (sex with either sex workers or business women who maybe needing transport for their goods). He says he normally negotiates privately the price of carrying the goods and most of the time they pay with their bodies. When told that the practice might be unhealthy, he only shrugs at it and declares that "I been away two weeks, madam. I'm human. I'm a man. I have to have sex" (McGeary 2001:143). Though he knows that his choice of commercial sex is a high risk of infection; that his promiscuity could carry the disease home to his wife and that people die if they get it. He says, "Yes, HIV is terrible. But sex is natural. Sex is not like beer or smoking. You can stop them. But unless you castrate the men, you can't stop sex and then we all die anyway" (2001:43). The response of the truck driver reveals a lot about his attitude towards fidelity and condomization. He is aware of the dangers of unfaithfulness and unprotected sex and at the same time he is caught in the whole idea that sex is natural and that he has to do it. He does not even give a thought about his wife, the various women he sleeps with and the children that might be orphaned if he gets or spreads the virus. Some African societies regards extramarital sex as socially acceptable, which makes difficult it to promote faithfulness among married couples, many of whom (despite having one partner) sees themselves as "protected" by the marriage bond. All these gendered constructions do not help HIV/AIDS prevention, especially among women.

In addition to poverty, violence and stigma have an impact on women. The story of Sinah, who contracted HIV/AIDS after she had been raped, will illustrate the point. Sinah, a 24 year old young lady was raped at age 16 when she was returning home from school with three schoolmates, a man attacked them. He threw stones at them and while others managed to run away, he caught up with Sinah and dragged her to a nearby bush. Sinah was raped and stabbed with a knife. By the time her friends, who had gone to ask for help, came back, she was unconscious. When she began to be sick, her mother was worried about her. In desperation, her mother confided in the headmaster of the school Sinah was attending, who in turn told Sinah's class teacher what had happened to Sinah. "My mother just wanted to protect me. But the teacher told other people and soon the news was all over the school. Then they started to isolate me. As I often fell asleep in class because of my restless nights, they would give me a chair away from others. Some of the parents said I shouldn't be at school because I would infect their children" (UNICEF 2001). This is an example of violence and social stigma. She was exposed to HIV/AIDS through violence that she socially isolated because she was HIV positive. She is at greater risk of developing anti-social behaviors and of being less supported by the society, especially the school that should have played an important role in giving her support. Stigma often occurs both in settings not covered by human rights legislation.

The question that I now wish to address is: is there a biblical perspective that gives us a mandate to resist illness-based stigma?

An HIV/AIDS Deconstructional Reading of John 9:1

Scene 1: Jesus and the Disciples, John 9:1-5

Scene 1 opens up with the disciples asking Jesus to make judgment concerning the cause of the man's blindness. Jesus prefers not to answer the question; instead he gives the purpose of the man's blindness (Resseguie 1993:116). The blind man becomes the main character and focus in the narrative. He is the infected and affected man in the narrative. As an infected person he is the one who bears the stigma, he is the one who bears "an attribute that is deeply discrediting" (Goffman 1964:114). Goffman asserts that there are three types of stigma that a stigmatized person may fall unto. These are:

i) abominations of the body – the various physical deformities

ii) blemishes of individual character perceived as weak will, domineering or unnatural passions

iii) Tribal stigma of race, nation and religion, these being stigmas that can be transmitted through lineages and equally contaminate all members of a family.

The blind man can be said to be falling under two of Goffman's division of the types of stigmas, that is the first type because he possesses a physical deformity that is an abomination to the body, and the other type is the third one, which is a tribal stigma, that has been transmitted through lineage and equally contaminates him because he has inherited it, as thought by the disciples.

Let us now turn to the question that the disciples put to Jesus. Their question is *"who sinned, the blind man or his parents?"* This question is a revelation of how the disciples treat the blind man. The question reveals his marginalization in that they assume that it is either the blind man or his parents that sinned against God that he has been born blind. And on the other hand, they use the blind man to "settle an obscure theological debate" (Resseguie 2001:139) which enhances his marginalization. Resseguie gives a synopsis of marginalized characters as characters that are

> at the margins of the dominant society. They are socially expendable avatars of law status, plebeian figures such as the poorest values, sick, lame, blind, paralysed, beggars, prostitutes, tanners and so forth. Women also were low on the status hierarchy, along with children. They have no voice in the dominant culture, and often are nameless-objects rather than subjects in there own right. They are relegated to the margins of the text: by pools, in tombs, at wells, outside the city, at hedgerows. They are the living dead – socially and culturally – and many have physical ailments that make them near dead (2001:134).

The question that the disciples ask reveals that it was a common belief in the society that being born blind was a result of sinful nature. It shows an accepted norm in the society, it again reveals a societal ideology about the concept of sin, suffering and sickness, but it must be kept in mind that such a stigma is passed from generations to generations and is a societal construction. The idea that sin caused suffering was common and was a well-known factor in the New Testament period, as attested by the disciples' question. The Pharisees respond when they say to him, "you were born in sin", and indicate that they also subscribe to the same opinion.

According to Malina and Rohrbaugh, blindness was another form of stigma; namely because

> To be blind was to have eyes from which darkness emanated; darkness was the presence of dark rather than the presence of light. Blind people were those people whose hearts were emanated, hence, from whose

eyes "dark" emanated. The blind were often suspected of having the evil eye. The text is not really silent on the way the blind people were treated nor is it not silent on the attitude of the society. This is shown by the first question that the disciples throw at Jesus; already they bring out what is a gross generalization of the society towards blind people. From the Pharisaic perspective, blindness was a bodily sign that exposed something unusual and bad about the moral status of the signifier (1998:169).

The suspicion that surrounded the blind people showed that somehow they were stigmatized. It reflects a social ideology. His blindness is negatively valued since he is viewed as a sinner because he does not have an attribute that society has termed as the acceptable, good, moral and normal. He has a "disability," a trait that is abnormal.

As I read the text and bring meaning to it, I sense an ideology of power relationships that emerge between the society of the normal people who are placed at the center and the marginal who are at the periphery. One perceives modes of privilege, modes of valuing and devaluing and of health-based dominance. The ideology that associates sin with suffering is evident. The disciples bring preconceived ideas in wanting to understand why the man has been born blind. They believe that for him to have been born blind he is paying for the sins of his relatives. It is a prevailing theology of sin of their time and day. Their judgment can be summed in the words of Catherine Belsey, who argues that ideology is "the sum of ways in which people both live and represent to themselves their relationship to the conditions of their existence" (cited in *The Postmodern Bible* 1995:275-276). The question represents a one perspective by which the ideology of sin is represented and reproduced in the Jewish religious society. According to Malina and Rohrbaugh the "question has a long history behind it, stretching far back into the dim beginnings of human thought" (1998:169). In the question we hear and listen to the ideological stories that the Jewish religious society has been telling about blind people.

What is embedded in the theology of sin is that "what we have been makes us what we are" (1998:168). All the physical challenge that beset us arise from our past mistakes and wrongdoings. We have no possible grievance against anyone or anything. It is all self-inflicted. The notion that sin caused suffering was thus common in the New Testament. Stereotypical thinking at the time would have Israelites perceive that given the justice of God, suffering could only be the result of some sin, whether conscious/unconscious. Pharisaic tradition put it this way "there is no death without sin and no suffering without iniquity. It is said that Israelite scribal teachers offered two possibilities. On the basis of Exodus 20:5, some argued that the sins of the fathers occasioned the suffering of the children. A child could be born blind thanks to his/her parents' misconducts. Whereas others argued that it was prenatal sin on the part of the child that brought on such calamities" (1998:170). Whereas Johanna Stiebert differs and argues that, "first of all the catalyst of divinely caused illness, disease or plague is by no means inevitably moral or disobedience but it is to make a theological point, to illustrate God's power and control" (2001:78). Thus Christ asserts the man born blind did not sin nor did his parents but that the works of God might be displayed in him. It is sometimes aimed at demonstrating God's grace and power so as to make a theological point, God's supremacy. Whereas Maluleke asserts "the air of taboo and stigma described above leads to a massive air of suspicion and distrust. Ironically this is a vicious style: taboo and stigma leads to massive distrust and suspicion and the latter leads to the former" (2002:19).

Still on the question that sets the unfolding of the narrative, the blind man has no name. He is "a waif of society, at the margins of both the culture and the text. He is nameless with identifiable traits of the marginalized; blind and sinner" (Resseguie 2001:139). He is labeled as a Blind Man, the "name" signifies his trait and attribute.

Scene 2: John 9:6-12 - The Healing

This is the part where Jesus begins the healing process of the blind man and the restoration of sight in Christ is the purpose. He begins the work in two stages, which seem very absurd. Firstly he deals with the prevailing social stigma associated with blindness. He answers the disciples by saying that the man was born blind not because he had sinned or his parents had committed any sin, but the works of the Lord may be seen and God be glorified. This shatters the belief that illness results from sin or lineage. In his answer Jesus indicates innocent people can get ill. He demonstrates that it is wrong and it is a misconception to assume that one has sinned. Second, he begins to heal him physically by anointing his eyes with clay. It is a process that tries the faith and obedience of the blind man. It is amazing how he instantly obeys Jesus and he breaks through every obstacle when he decided it was safe to trust Christ. He is not afraid of what will the people think of him, he is not even afraid of their stigma nor their looking down upon him, for he knows that he is the one who will be benefiting from the healing. The spittle from his mouth denotes the divine essence of the Word." Malina and Rohrbaugh assert that "Jesus' use of the saliva reflects the widespread belief that saliva afforded protection, especially from the evil eye (which many would have assumed the blind man possessed)" (1998:170). The place where he sent is called Siloam; meaning or rather translated "sent" (Calvin 1890). Beggars in Palestine were even more stigmatized, as they were not allowed to live in the city; they were forced to live outside the city but only came into the city streets during the daytime to beg. And although he is now a healed man, the people still do not trust the once blind man, no wonder they still interrogate them. Maluleke argues, "distrust like its twin brother suspicion is not rational dispositions" (2000:62). Even if he might reason and give information, even if the Pharisees have seen Jesus healing the man with their naked eyes that will not erase their suspicion and distrust. The blind man was known not only to the neighbors but also to all the inhabitants of the city, since he used to sit and beg at the gate of the temple. Although his eyesight is restored, the minds and hearts of the Pharisees are not softened. The Pharisees are more zealous than the others to maintain the status quo. Are not most of the stigmatizes more zealous in stigmatizing those who are HIV positive, are not the stigmatized viewed as untouchables, if they are being taken care of at home, do we not dictate to them what not to touch and what to touch.

Scene 3: John 9:13-17 – The First Interrogation

The Pharisees pose a question to the man asking, "how can a man who is a sinner perform such signs?" Malina and Rohrbaugh make the statement that according to the "ideology of reward and punishment, a sinner should be suffering and not performing miracles and signs. A sinner is someone grossly wicked and a despiser of God" (1998:169). The Pharisees inferred this from Jesus' breaking and violation of the law of the Sabbath. They are already passing judgment, they view him as someone who is not even worthy to heal, or even to perform miracles, they view him as a sinner, a breaker of the law. Similarly we tend to make judgments upon the HIV/AIDS sufferers, we never see any good in them; we tend to view them as sinners, as people who have broken the law of God and as people who can do no good to us as a society. But those who have received mercy; those who have themselves suffered from stigma judge more fairly, however, decide that Jesus is a godly and religious man, who is equipped with a remarkable power of God to work miracles.

The Pharisees interrogate the blind man for his opinion. It is not because they want to abide by his judgment, or think it has the slightest value, but because they hope the man will be frightened and give them the answer they want. But the divided opinion leads to the newly sighted man's next stage of enlightenment and he now identifies Jesus as a prophet. But he is full of courage and confidence, he refuses to be pressurised on how to answer them but rather, though he did not yet know that Christ was the son of God, courageously and freely overturns the table and answers that Jesus is a prophet. What is evident here is that even when the blind man had now fully found his sight, they still want to prescribe how he ought to live. This highlights the prescriptive nature of the healthy oppressor: s/he wants to dictate to the blind man/the sick on how s/he ought to live her/his life and answer their question. In most cases, the stigmatize will often want to dictate how the stigmatised ought to live.

Scene 4: John 9:18-23 – The Parents are Interrogated

The Pharisees still do not believe that the once blind man has now been healed; they continue to interrogate him and even go to the extent of interrogating his parents. The whole series of interviews dealing with the occurrence of the miracle reveals an acknowledgement of the legitimacy of the miracle. When the Pharisees interrogate the parents, they do not simply ask one straightforward question, but cunningly wrap up several all together to prevent a reply. But out of this entangled and captious interrogation, the parents select and partially respond. They are terror struck. They put their son in their place as witness to explain the whole affair as it happened, with less ill will and more credit. Firstly they refuse to accept the legitimacy of the miracle on the basis of a broken law. Secondly, the stigmatizer's non-acceptance approach turns the table around, revealing them to be psychologically unwell.

In their interrogation, two things should be noticed here, the Pharisees do not believe a miracle has been performed, and because they are apparently blinded by their antipathy for Christ, they do not see what is plain.

Scene 5: John 9:24-41, The Second Interrogation, Jesus and the Pharisees

In this scene the blind man becomes a deconstructionist in the way he addresses the Pharisees. He publicly challenges them by asking a question that becomes "sharp public honor challenge" (Malina & Rohrbaugh 1998:173). There is total subversion, a displacement and a destabilization of the hierarchy of binary coupleting of Pharisee/blind man, sinless/sinner, innocent/guilt, normal/abnormal, ability/ disability, upper class/ lower class, fully sighted/blind. Thus now the blind man is the one who is in control, who brings about challenges and makes them very uncomfortable. One way of dealing with such challenges, especially if the challenger came from a lower social status, was "to pour sarcasm on the challenger and thereby implying that he is of sufficient to warrant a direct answer" (1998:175).

The Pharisees have now lost the game and they resort to violence by throwing out the once blind man and emphasise by saying that he was entirely born in sin and who does he think he is to them? And in their resort to violence, they are admitting that their wits have failed and the challenge is lost. More tragically, their last word indicates that they still hold on to the stigma that associate physical challenge/ disability with sin. Their perspective has prevailed in many societies demonstrated by HIV/AIDS stigma.

Conclusion

John 9 is a deconstructionist text that directly asserts that there is no relationship between sin and suffering/disease. The blind man sat begging where people passed by, people thought his blindness was due to his own sin or that of his parents, and even his parents are constrained to admit his blindness from birth (and hence their probable sin), these are also very irrelevant. So the text indicates that rather than viewing physical infirmities as "sin" it indicates that some sickness and physical challenges may be understood to exist in order that the works of the Lord may be made manifest in those who are suffering (Sherwood 1998:122). This does not mean that God is responsible for the man's blindness; God is not responsible for the HIV+. What would be the testimony in the case of someone who is HIV+? Will it be that the works and glory of God be made manifest and that, "the possibility that some illness could be in accord with the divine will no doubt help us ask, why Africa has been hit like no other continent in the whole world"? (1998:152). The whole notion of sin and suffering/sickness having no causal relationship seizes and creates meaning through what Sherwood says is "an inappropriate violence that is subversive, unexpected, undermining, deconstructive (1998:153). But theologically, the presence of the sick amongst us should not lead us to stigmatizing. Rather to manifest God to them. In a way God's story is revealed to us and to them.

As a deconstructionist text, it is an "interrogation of being and an attempt to deconstruct the fundamental binary opposition between what is and what is not" (1998:164). It helps us see that in accepting and believing that there is a causal relationship between sin and suffering and sickness, between sin and disease, involves "a certain view of the world, of consciousness, and of language that has been accepted as the correct one and if the minute particulars of that view are examined, a rather different picture emerges," (Gayatri Spivak as quoted by Sherwood 1998:166). John 9 helps to show and expose a social rather than an individual myopia, and demonstrates that "what a society creates is systematically related to what a society does not see" (1998:167). Lastly, it helps readers of the bible to rather "discover" the contradictions that have been already been produced within the language of the text.

John 9 deconstructs the whole ideology of sin causing suffering and illness and deconstructs the stigma that surrounds the conception of sin and suffering. Jesus is a deconstructionist in the sense that he subverts the whole notion of the relationship between sin, stigma, suffering and sickness. He undermines and disrupts the concept that sin causes suffering. It helps to make us see that once we socially create a relationship between sin and suffering, we create a worldview of stigma. It helps us discover that in the construction of sin and suffering, of stigma and HIV/AIDS contradicts that have been produced within society. It again offers a theoretically response and a displacement of HIV/AIDS stigma.

As a narrative, it does not only portray something neutral, objective, something that is uncontaminated, by telling us of the formal characteristics of story telling which convey something about HIV/AIDS stigma, but says something about life itself, about sufferings that are independent of the content of the narrative. John 9 disrupts the concepts of boundary, the distinction between "inside and outside", the concept of boundary between sight/blind, stigma/non-stigmatized. It has helped to problematise the relationship of power by showing how stigma is a strategy for constructing and regulating power relations and how who has been given the power to speak and to dictate. The Pharisaic ideology of "no-mixture," "exclusivity," and "purity" is also deconstructed in the sense that Jesus subverts their ideology at the end of John 9 by saying that once they think they see, their sin remains, the sin of stigmatization, the sin of judging others. Since the pure are also sinful, we really have no business labeling each other. As demonstrated in John 8:1-12, no one is sinless.

In conclusion, HIV/AIDS is in our midst, digs deep within us that the "hour has struck" for a genuine Christian response. It is not the flail of God, nor is the world His threshing-floor as the sermon of Father Paneloux held. We must not be judgmental of those who suffer from AIDS, but must try to take this matter to reveal God's love for us as Thus even the blind man finds compassion, healing, acceptance, embracement and love from Jesus Christ. He does not distance himself from the blind man. Throughout the New Testament, Jesus welcomes the waifs of the society; he welcomes the so-called outcasts, regardless of whether or not they were branded as sinners, sick, lame and sex workers. This is the revelation of God's glory in our broken world and societies – one that does not groom any form of stigmatization.

Endnotes

1.   Rev. Canon Gideon is Canon of the Anglican Church in Uganda; he is HIV+ and has been an HIV/AIDS activist since he was diagnosed with the disease twelve years ago. The words are quoted in the *Plan of Action: The Ecumenical Response to HIV/AIDS in Africa*. 2000:53-54

Bibliography

Ainlay, S. C. et al. (1986). Stigma reconsidered, in Ainlay, S. C, Becker, G & Coleman, L. M. (eds), *The dilemma of difference: A multidisciplinary view of stigma*, 1-11. New York: Plenum Press.

Anderson, J. C. (1992) Feminist Criticism: The dancing daughter, in Anderson, J. C. & Moore, S. D. (eds), *Mark & method: New approaches in biblical studies*, 103-134. Minneapolis: Fortress Press.

Coleman L. M. (1986). Stigma: An enigma demystified, in Ainlay, S. C. Becker, G. & Coleman, L. M. (eds), The *dilemma of difference: A multidisciplinary view of stigma*, 17-35. New York: Plenum Press.

Crosby, F. & Ainlay, S. C. (1986). Stigma, Justice and the Dilemma of difference, in Ainlay, S. C. Becker, G. & Coleman, L. M. (eds), *The dilemma of difference: A multidisciplinary view of stigma*, 212-227. New York: Plenum Press.

de Bruyn, T. (1999). HIV/AIDS and discrimination. A discussion paper for the Canadian HIV/AIDS Legal Network and the Canadian AIDS Society.

Dube, M. W. (2001). Culture, gender and HIV/AIDS: Understanding and acting on the issues, *Special report: Methods of integrating HIV/AIDS in theological programs: Training of trainers workshops, South Africa and Botswana*, 113-130. Gaborone/Johannesburg: World Council of Churches.

Freire, P. (1970). *Pedagogy of the oppressed*. New York: Penguin Books.

Gupta, G. R. (2000). Gender, sexuality and HIV/AIDS: The what, the why and the how. Plenary address at the Thirteenth International AIDS Conference, Durban.

Lovegrove A. (1996). AIDS: Some theological reflections, in Almond, B (ed), *AIDS: A moral issue: The ethical, legal and social aspect*, 139-144. 2nd ed. London: Macmillan.

Luchetta, T. (1999). Relationships between homophobia, HIV / AIDS stigma, and HIV/AIDS knowledge, in Pardie, L. & Luchetta, T. (eds), The *construction of attitudes toward lesbians and gay men*, 1-9. Binghamton: Haworth Press.

Lulama, N. (2002). I watched my sister die of aids. *True Love Magazine* May, 114-116.

Maduna, B. (1997). Women sex workers and the HIV pandemic: Stigma & blame in context. *SAFAIDS* 5, 8-10.

Malina, B. & Rohrbaugh, R. (1998). *Social science commentary on the Gospel of John.* Minneapolis: Augsburg Fortress Press.

Maluleke, T. S. (2001). Towards a Christian theology of healing in the time of HIV/AIDS: Healing for the wretched on the earth, in *Special report: Methods of integrating HIV/AIDS in Theological programs: Training of trainers workshops, South Africa and Botswana.* Gaborone/Johannesburg: World Council of Churches.

Molebatsi, C. & Mguni, B. (1999). *Kweneng East comprehensive district plan on HIV/AIDS: Phase I: Situation analysis and responsive analysis.* Gaborone: UNDP.

Odell-Scott, D. W. (2000) "Deconstruction" 55-62, in Adam, A. K. M. (ed), *Handbook of Postmodern Biblical Interpretation.* St. Louis, Missouri: Chalice Press.

Page R. (1984). *Stigma.* London: Routledge & Keegan Paul.

Stiebert, J. (2003). *"Does the Hebrew Bible have anything to tell us about HIV/AIDS,"* 24-34 in Dube M.W., HIV/AIDS and Curriculum: Methods of Integrating HIV/AIDS in Theological Programs. Geneva: WCC Publications, 2003.

The Postmodern Bible: The Bible and culture collective. (1995). New Haven: Yale University.

Resseguie, J. L. (1993). "John 9" in Stibbe, M (ed), *The Gospel of John as literature: An anthology of 20th century perspectives,* 115-122. New York: E S Brill Publishers.

Talbert, C. H. (1994). *Reading John: A literary and theological commentary on the Fourth Gospel and the Johannine Epistles.* New York: Crossroad.

Thomas, J. C. (1998). *The devil, disease and deliverance: Origins of illness in New Testament thought.* Sheffield: Sheffield Academic Press.

Time (12 Feb 2001). The story of AIDS in Africa.

Sherwood, Y. (1996). *The Prostitute and the Prophet: Hosea's marriage in literary-theoretical perspective.* Sheffield: Sheffield Academic Press.

Sozi, C. (2001). A Presentation focusing on the role of faith-based and healthcare workers. Presented at the Twelfth International Conference on AIDS and STDs in Africa.

UNAIDS. (2001). *United Nations special session on HIV/AIDS.* New York: UNAIDS.

UNICEF. (2001). *Botswana's children leading the battle against HIV/AIDS.* Gaborone: UNICEF.

World Council of Churches (2001). *Facing AIDS: The challenge, the churches' response.* A WCC Study Document. Geneva: WCC.

Chapter Seven

Allow Me to Cry Out:
Reading of Matthew 15:21-28 in the Context of HIV/AIDS in Tanzania

Anastasia Boniface-Malle, United Bible Societies

Introduction

For the purpose of this paper, I have chosen as a case study, the story of the Canaanite woman whose daughter was demon possessed. My intention is to show how often a woman is victimised, suffer the stigma of HIV/AIDS and carry a load of suffering in the African society, with particular reference to Tanzania. The focus of the story is on the cry of this woman for help. Her daughter is severely attacked by an unclean spirit. This story is a good model of what the Bible says, or should say and should not say, about HIV/AIDS and its implication for women in East Africa.

Before I probe further into a lengthy discussion of this study as related to the HIV/AIDS and women in Tanzania, it is important to familiarise ourselves with the story as narrated by Matthew 15:21-28. This reading of the story is from one African woman's perspective.

Background to the Text

In the synoptic gospels (Matthew, Mark and Luke) Jesus' ministry was mainly focused on proclaiming the good news of the kingdom of heaven, teaching and healing the sick. Scholarly research on the Gospel of Matthew indicates that the healing ministry of Jesus is intertwined between the five blocks of teachings. These are: the Sermon on the Mount, chapters 5-7; teachings on discipleship, chapter 10; teachings on the kingdom of heaven through parables (chapter 13); teachings on humility (chapter 18) and discourse on end times – eschatology (chapters 24-25). The healing ministry is portrayed more vividly in the context of Jesus' teaching. Matthew hemmed together these discourses in the five blocks of Jesus' teachings to demonstrate the fulfilment of the prophetic promises of God and through his ministry and what it implies to humanity. According to Matthew, faith and praxis, that is, proclamation and healing are inseparable. They go hand in hand. In this respect, Matthew's Gospel alters the notion of dualism. In most of our churches it is not surprising to see or hear the emphasis on teaching and preaching for the soul's deliverance alone rather than the whole person, that is, body, mind and soul. We will discuss the implication of this division in detail in our analysis.

Before the story of Matthew 15:21-28, Jesus had finished his third discourse on the kingdom of heaven. His teachings arouse great controversy on his credibility in his own country; "Is not this the carpenter's son? Is not his mother called Mary?" (Matt. 13:53-58). Regardless of opposition and rejection, Jesus continues his ministry to humankind; feeding the hungry (14:13-21); calming the chaotic sea (14:22-33), healing many sick (14:34-36) and correcting the teachings and the understanding of the religious leaders on the ceremonial and real defilement (15:1-20). In the context of his second rejection and the hard-heartedness of the Pharisees, Jesus envisioned threat to his life (Herod supposedly thought John the Baptist has been raised from the dead [14:1-12]). Therefore, Jesus withdrew from his own territory to the Gentile province. Matthew calls it the "district of Tyre and Sidon" (15:21). It is in the Gentile territory that the encounter between Jesus and the Canaanite woman took place.

Again, after this episode, Jesus continues to minister to many, healing the sick and feeding the hungry (15:29-31 and 32-39). By preaching, teaching, healing the sick, and feeding the hungry, Jesus showed in practice that his ministry is one that meets the needs of all human beings holistically.

Narrating the Story: Matthew 15:21-28

Foreign lands in God's scheme

As mentioned above, the story shows that Jesus went away from Nazareth to the Gentile region. The author of Matthew identifies the place as the 'district of Tyre and Sidon". Perhaps his purpose of withdrawal to the foreign land was to find solace from overwhelming demands of human needs as well as avoiding the steaming chaos and threats of the religious leaders, the Pharisees and Scribes.

However, in everything there is God's purpose. Foreign lands have always been the refuge and solace for Israel and for Jesus.[1] Apparently, in this episode, God used this opportunity to extend the benefits of God's reign across the geographical and cultural boundaries. Both the foreigner (Jesus) and the native (the Canaanite woman) benefited.

Meeting en route: cry for justice and wholeness

The story introduces the woman with a sense of urgency, *"And behold, a Canaanite woman from that region came out and cried"* (Matt. 15:22). This happened as soon as Jesus entered Tyre and Sidon. In Mark's version (7:24-30) this encounter took place after Jesus had entered an unidentified house (Mk. 7:24). The woman is nameless as in most biblical stories. Her identity is "a Canaanite/Gentile and a woman." In Mark's gospel she is identified as a Greek, a Syrophoenician by birth (7:26). Her identity as a foreigner in both gospels is unquestionable.

The woman came out without shame and/or fear and cried out! The Greek has *ekrazen,* which means "cried out."

This was both a cry of pain and a plea for help. It implies helplessness because she was unable to heal her severely demon possessed daughter. It also implies power on her ability to seek and express her ordeal. The woman knew her limits. Yet, she immediately sees an opportunity; someone who is able to restore her child's health has come to her homeland. Matthew does not tell us that his woman had a prior knowledge of Jesus. We can only assume that she has heard of him. So when she sees him, she cries to him for help.

In the Hebrew Bible, the word *qarah*, which means cry or call out loud, is frequently used as a cry of pain and a plea for help. The Psalms of Lament often use this word *qarah* as a prayer of the needy[2] (see also Pss. 4:1; 5:1-2; 17:1, 6; 22:2; 27:7; 28:1, 2b; 40:1; 57:2; 77:1; 86:3; 88:1, 2; 102:1b; 119:145,146,169; 120:113; 141:1; 142:1). In these Psalms of Lament, the cry of pain and plea for help is found mostly in the individual laments. The quick reference to these Psalms shows that this word appears mostly in the first part[3] of the complaint prayers, that is, an address section. The cry is always directed to God, the source of power, mercy and giver of justice and wholeness. It is the same cry uttered to Jesus by the woman in our story. Out of desperation she seeks Jesus!

Cries of help are verbal expressions of pain and helplessness on the part of the petitioner. Here the woman cries *eleeson* (have mercy on me). Mercy is an attribute to God. In the Hebrew Bible, the word *rehem* indicates both the emotion and location of mercy (the womb). As God's character, it is primarily used directly or indirectly with reference to God. In rare cases it is used in reference to human subject (see for example Isa. 49:15 for a mother; Psa. 103:13 for a father and 1 Kgs. 8:50; Isa. 13:18; Jer. 6:23; 21:7; 42:12; 50:42 for an enemy) (Jenni and Westermann 1997: 1227). Even with reference to human beings, it means a "soft place" full of compassion (1226). Various meanings are given for *rehem*: 1) may indicate a womb as a point of origin for all human and animal life; assuming that cry to Yahweh or to Jesus "have mercy" means an acknowledgement that God/Jesus is the Lord of birth or life. 2) *Rehem* means an appeal to soft place/emotion of action to find mercy from someone. 3) With respect to human beings as subjects of *rehem*, it does not necessarily mean an appeal to "soft place/emotion". Jenni and Westermann remark that "This love does not concern an emotionally rooted fatherly tenderness but a volitional acknowledgement (or rejection) of paternity involving the resultant duties of providing security and protection for a child" (1227). 4) When *rehem* is used in combination with *hnn* (*hen* or *hanan*) to be gracious to someone") then the emphasis is more on God being gracious, that is rendering the petitioner undeserved mercy (see for example Ex. 33:19; 2 Kgs. 13:23; Isa. 27:11; 30:18; Ps. 102:14). 5) Like *qarah*, *rahamim* (noun) occurs more often in the language of the Psalms and prayers (1229). However, since most occurrences of *rehem* have God as their subject, the focus is on the re-establishment of the damaged or installation of new relationship (1229). Re-establishment or installation of new relationship includes rectification of injustices in all their manifestations.

While the cry *eleeson me,* may carry several of the above meanings, in this story it is a cry to the mercy/heart ("womb") of Jesus in search for help from intensive suffering of the Canaanite woman's daughter. The suffering of the child is the suffering of the mother. Therefore, the mother pleads on behalf of her helpless and demon possessed child. She does this because her maternal womb aches for the child's situation and in her own capacity she is powerless to alleviate the problem.

Like the Hebrew Bible Psalmists, the woman does not cry in the vacuum, she directs her cry to Jesus. She approaches Jesus and addresses him with titles that definitely testify to his Lordship and Kingship: "*Have mercy on me, O Lord, Son of David!*" (v. 22). Jesus is the Lord, in the pattern of the Hebrew understanding of Yahweh, although the Greek has *kyrios*. Yahweh is the God revealed to the Israelites through Moses. Yahweh is the Creator and Redeemer God of Israel. Since Matthew's audience is mostly Jewish Christians, he uses titles that are familiar to his people. The Messiah/Christos has to be the Son of David (2

Sam. 7:1-14). God promised David and his offspring an eternal throne.

By addressing Jesus *"Lord, Son of David,"* this Gentile woman realizes the Lordship of Christ and discovers powers inherent in him. In coming to Jesus, she realizes the divine presence in him. Again, the pattern of her prayer is that of the complainant of an individual in the prayers of Israel. Before she starts narrating her complaint, she addresses Jesus, whom she will direct her complaint to.

Her complaint, which is in form of a request, is brief and poignant: *"My daughter is severely demon-possessed."* This description of the plight of her daughter is brief yet sufficient to show its intensity. The description is enough to state the situation, which is heartrending and heartbreaking. The child is under severe attack of the evil spirit! The woman does not waste time dwelling in her complaint that is why we said this is a complaint in form of a request. Her statement shows the suffering, but does not dwell on that. She moves to her request. In essence, the woman is asking Jesus to help; the complaint and petition are mingled together.

Request suspended through disciples' interference "send her away"

One would have expected Jesus' response at once. But Jesus' response is suspended in my view to invite the response of the disciples who will, in future, be commissioned to serve among the Gentiles. The disciples have seen Jesus' attitude to people especially among the Jews. Now it is time for Jesus to demonstrate to them that his ministry is for all people. In other words, Jesus wanted to make clear that God's reign is not confined within the geographical boundaries of Palestine.

In verse 23, the author of Matthew writes in such a way that he gives time dimension to the story: *"His disciples come and urge him."* In reading this text, the gap is already seen.

The disciples are watching this drama, but they cannot stand it: a Gentile, who is also a woman, approaches the master with a loud cry. She is disturbing Jesus. Yet, they are in no position to send her away. They request him to: *"Send her away for she cries after us."* Now the cry is not directed to Jesus according to Jesus' disciples. It is "she cries after us," indicating that Jesus and the disciples are one, yet they do not seem to share the same visions and goals. But, the cry of the woman was *"Lord, Son of David, have mercy on me."* The reaction of the disciples to defend Jesus against people "disturbing" their master is not unique to this incident. The disciples also wanted to send the children away (Matt. 19:13-15; Mk. 10:13-15; and Lk. 18:15-17) since children and women were not public audience that had any significance in the world of men in those days.

Request suspended through dialogue: another opportunity

Closely connected to the first dialogue is the one between Jesus and the woman (15:23b-27). The harsh criticism of Jesus to this Gentile woman is counteracted by her persistent and intriguing claim that she deserves love and grace in God's plan. Furthermore, as the story indicates, at the end Jesus' harsh responses are overpowered by the gift of faith and healing that he bestows upon her. These two contrasts heighten Jesus' objective: the good news of the kingdom pervades human made boundaries.

Jesus does not respond to the disciples verbally. His initial response to the woman and the disciples' reaction to send her away due to her out-cry aim at one thing, discouragement! Jesus says, *"I was sent only to the lost sheep of Israel"* (v. 24). Jesus' response begins the dialogue with the woman. His response does not discourage her, but it invites her to the heart of the savior where she sees "mercy". She does not go away offended, *"she comes and kneels before him, saying, "Lord, help me"* (v. 24). The realisation of this divine presence compels her to bring her plight to Jesus, *"Lord, help me"*. As with *"have mercy on me,"* the narrator shows that the plight of a child is equally an agony of a mother. She does not say, help my child directly, but "help me."

Jesus seems to be unmoved with this petition. Again, using offensive language he responds, *"it is not fair to take the children's bread and throw it to the dogs."* Israel and other nations used such language when they referred to each other as enemies. Animal imagery was a common literary technique of the ancient Near East, although it seems offensive and comfortable for us. The woman is not silenced by this response, which seems insensitive. She has heard clearly what Jesus had just said and she responds in the same line of argument: *"Yes, Lord, yet even the dogs eat the crumbs that fall from the masters' table"* (v. 27). Like the woman who comes from behind or from the side and touches Jesus' garments, this Canaanite woman does not claim a great place! She asks only a small favor, which eventually turns or transforms her whole life.

As the story reveals, the disciples and Jesus are challenged by the reality of the woman's cry. Jesus' ministry was twofold: First, his ministry involved the healing of humankind in all aspects: physically, spiritually, psychologically and socially. He did this through word and deed. Second, his task was to prepare those who will continue this healing ministry. The disciples were chosen not for privilege. They were chosen to be instruments of justice and wholeness for all people. Conversely, the story does not give a hint as to how much this was comprehended by the disciples. At the end the focus is on Jesus and the woman.

The woman invited Jesus to experience faith outside Judaism. Both Jesus and the woman were drawn into each other's experiences. Jesus entered her life and was drawn into her both personal and social experiences of suffering and her faith in Jesus as a healer. He saw her predicament; but he also saw that this is God's child whose image and dignity cannot be diminished by weakness, dependency, suffering or stigma associated with the disease of her child. The woman was also drawn into the experiences of love and grace. She was able to see the difference between Jesus and the disciples, between Jesus and her community that stigmatized and ignored her. The community did not possibly cry with her in her sorrows and helplessness. The community is absent in this story except the disciples who seem to be a hindrance to her fortune: *"send her away, for she cries after us."* The woman has her request granted plus receiving a greater portion, the gift of faith. This faith was revealed and nurtured through the encounter and dialogue. "Her persistence based on her faith in a God who can change things for the better is rewarded" (Hare 1993:179). Healing comes as a process of the realization of the divine power. *'O woman, great is your faith! Be it done for you as you desire.'* *"And her daughter was healed instantly"* (v. 28). The Gentile, who is a woman, has received the gift of healing for herself and cure for her daughter. What she has received has far greater significance from both personal and social level than simply the cure for her daughter. She has a social recognition; her dignity has been restored. She is commended for incredible faith where she has seen the extent of God's work through the Messiah as extending to the Gentiles.

Narrative Interaction with Tanzanian Women on HIV/AIDS

From the outset, this story raises several critical questions: Why does she run around with her sick child all by herself? Why did her husband not accompany her? Where was he? Where are the relatives, friends and neighbors? Where is the community? Does she not deserve the sympathy or empathy of others? Where is compassion? Where is love? Where is biblical imperative to love your neighbor as yourself? Where is the African belief in community?

Nobody can underestimate the reality of HIV/AIDS crises in Africa especially its implication on women. AIDS has claimed and is claiming and will continue to claim lives of millions of people in the world, the majority of these live in Africa. To show this reality, see the HIV and AIDS Statistics in Africa where in every country the number of women infected outnumbers that of men.

Across the countries of sub-Saharan Africa a total of 28.5 million adults and children are estimated to be living with

HIV and AIDS (UNAIDS 2002:8). This is (up grade status) approximately 8 percent of the total adult population.

In East Africa, approximately 1.6 females to every male are infected (Ranaivoarisoa and McIsaac 1995:10). According to research in Tanzania, 670,000 women were infected with the virus as opposed to 530,000 men. That means AIDS claims the lives of more women than men in East Africa. This tragedy has implications also for the children, society and the church where women play a major role.

Culture and economics are major forces in intensifying the high risk of infection and deaths of women from AIDS. I will simply give a brief, non-exhaustive summary.

◆ Knowledge and perception about AIDS: The majority of women in East Africa live in rural areas where access to media and communication are limited. Most of these women have no formal education so that even news from media is not accessible to them. Studies done in Nairobi confirm this statement. "Current knowledge about attitudes and behaviors related to HIV/AIDS is limited especially when related to gender issues.... Knowledge and communication are usually higher in cities, in youth, and in individuals with higher education" (Cabrera 1996: 63).

◆ Women are less likely to discuss HIV and AIDS related issues. Culturally, women are not quite comfortable to seek help from sex related diseases. "Because of the stigma attached to AIDS, some HIV infected individuals and their families have sought to conceal or deny their illness" (Kusimba *et al* 1996:28). This increases risks of immature deaths.

◆ Women are not initiators of sex in East Africa. Sex and marriage are largely domains of men. This fact possesses some implications. One is the use of condoms in casual and in commercial sex. Men decide whether they want condom or not. In commercial sex, it is sometimes not easy for a woman to refuse because of economic constraints on her.

◈ Practices like female genital mutilation are among cultural practices that increase the danger of HIV/AIDS for East African girls and women, from some ethnic groups.

◈ Polygamy, which is prevalent in some East African societies, can facilitate the infection of many women and children.[4] Polygamy apparently intensified two risk factors: the man's accumulation of several sexual partners and of women's likelihood of having been in other unions (Cabrera 1996:67).

◈ Economically, the rapid spread of AIDS is rampant among sex workers. Observations done in urban areas of Rwanda and other cities of East and Central Africa demonstrate that sex workers have between 500 to 1500 clients per person and that there is a prevalence of STDs among their clients (68).

◈ Poverty among rural East African women increases risks of death since AIDS drugs are very costly.

Unearthing the Story

All these contributing factors confront us with issues of suffering and justice. How can we interpret the story of the Canaanite woman in this context? Some of the unanswered queries and ambiguities in the story make this story open to many interpretations. The story allows us to see multiple images of women.

In relating the story of the Canaanite woman to the HIV/AIDS problem, let us pause and look at different images of East African women as related to HIV/AIDS epidemic. We shall use four different portrayals of women from Tanzania: 1) a widow, 2) unwed mother, 3) a sex worker with a child, and 4) a woman in a polygamous marriage.

The first example: The first story is of a widow whose husband died of AIDS. She is left with children and one is severely sick. The mother feels compassion; she is worried about the state of her child. She could follow her father soon. Would this reality of death silence her crying out? The woman is not content with the fact that AIDS kills since it has no treatment. She is not afraid of being stigmatized. She is convinced that her daughter deserves to be given a chance of living a normal, healthy and productive life. Yet she knows her situation is critical.

A widow, who is probably weak from sickness, is among the poorest people in the East African community in the HIV/AIDS era. She has no access to money to buy expensive medication for her child. She seems to have no other support from her in-laws or her own family. They are either angry with her or blame her for the death of their son. They seem not to know what to do with supposedly two dying people. They are poor and have no resources to help them. They are alienated. She does not seem to have mercy from the community. The Non Governmental Organisations in her area do not seem to notice her as well. They are focusing on those children whose both parents have died of AIDS. AIDS has changed the family pattern in East Africa. "Orphans, traditionally, were almost unheard of in East Africa. By tradition, the extended family or the clan takes care of orphans, but the impact of AIDS has placed a severe burden on their ability to care for all the needy children (12).

The second example is that of an unwed mother in the East African HIV/AIDS context. It is not important that the father of her child died; perhaps he is dead, she does not know. She also faces another dilemma she cannot reveal the identity of the father of the child. Therefore, her image is extremely low in the society. She has no education, no job so she has no income at all. Life is unbearable. She is already facing family criticism and rejection because she is not officially married. From that point of view, she has no one to cling to except her daughter. But her daughter is severely ill; her hope is fading out. This is a sad story; she does not have remedy for her situation, and her parents/relatives (if any) are not supportive in helping her child. Anxiety, frustrations and fear of the inevitable death of her daughter surround her.

The third image is that of a sex worker in the East African HIV/AIDS context. She is involved in unsafe sex. Her client is HIV positive. She got pregnant and gave birth to a baby girl who is also infected by HIV. In a course of time, she fell sick. She went to the hospital with her meagre resources. Her test results showed that she was HIV positive. A state of confusion began after learning that she is a victim of the incurable and deadly disease AIDS. She is afraid to reveal her situation to friends. But because of this situation, she is down so that people started to speculate that she is HIV positive. In her state of confusion, she shared her ordeal with one of her friends. Unfortunately, the friend she confided in was not faithful. She started to spread the news. The sex worker started to experience rejection, isolation and loneliness. Her clients started to run away from her. Her income deteriorated. As in the above case, she can foresee the death of her little girl. This also intensifies her agony.

The last example is of a woman in a polygamous marriage in the East African context. She is the youngest (the fifth) wife. She was the favourite wife to her husband. He loved her so dearly. In their marriage, she had only one child, a daughter who is four years old. After the birth of her daughter, her husband died of AIDS. Immediately after her husband's death, the problems started. She was denied her husband's property because she has no son to inherit. Her in-laws turned against her and took everything. She experienced malice, blame for her husband's death and rejection from all family members. In the middle of all this, her only daughter got sick. With her meagre income, she took her to the hospital where she was diagnosed with HIV. Her condition was getting worse day by day. Her resources are exhausted; where does her help come from?

In all these different images, the woman cries out for help. She asks "why" (justice question) and "how long" (suffering) to the place of encounter (community, family, church) where she assumes she can bring her suffering. Does anyone hear? Are they comfortable with this kind of language? She is an East African Christian who knows that her tradition allows her to pour out her grief. She understands that in times of suffering, the community stands by her and gives her both the verbal and symbolic language to express grief (through songs of lament, wailing and rituals to alleviate the problem).

She comes to Church with this understanding to seek help but could not find any. The Western civilization and theology impact has changed the East African cultural values and practices by looking down on them, undermining and labeling them as primitive and un-Christian (pagan, animistic). Because of this line of thought, these ways of alleviating grief are not entertained by the East African Church especially main line churches. In other words, the church will not accept wailing, lamenting and crying women as Christian ways of expressing grief and suffering. It silences the lamenting woman who comes to church seeking help.

PLWHA (People living with HIV and AIDS) are silenced to speak out their predicament. Why is this so? Of course, there are many answers to this question. One is that HIV/AIDS is considered to be one of the shameful diseases because it is associated with sex. One might be looked down upon as sexually promiscuous. PLWHA are stigmatized with shame, guilt and alienation. Another reason why people do not speak out pain is because they have been taught that complaining is against the conventional faith. In other words, complaint shows lack of faith; it is a sign of unbelief. Because of these misleading teachings, PLWHAs ought to keep silent. Even when they try to speak, the family, church and community silence them.

Silence is one of the "virtues" of Western Christianity, which has also been adopted by the main line East African Christians. Silence is especially seen on the issues of sex, and sex related diseases or problems and silence over the immense suffering of the people. When we do not know what to do about the situation, we either keep quiet or resort to some spiritualized answers from our religious resources.

Biblical/Liturgical Resources to Confront Suffering

Allow me to cry: breaking the silence

Matthew puts emphasis on the dialogue and delays the healing as the last step in meeting the need. Matthew portrays Jesus as one who listens to the cry before rushing into giving answers or solutions. We also learn this fact from the Canaanite woman. The woman was not afraid to bring her predicament to Jesus. She insisted and she was finally granted what she wanted and much more, "woman, you have a great faith!" (v. 28). The disciples wanted to silence her outcry. But she comes from a different background where crying and the expression of feelings and grief are permissible.

Like her Hebrew neighbours, her religious/liturgical settings created a source of encouragement. In these traditions she found a language (the lament language) to express her pain. She was not afraid to cry out, nor did she shun or run away from suffering. She faced it with boldness. Her faith in Christ gave her a language to cry out her pain *"Lord, Son of David, have mercy on me, my daughter is under severe attack of the demons."* [5]

With the current threat of HIV/AIDS on the lives of many people, especially women and children, how does the church help women to express their cry of suffering? How do the church and community enable people to break the silence?

How does the church deal with these existential realities? How does the Church explain the existence of suffering and its remedy? "Our Christian practice has created an euphoria, a sense of well-being that, on the one hand, narrows and deflects our understanding of life into a straight, one-dimensional adventure, and on the other hand, gives a permanent numbness to the pain and suffering that people face from day to day. Christian teachings have claimed that the harsh realities are only temporary, deluding its believers to masochism, in hope of that otherworldly and permanent life.... As a result, "faith and worship become lethargic and less authentic" (Boniface-Malle 2000:128). We need Christian practice that prays "let your will be done on earth as in heaven" (Matt. 6:10).

One of the important theological challenges that these prayers offer to us is that they do not mention sin. Except for the Penitential Psalms, both the individual and communal lament do not refer to sin as the cause of their suffering. These are a primal cry, a prayer of a human heart made to God who is liberator, protector and initiator of justice. "An important theological phenomenon is that the lament is in the whole worship and religious traditions of Israel. While prayers of agony flow from the heart both individuals and community find expression of their grief within the religious patterns of Israel. The distress and suffering of the individual is expressed in the personal laments that pervade the whole of the Old Testament. Psalm 130 begins: "Out of the depths I cry to thee, O Lord!" (See also Psa. 113). All the Psalms of Lament in the Psalter revolve around this cry out of the depths, and Psalms of praise declare that God has heard it" (Boniface-Malle 2000:132). This challenges us as a church to mediate on this question: "Where is the place of lament in our worship and liturgy? Do we have language and space by which sufferers and their families can appropriate their groaning before God and before the worshipping community? Do our faith, worship and liturgy offer real support and encouragement to persons suffering from HIV and AIDS? While this will be answered differently, the story of the Canaanite woman gives us mandate to insist on making our laments heard, even if some male disciples try to dismiss us.

Endnotes

1.   For example, Abraham in the land of Gerar (Gen. 20:1), Isaac in the land of Gerar (Gen. 26:1), Children of Jacob in Egypt (Gen. 46:1ff), Moses in the land of Midian (Ex. 2:1-15ff), Jeremiah in Egypt (Jer. 43:1ff) and Jesus in Egypt (Matt. 2:13).

2. See the superscription to Psalm 102: "A prayer of one afflicted, when she is faint and pours out her complaint before Yahweh."

3. Form critics have divided the Psalms of Lament into these sections: 1) An address to God; 2) Lament (description of pain); 3) petitions (plea for help) and 4) confession of trust/ vow to praise.

4. Women who have more than one union are affected more than those in single union (31.4% versus 5.3%). These women were more often in polygamous unions (20% -30%). This information is found in Cabrera *et. al. AIDS and the Grassroots: Problems, Challenges and Opportunities*.

5. The translation is mine.

Bibliography

Boniface-Malle, A. (2000). *Interpreting the Lament Psalms in the Tanzanian Context: Problems and Prospects*. PhD. Thesis, Luther Seminary: St. Paul, Minnesota.

Cabrera, C. et al. (1996). *AIDS and the Grassroots: Problems, Challenges and Opportunities*. Nairobi: Ipelegeng Publishers.

Hare, D. R. A. (1993). *Matthew Interpretation: A Bible Commentary for Teaching and Preaching*. Louisville: John Knox Press.

Jenni, E. and Westermann, C. (1997). *Theological Lexicon of the Old Testament Vol. 3*. Massachusetts: Hendrickson Publishers.

Kusimba, J. et al. (1996). "HIV/AIDS Within Family: Women's Responses and Needs" in Forsythe, S. and Rau, B. (Eds) AIDS in Kenya: Social Economic Impact and Policy Implications. Nairobi: Family Health International AIDSCAP.

Ranaivoarisoa, E. S. J. and McIsaac, P. S. J. (2000). *AIDS Ministry in Kampala, Uganda: Pastoral Placement and Reflection*. Nairobi: Hekima College, Unpublished Manuscript.

Chapter Eight

Twenty-Two Years of Bleeding and Still the Princess Sings!

Musa W. Dube, Scripps College

Introduction

This paper is based on three stories. The first one is about an African princess, who gets invited by her friends to fetch wood in the forest, where they invite her to play a game of jumping the fire. But then they push her into the fire and bury her there. One day she hears someone cutting logs and she begins to sing, telling her story. The second one is the biblical story in Mark 5:21-43. It says Jesus was on his way to heal a very sick twelve-year-old daughter of Jairus. But on his way, he met a woman, who had been bleeding for twelve years. She had gone to many physicians and lost all her money, but she did not get healed. When she heard that Jesus was passing by, she said to herself, "If only I can touch the garment of Jesus, then I will be healed." The third one is the story of women and HIV/AIDS in Africa, personified in the character of Princess Africa Izwelethu (henceforth PAI). The combination of these stories highlights the many trying experiences that Africa and African women have undergone in the HIV/AIDS epidemic – meeting with many doctors who could not heal them, but took all their money. Nonetheless, despite being buried alive, they sing even in death, thereby underlying their will to arise and live. This singing is the stretch of the bleeding woman (PAI), who seeks to touch the garment of Jesus. *After twenty-two years of bleeding (of HIV/AIDS) "If only she can touch the garment of Jesus!"*

Once. Upon. A Time: A Time! A Time! A Time!

Ngubane o gamla lapha? Nqo
(Knock, knock, who is there?)
Yimi e ngamla lapha. Nqo
(It's me. I am around)
Ufike Otsele uMama lo Baba
(Go tell My Mother and My father)
Uthi Untentelezanhlane ka sekho
(Tell them I am no more)
Ngoba ba nqibela emhlathini we bonhla ka kusaiwa
(For they buried me here, and they don't come here any
more.)

Scene I: 1960-80:[1] The Dawn: Dr. Independence & Birthday Celebrations

Once upon time, a long time ago, yet not so long time ago, a child was born to Africa. Her parents gave her the name Princess Africa Izwelethu (Africa our land). She was born in the 1960s. She was, by far, the most beautiful daughter to be born to Africa in the contemporary times.

When she was born her parents named her Princess Africa Izwelethu (henceforth PAI) for she came from her mother's womb arrayed by the golden rays of a rising sun. She was born wearing a sun crown on her head. She came holding a scepter of peace in her hand. She came wearing a coat of shining stars, that kept rising and shining on her coat as the years passed. She was named PAI, for the day of her birth was a day like no other day in the modern history of Africa.

It is said that on the day of PAI's birth, the sun refused to go down. God's billion stars in the sky and the graceful moon said they would not wait for the sun to go down. And so it was, on that day, a day like no other day. It was a day with a bright shining sun. A day with a billion stars twinkling and dancing in the wide blue skies of Africa. It was a day when the moon smiled and showed its wide, broad and peaceful face in the company of the sun and the stars in the same sky.

It is said that on the day that PAI was born a sweet breeze from the south swept across the land, touching everything and touching everyone. Trees stretched to the heavens. They raised their branches up high. Their leaves turned, twisted, and danced in the music of the sweet breeze from the south.

It is said that on the day of PAI's birth you could hear the flowers of the mountain and the flowers of the valley, the flowers of the field and the flowers of the hillside, opening, stretching and raising all their petals to the skies. On that day, the flowers looked up and said, "Hello," to the sun, the stars and the moon in the skies. Joining the sweet breeze that was floating from the south, the petals danced and poured the sweetest perfume on the whole face of the land. On that day you saw all the colors: yellow, violate, red, white, you name it, all colors, of all flowers gracing the landscape, than any artist could ever capture natural beauty.

It is said that on the day on which PAI was born, you could hear the butterflies, breaking open their cocoons. You could see their wings stretching out. You could see a thousand butterflies of various colors, flying slowly, lazily greeting and saluting each flower. You could hear the bees buzzing in and out of their beehives, flying and landing from one flower to another, the bees carried and made so much honey that began to flow on the face of the land.

It is said, that on the day of her birthday the birds gathered in the branches of every tree. They took their place among the dancing leaves, and began to sing their songs – adding to the breeze. It is said that the sound of their songs was like the song of a million angels, coming down, escorting God down. Angels bringing God to dwell in Africa with humankind. It was a day God's will was being done on earth as it is done in heaven.

It is said that on the day that PAI was born, although some strong winds tried to rise and shake the beauty of the day, and although some dark clouds tried to rise from the west and some rain tried to pour-but no, nothing could stop the light of the day of her birth. No nothing, for the light was not in the skies – the light was in her. She was the light of Africa, and her light was the life of all her people.

I can tell you all this, for I was there on this day. I was there when PAI was born. I heard and I saw, I felt and I smelt the dawn of her day. I can still hear the sound of drummers drumming; I can still hear the dancers dancing and thumping their feet. I can still hear the sounds of laughing children ringing across the land. I can still hear the voices of women ululating, *"lelelele".* The men were whistling and blowing horns of joy. I can recall all the songs and the sounds of joy that filled that day. People singing and saying, *"Fatshe leno larona ke mpho ya Modimo.* (This land of ours. It is God's gift/blessing to us). *Ke boswa jwa bo rraetsho* (it is the inheritance of our ancestors). *A lenne ka kagiso* (let this land dwell in peace). I tell you, I felt and saw the warm blanket of peace and hope falling upon the land.

Yes, I was there when PAI was born. So beautiful were the birthday celebrations. I was there. It was in the 60s, 70s and the 80s. It was the day, the age of the struggle for Independence, when hope was born, screaming and thrusting out of the womb of the struggle with a powerful force of life. I was a witness to the birth of Mozambique, the birth of Zimbabwe, the birth of Namibia. I was to become one of the midwives in the birthday pangs of South Africa.

And so beautiful was the day of PAI's birth. We walked in the power of her dreams – dreams so crystal clear. We walked in the promise of Independence. We walked in her hope for peace, justice, autonomy and life. Those were the days of Dr Independence, who cured his own PAI with the medicine of a beautiful future. But when the birthday celebrations ended in the 1980s, PAI was visited by different physicians. In fact, she found a new physician, Dr Cold War.

Scene II: 1980-90: Dr. Cold War and the Long Freezing Winter

PAI was growing into a beautiful young woman. Many suitors came from many different lands courting her. Finally, there came a suitor, riding a bicycle with many mirrors and wearing sharp pointed shining shoes. He was a 'Mojita,' one who had just landed from 'Makgoeng,' the mines. They married. Two weeks later her husband went away to the mines where he was a labor migrant and a contract worker.

But when we gave PAI's hand away to a husband, a dream so beautiful began to be blurred. She caught a disease of irregular bleeding.

She lived with her mother-in-law and worked hard in the fields to grow food for the children, for her husband sent very little or no money. Her husband came home once every year, during Christmas time, and every time he left her pregnant with a child. PAI was married to an absentee husband, but within ten years she had ten children and looked much older than her age. After the tenth child, he stopped coming home. He did not write. PAI's bleeding was increasing.

But other visitors came to see PAI. Some came from the east and offered her the medicine of communism. Some came from the west and prescribed capitalism to her. Soon a cold war was fought on her body. Dictators like Mabuto Seseko, Jonas Savimbi found many sponsors, who did not want the medicine communism. Cold wars were fought in Mozambique, Angola and Liberia. Independent Zimbabwe was threatened by the same. Things became worse with time.

> Now the sons of PAI were fighting amongst themselves....
> Young children took arms, went to war and killed. The Genocide of Tsutsis in Rwanda and Burundi claimed millions. Princess Africa's Somalian children starved until they were skeletal bones, while warlords made war, not love. Land mines were planted, and playing boys and girls lost their limbs and legs until they learned how not to play. Princess Africa could not plant anymore crops, for fields had already been planted – with landmines. Princess Africa Izwelethu could not walk freely again, for her body was full of explosives. She was confined, afraid to set one foot outside her yard lest she steps on a minefield (Dube Shomanah 2001a:56-57).

The sun itself was fast fading from her skies. The stars became too shy to shine their light. The moon was too sad to show its face of peace. Trees lost leaves. Flowers and grasses dried up in the cold war. The birds were too hungry to sing. Flowers closed their buds and dried up. Butterflies turned themselves into dark hard cocoons and dug themselves in the soil – waiting for the long cold winter of the cold war to end.

People were too afraid to plough and feed themselves. Cholera struck. Malaria killed. Kwashoko reigned. Children's laughter ceased, for they were too hungry and too afraid to run around playing. You could hear the sound of their silent tears rolling down their bony cheeks, crying for food.

I was there when all these things happened. I am sure you were there too. I am sure you will remember how we heard songs of intervention from distant lands saying as other people began to say:

> We are the world,
> We are the children
> We are the ones to make a better day,
> So let us start giving
> There is a choice we are making.
> We are serving our own world
> It's true we make a better day,
> Just you and me!! (USA for Africa)

You remember that? I am a witness.

But the worst was yet to happen. PAI's husband was brought home from the mines very very sick. He needed to be washed and to be fed. Nobody had ever seen such a disease. He was sick for a long time and the PAI was confined to nursing him for months. She could not go to the fields anymore. Hunger intensified for her children.

When he finally died, the relatives of her husband cut a long black mourning dress for her, and put it on her for one year. Because of her mourning status, PAI could not walk in the fields and in the midst of cows, for she could easily suppress their productivity and the rains. Her bleeding was becoming heavier.

The dark frightening clouds were gathering ferociously. Poverty and disease were the order of the day. But one day she heard the sound of someone chopping at a distance. And she cried out saying:

> *Ngubane o gamla lapha? Nqo?*
> (Knock, knock, who is there?)
> *Yimi e ngamla lapha. Nqo*
> (It's me. I am around)

Ufike Otsele uMama lo Baba
(Go tell My Mother and My father)
Uthi Untentelezanhlane ka sekho
(Tell them I am no more)
Ngoba ba nqibela emhlathini we bonlha ka kusaiwa
(For they buried me here, and they don't come here any
more)

And, indeed help came. Relatives came in, and said her
mourning period was over. They took off her black clothes
and gave her a new husband, the brother of her late
husband.

Just then a great bang was also heard. The Berlin Wall
had collapsed and the cold war had to leave. Hope touched
the horizon of her skies. The sun dared to show part of its
face through the thickest clouds. A few stars glimmered
and the moon laughed through the clouds. 'International
organizations arrived. Church organizations arrived to
facilitate reconciliation. Even Princess Diana mobilized the
international community against landmines. International
bodies arrived to lend money. They were ready to resuscitate
her devastated economies. PAI was ready for a much needed
rest. That is how she came to meet her new Physician: Dr.
Neo Colonialism, who also goes by the name Dr. Global
Village" (57).

Scene III: 1990-1995: Dr. Global Village: Opportunistic Infections and Profits

Still bleeding, Princess "Africa heard about the miracle of
external aid, which would bring to an end poverty that had
befallen her land and children. The qualified players and
planners were numerous, among them the International
Monetary Fund and the World Bank. Soon Mama Africa
(PAI) was receiving millions of dollars. She was even wearing
the imported garments of Democracy" (57).

For her to be healed, Dr. Neo Colonialism's prescriptions
were that she must undergo structural adjustment and
democratize. She took the prescriptions. But her bleeding
increased. Foreign aid turned to debt. PAI had received

millions of dollars to alleviate poverty and now she owed billions of dollars. Now everyone in her land worked only to repay the debt to Dr. Neo Colonialism. The debt was ever increasing as the interest rates escalated. Everyone, all her children, were working to repay the foreign debt. Her economies plumbed. Poverty worsened.

Just then Princess Africa heard there was a deadly disease on the loose: HIV/AIDS. What does this deadly disease look like? How does it kill? she asked, for no one had ever seen it. The Information campaign put up pictures of thin bony looking people and Princess Africa and her people recognized that what causes such a disease is poverty.

But the leaders said knowledge is power. The information campaign was intensified. Posters sprang everywhere saying, "Parents talk to your children about HIV/AIDS." On stickers, radio stations, t-shirts, TV stations, newspapers, billboards, public meetings – everywhere, the loud chorus was the same everywhere: *Defeating HIV/AIDS is as easy as ABC.* "Abstain, Be Faithful and Condomise," was the prescription the information campaign offered against the disease that made people thin.

But then how could PAI abstain if culture expected her to be a child bearer? How could she say, "No" to sex if she had no property rights, if she had no decision making powers, if she had no control over her body and if she was afraid of violence in the home and public? How could talking to her children help while adult and older men believed that having sexual intercourse with young girls cleanses their blood? How could the young girls abstain when they were too poor to refuse the little money offered by the Sugar Daddies? How could being faithful to one's partner help, when some cultures tolerate multiple partners amongst married men? And how could her daughters ask men to condomise without being thrown out by angry husbands? How could they insist on the condom without risking further poverty? And so the chorus continued: "Defeating HIV/AIDS is as easy as ABC." But defeating HIV/AIDS was not as easy as ABC. Neither was knowledge alone power to PAI and her children.

Poverty intensified. More people became thin and sick. Her children were dying. When PAI turned to the church, for help, she met hostility. "Those who have AIDS are immoral. They fail to abstain and to be faithful. Those who are suffering from HIV & AIDS deserve it. God is punishing them for their sins." Moreover, the church said, "Condoms are not hundred percent safe and they promote promiscuousness." The church said the only medicine that heals was abstinence and being faithful. PAI's bleeding intensified. She knew that neither the medicine of culture, church or information campaign healed this disease.

Then there appeared a new Physician: Dr Globalization. This physician said the healing medicine was in building a global village. This village would end poverty by offering unlimited access to trade across the boundaries. It would create more jobs and massive profits. PAI took the prescriptions of Dr Globalization. She made her last bet, and bought shares in the Global Village market.

And indeed, national boundaries seemed to fall down. There appeared chain stores and products: KFC, CNN, BBC, Hyundai, Wimpy, VISA cards, MacDonald's, American Express Cards, Coca-Cola all over her land. Everything was in the Cyber space, where distance and time was no more. The world had shrunk, so she heard! PAI and her children began to work for Dr Global Village. But globalization also demanded deregulation and privatization. Social services that were offered by the state, such as education, health and water were sold to private companies, until big transnational companies owned everything in her land. Social welfare services became expensive.

When Dr Globalization brought his computers, PAI and her children were retrenched. Just then the world market collapsed and the Princess lost all the money that she had invested in international markets. They were home, unemployed, sick, hungry and poor. Princess Africa and her children began to do day jobs that offered no security.

Just then her second husband fell ill. He was sick for a long time. He was in and out the hospital, until the hospital people said he must be taken care of at home. Home-based care was the medicine they offered. She started nursing him. Now Princess Africa could not even go and search for day jobs from the transnational companies, for she had to nurse her husband twenty-four hours a day. Social workers, spiritual leaders and volunteers dropped in and checked on her and her sick husband. Dr Globalization, however, amazingly held on to boundaries and would not allow PAI the copyrights to produce affordable and accessible anti-retrovirals.

Opportunistic infections were competing on her body. They came, one after another, day after day. PAI kept on trying to manage the infections, visiting private hospitals, traditional healers, spiritual healers, herbalists, counsellors and social workers. In the process, they had used all the money and sold all their cattle trying to find help. With privatization and deregulation, social welfare services such as paying hospital and school fees were higher.

When money became very scarce, PAI had no other choice, she decided to take her secondary school, Lorato, out of school to help with the nursing – so she can try to find some jobs. But her sick husband said it would even be better, if Lorato was married away so they could get the bride price, which would solve their material crisis. And so they married her away to an older and richer man in the village. He paid a good head of cattle, but the medical expenses were so high that soon they had finished the money.

Her married daughter fell pregnant and gave birth to a sickly child and her husband was beginning to visit the hospital frequently. PAI's other children were also doing badly at school. The children were hungry. They were afraid that their father would die and they were worried because other children stigmatized and marginalised them. PAI's pain was never ending and she was becoming weak herself. She had caught a harsh cough and the hospital said it was TB. What shall I do? She was sitting there feeling like someone buried alive, when she heard someone chopping from a distance. Shaking and still bleeding, she stood to call out

> *Ngubane o gamla lapha? Nqo?*
> (Knock, knock, who is there)
> *Yimi e ngamla lapha. Nqo*

(It's me, I am around)
Ufike Otsele uMama lo Baba
(Go tell My Mother and My father)
Uthi Untentelezanhlane ka sekho
(Tell them I am no more)
Ngoba ba nqibela emhlathini we bonlha ka kusaiwa
(For they buried me here, and they don't come here any
more)

There was good news. The donor community had decided
to intervene and Pharmaceutical companies had created
helpful drugs. These drugs could clear the body of the HIV/
AIDS virus completely. This is how PAI met her New
Physician, Dr Pharmaceutical Companies and the Donor
Community.

Scene IV: 2001: Dr Pharmaceutical Companies and Anti-retroviral Cocktails

Still shaking and bleeding, there was hope for PAI. The sky
turned blue. The sun, the stars and the moon smiled, a
little. The donor community had given money for caregivers.
Melinda and Bill Gates, the couple that gives more money
than all super powers combined, had given massive
amounts of money for the drugs.

Indeed PAI and all other caregivers were given income-
generating projects. They could bake and sell bread to raise
money for their families. What a great help. Some volunteers
from Home Based Care, a Community Based Organization,
would come in and talk to the sick people while they did
business, raising money for their families. PAI and her
daughter and many other caregivers joined the income
generating projects.

But the volunteers were not consistent, for they also had
other business to take care of. They too had sick people
and troubled children. PAI herself was tired and becoming
more weak. Her husband was now just a skeleton –
devastated by continuous diarrhoea. The children and
everyone looked up to her. So she stayed home and could
not use the income-generating project put up for caregivers.

She began to depend entirely on the social welfare government food rations, although they were not enough for the whole house. They ate only one meal a day.

Finally her second husband threw in the towel. He died. People came and the funeral was arranged. Her children were fearfully holding her hands. PAI did not cry, for no tears were left in her eyelids. The cause of death was named: witchcraft, although the witch was not named until after the funeral. The relatives met to say, "Who shall take care of the widow?" They wanted a Third Husband for PAI. It was then that she said, "I cannot possibly take a third husband, for my husband died of HIV/AIDS. I am HIV/AIDS positive myself." There was silence. Then anger. "You killed our child. You killed both of them. You witch."

They kicked her out of her house. She was dispossessed and separated from her growing children. She found home with her married daughter, helping her nurse her sick husband and the sick child. PAI's sickness is getting worse. Her cough was getting harsher. Each day she is anxiously waiting the Melinda and Bill Gates money to bring the drugs that can clean the body free from the virus. But this money, it is said, involves many talks and negotiations that are taking forever. "Pharmaceutical companies are selling these drugs for too much money, so there has to be negotiations, to try and persuade them to drop the prizes, otherwise Bill Gates money will not last." Further, they are other debates such as does she have enough doctors and health centers to administer these drugs; does she have enough equipment. There are many unresolved misgivings, fears and concerns. PAI's bleeding is, however, getting worse.

Scene V: The Time is Now: 2003 Gaborone: If Only, I Can but Touch!

As I speak, PAI is still bleeding and waiting and praying for the Pharmaceutical companies to be persuaded that saving life is more important than profit. Together with her daughter "she runs home based care centers for her dying children and people. She washes them, feeds them, holds them in her arms and rocks them, singing a little song, while she awaits their death. And when they finally die, she rises to close their eyes, to wrap them and bury them. PAI (Mama Africa) bears in her own flesh the wounds of their suffering. And they die in her loving arms (Dube 2001a: 61-62).

PAI was burying this morning and this afternoon she will bury again. And tomorrow morning she will put away yet another of her precious gems. She will bury again. At this moment PAI/Mama Africa is nursing a sister, an uncle, a brother, a son, with one hand; and with her other hand she is holding a dying child and feeding many, many orphans. She has closed many homes and villages, and she will close many more. Princess Africa is once more confined: caring for the sick and dying (61-62).

Just a few minutes ago, she was sitting here in her homeland, feeling like a motherless child, when she heard a crowd in the distance streaming into Gaborone, Botswana, the best democracy in the Africa! PAI in dire straits began to call out singing;

> *Ngubane o gamla lapha, Nqo?*
> (Knock, knock, who is there)
> *Yimi e ngamla lapha. Nqo*
> (It's me, I am around)
> *Ufike Otsele uMama lo Baba*
> (Go tell My Mother and My father)
> *Uthi Untentelezanhlane ka sekho*
> (Tell them I am no more)
> *Ngoba ba nqibela emhlathini we bonlha ka kusaiwa*
> (For they buried me here, and no one come here anymore)

'When she called out, "Who is there? Who is there?" she was told, "Jesus Christ the healer of all is passing through Botswana. She heard that Jesus is on his way to heal a little girl who is already dead, the daughter of Jairus" (60).

PAI is not waiting. "She is standing up. She is not talking. She is not asking. She is not offering anymore money – for none is left." PAI is coming behind Jesus. She is pushing through a strong human crowd of Botswana that are thronging Jesus. "Weak and still bleeding, but determined to live, PAI is stretching out her hands. *If only she can touch the garments of Jesus, Christ..."* (60)

Endnotes

1.   African women's experience cannot be assumed to be uniform, for it differs from one woman to another according to age, ethnicity, culture, race, class, health status and national and international status.

Bibliography

Dube M. W. (2003). *AfricaPraying: A Handbook on HIV/AIDS Sensitive Sermon Guidelines and Liturgy*. Geneva: WCC.

_____ (2000). *Postcolonial Feminist Interpretation of the Bible*. St Louis: Chalice Press.

_____ (2001). "Preaching to the Converted: Unsettling the Christian Church," pp 38-50. In *Ministerial Formation 93*. Geneva: WCC Publication.

_____ ed. (2001a). *Other Ways of Reading: African Women and the Bible*. Atlanta: SBL.

Dube Shomanah, M.W. (1998). "An African Woman Reflects: Five Husbands by the Well of Living Waters," pp. 6-28. In Musimbi Kanyoro and Nyambura Njoroge, eds. *A Decade in Solidarity with the Bible*. Geneva: WCC.

_____ (2001b). "Fifty Years of Bleeding: A Storytelling Feminist Reading of Mark 5:24-43," pp. 50-62. In Musa W. Dube, ed. *Other Ways of Reading: African Women and The Bible*. Atlanta & Geneva: SBL/WCC.

IPS. (2001). "Rights for Women Can Stem HIV/AIDS." *Shaan: IPS Magazine on Gender and Human Rights*. Harare: IPS.

Njoroge, N. and M. W. Dube eds. (2001). *Talitha Cum! Theologies of African Women*. Pietermaritzburg: Cluster Publications.

UNAIDS. (2001). *Investing in Our Future; Psychosocial Support For Children: A Case Study in Zimbabwe and The United Republic of Tanzania*. Geneva: UNAIDS, July.

UNDP. (2000). *Botswana Human Development Report 2000: Towards an AIDS-Free Generation*. Gaborone: UNDP & Botswana Government.

_____ (2001). *Fact Sheets: United Nations Special Sessions on HIV/AIDS*, New York: 25-27 June.

_____ (2000). *HIV/AIDS Best Practices: The Experiences From Botswana*. Gaborone: UNDP/Ministry of Health.

Postscript

In Dialogue
and Solidarity

Chapter Nine

Re-Imagining the Bible in a Pandemic of HIV/AIDS

Letty M. Russell, Yale University Divinity School

In the later 1980's, when HIV/AIDS was still only called an "epidemic," a book was published in the United States concerning the social response to the biological threat entitled *Thinking AIDS*. The authors asserted that one of the things the crisis was teaching us was to use our imagination as a means for overcoming the stigma of the disease and sexual discrimination against homosexuals. In the midst of ignorance, fear, denial, lack of health care, and blaming the victim the writers asserted that the tragedy can teach us to use our imagination to work against all the cultural, political, economic, and sexual issues involved, "...for the imagination of AIDS is the imagination of a human unity, intimately held in the interdependent web of life." [1]

The African women writers in this volume have been sharing in the *imagination of AIDS* by re-imagining biblical texts so that they can help to provide strength and hope in a pandemic of HIV/AIDS. With courage, care and solidarity they have used their biblical and theological scholarship to address the ways religious and cultural practices need to change to promote gender justice. They have taken up the challenge voiced by Musa Dube and addressed to church leaders in South Africa: "That as long as men and women are defined as unequal, the control of HIV/AIDS will prove to be a challenge." [2]

I am excited to be part of this work on re-imagining biblical texts in the midst of the struggle for life and I know that the work shared here will be important for readers around the world who are concerned to address the HIV/AIDS pandemic. This book is just a small part of the work women theologians in Africa are doing in re-imagining the traditions of their communities that are death dealing to women and their families. My contribution is from the perspective of an Anglo North American woman who has had years of opportunity to teach and learn about the imagination of theology. In those years I have learned that action/reflection in each context brings new imagination and new ways of living our faith and I am honored to be included in the global network of those calling out with so many women, "grant me justice" that I may live! [Lk. 18:1-8]

In this "Postscript" I would like to join both writers and readers in talking about *Re-imagining the Bible in a Pandemic of HIV/AIDS*, reflecting first on how these African feminist scholars work with issues of gender, social injustice, and sexuality as they do both biblical and cultural hermeneutics. Then I will join the writers in discussing the importance of *Re-imagining Resurrection* in the face of suffering and the stigma of death.

Re-imagining the Bible

To talk of the *imagination* of AIDS is not to talk about *imaginary* things! The presence of God in the midst of this pandemic is real and so is the life-denying situation of so many women, men and children on this continent. As one book on *African Feminism* has put it: "Links to sex, reproduction, and death endow AIDS with extraordinary symbolic power." [3] The contradictions of this religious and cultural power need re-examination to see what is life giving and what needs transformation because it is death dealing.

The contradictions found in the Hebrew Scriptures and the New Testament are also just as dangerous. As Musa Dube points out in her "Introduction," the texts and their traditional interpretations are often used as the religious authority for patriarchal practices that increase the

likelihood that women will become HIV positive. Thus
Sarojini Nadar re-reads Job from the perspective of a poor
African woman. She points out that the woman and her
children do not deserve to die and says the argument that
HIV/AIDS is a punishment from God sounds like the advice
of Job's friends that tells us "How Not to Talk of God."

> If, however, we listen carefully enough we can discern
> an alternative voice within the Bible, one that critiques
> the dominant ideology of retribution and reward (Nadar,
> 62).

Many persons will ask why it is that women have the
authority to re-interpret texts that have already established
interpretations both in dominant Euro-centric male biblical
scholarship as well as cherished interpretations coming out
of African religious and cultural traditions. Yet every time
we come to see our world in a new way and struggle to
change it, we bring new questions and insights to our
interpretations. This struggle to open our eyes to new
understanding has a long precedent in biblical
interpretation. For instance, it is Jesus himself who has to
interpret the scriptures to the disciples on the Road to
Emmaus [Lk. 24:13-27]. Cleopas and "Ms. Cleopas" [who
remains unnamed in the text] cannot see that the scriptures
point to the ministry of the one walking with them because
they are only looking at them with pre-resurrection eyes.
Opening our eyes to see God's presence in the world around
us is the continuing struggle of those who seek to "open
the scriptures."

Women writers in Africa have more than one strike
against them because they are assumed to have "less to
say" because they do not usually come from the universities
of the dominant nations of the North. They also struggle
against great odds of racial, social, political, economic, and
gender injustice. Just because of this, however, they have
a lot to say to those of us who need to know how the Bible
looks from the perspective of suffering and injustice, and
plenty of scholarship to back it up.

Along with other feminist writers that advocate the full
humanity of all women together with all men and the dignity

of the whole creation, they have taken on three areas of interpretation and related them to the HIV/AIDS pandemic. The first is addressing "texts of terror" that are to be found both in the Bible and in their own cultural contexts. In this volume the story of the "Cry of Tamar and need to lament is lifted up by Denise Ackermann. The problem of stigma associated with HIV/AIDS is related to John 9 and the story of the man born blind is discussed by Malebogo Kgalemang, while Johanna Siebert shows how stigma and sin are related to women's sexuality in biblical texts.

The second area of interpretation is texts about women and healing that counteract the negative views of women in the Bible and in culture. Here we find Musa Dube's chapter on "*Talitha Cum*: A Post Colonial Feminist HIV/AIDS Reading of Mark 5:21-43." Dube helps us to re-imagine the story of Jairus' daughter as a story that exposes the colonial situation of Mark's time in relation to neocolonialism in Africa. In the same way the story of the Canaanite Woman from Matthew 15:21-28 is reinterpreted by Anastasia Boniface-Malle.

A third choice for re-imagining and interpretation is to emphasize the liberating aspects of a text that reveals God's love for the least of God's children and the desire of God to bring about the mending of creation. Sarojini Nadar introduces this theme in her re-interpretation of Job and the understanding of God, and Dorothy B. Akoto asks the question of Ezekiel 37:1-12, "Can These Bones Live?" while affirming that the Spirit raising the dry bones is a sign of hope in the time of the pandemic. In this same order of resisting the devastation of imperial conquest, global economic "underdevelopment," Musa Dube tells the story of Jesus' healing of the woman with a flow of blood and relates that to the healing of Africa's continual bleeding through exploitation.

In all these essays the use of gender analysis facilitates what Musa Dube calls a "Gender-sensitive multi-sectoral approach" that keeps the focus on the "double predicament" of gender and social justice in the text and in the community reading the text (Dube, 4). Recognition that gender is socially constructed rather than biologically determined has led feminist scholars to look carefully at the social norms for what it means to be a woman or a man both in the text and in the life of the interpretative community. This allows a critical voice to be heard in regard to what the story conveys concerning masculine and feminine gender roles and to critique it when this "gendered face" contributes to the continuing spread of HIV/AIDS. It also helps in reminding us to look at the ways gender interacts with other socially constructed roles such as those of race, class, nationality and economic location, and to include such perspectives along with more traditional forms of biblical interpretation.

Re-imaging Resurrection

Thinking about HIV/AIDS and thinking about religion is not easy and sometimes it is risky. People do not re-imagine biblical and theological interpretation unless forced to think about life and death and to search for the meaning of life that can transcend our finite and limited reality and customary views. In our time African women are really being forced to do just that; not only to do theology and speak about God's absence and presence, but to do it in a new way as women who care very much for life *after birth* and not just *life after death*. In the words of Mercy Amba Oduyoye, they are confronting this pandemic by "giving birth" to themselves and continuing to live out the theme of the first meeting of the Circle of Concerned African Women Theologians in 1989, "*Talitha Cum*: The Will to Arise!"[4]

In the face of suffering and death, the women of the Circle and in this volume join women and men around the world who search for the will to arise out of pain and loss. The poet, Julia Esquivel has described this experience of death and loss of loved ones through murder and war in Guatemala as being *threatened with resurrection*. Her poem, "They Have Threatened Us with Resurrection," describes the imagination of struggle in which those who have died as martyrs are still present to those who love them, saying to them, "*Presente!*" and bringing them courage so that they "...continue to love life, and do not accept their death."[5]

This happens with AIDS as well. For instance, during writing this short reflection, Ron and John, the two men living and dying with AIDS who helped me in editing a book on *The Church With Aids: Renewal in the Midst of Crisis*, have been present to me "threatening *me* with resurrection" in the sense that they are present with me urging me on and letting me know that their presence continues with me.[6] In the same way the spirit of Brigitte Symalevwe, a pioneer in speaking out about her own HIV infection who joined her husband to take their life and make it count for others through a ministry with HIV/AIDS orphans in Zambia, is still present among us urging her African sisters to cry out for justice!

One source of hope against hope as we confront the pandemic, then, is the presence of loved ones that continues with those who are affected and/or infected with HIV/AIDS. Although the death of persons with AIDS is a relief that the loved one is beyond suffering, it is always a time of sorrow at the loss, and a time of fear about infection and the future. This fear is real in the lives of African widows as they often lose the source of income, their homes and even, sometimes their children to the husband's family, and are themselves in danger from infection. For widows it is often like "living death" as they are cut off from their families and communities and they can only cry out to God like the widow in Luke 18:1-8, "Grant me justice" (Dube, 16).

In her article for one of the latest Circle books, *Talitha Cum! Theologies of African Women*, Nyambura Njoroge describes the courage to struggle against death as "a spirituality of resistance and transformation.[7] She urges us all to recognize that Jesus' death on the cross is not a justification of the endless suffering of women. Others like Virginia Fabella from the Philippines join her in calling this, "...a dead-end theology of the cross with no resurrection or salvation in sight."[8] Jesus died because he freely chose to oppose the powerful of his society on behalf of the weak and powerless and was killed. If we are to follow his example, to take up our cross is to join in resisting evil and injustice and to work for full human dignity. Nyambura urges us to follow the example of Rizpah in her resistance to the senseless killing of her sons when King Saul, their father, dies. Her vigil for her sons is a public resistance to the injustice of powerful rulers [2 Samuel 21:9-14]. Like Rachel weeping for her children, she joins us in a powerful reminder that neither God nor those we love are separated from us by death [Rom. 8: 35-39]. [9]

In the face of so much suffering the Christian idea of resurrection comes to be represented as a source of salvation and blessing after death when we are joined to Christ's resurrected body as members of the church. The difficulty with this is that more and more the comfort of knowing that we are in God's hands in death, leads church leaders to focus on the after life and to ignore the heartbreaking, and backbreaking reality of every day life. Along with condemnation of any one with HIV/AIDS as a sinner, this attitude that the world does not matter because we are saved after death contributes to the pandemic rather than providing a source for resistance to the medical and social causes of suffering. For this reason, this book is very much needed for people in all parts of the globe as they work to re-imagination of resurrection as a source of commitment to struggle for life together in community. Thus Dorothy Bea Akoto claims that the vision of Ezekiel works to create "an alternative consciousness" that "moves the community toward faith in God and God and God's promise ..." (Akoto, 109).

This re-imagining calls for what Paul describes in Romans 12:2 as a transformation of our minds: "...be transformed by the renewing of your minds, so that you may discern what is the will of God ...." From this perspective we can say that resurrection is not an escape, but rather God's **"No"** to evil, suffering and death. Confidence in God's continuing love for all of humankind and desire to mend the whole creation is the *impulse for change in the present*. In responding to that "no" we ourselves join those whom we have loved and lost by resisting the evils that feed the pandemic of HIV/AIDS. As Denise Ackermann so clearly says:

> HIV/AIDS is our *kairos*. It is a time when the ordinary
> rhythm of life is suspended. Will it be a time of doom or
> will we find a new unveiling of God's presence and love
> for us here and now? (Ackermann, 54).

Re-imagining resurrection also leads to a second clue to its meaning in our lives. In biblical terms *resurrection is about bodies*. There is no way we can ignore our bodies and just talk of our souls because we are created as one integration of soul and body that gives us our identity as children of God. In Romans 21:1 Paul urges his brothers and sisters to present their "...bodies as a living sacrifice, holy and acceptable to God, which is your spiritual worship." This passage is about more than just sacrificial language that has been used to justify the social construction of women's role as those born to sacrifice their lives, and talents for others. Paul connects our bodily work to our worship and declares that through the power of Christ's Spirit the whole community, both female and male, is made holy and is empowered to become part of the risen body of Christ.

Through baptism and eucharist we are already part of that risen body as the church. In faith we are both connected to the realities of this world and yet with a foretaste of what is to come [Rom. 8:18-21]. If this is so, bodies are also sacred and their need for healing cannot be ignored. As Denise Ackermann says, "Bodies are at the centre of this crisis, sick, poor and too often women and children's bodies" (Ackermann, 44). In order to open the eyes of those who are the leaders of religious bodies, women theologians such as Johanna Siebert, and many others are working to make it clear that sexuality is also of God and must be discussed and understood so that we can confront the domination of women and misuse of women's bodies that so often leads to infection.

A third clue to re-imagining resurrection that we find in these texts and in our own lives is that resurrection is not only something that happens at death. *Resurrection is a daily matter.* It happens over and over in our lives as we catch glimpses of wholeness and joy in the midst of our struggles. In her book, *Out of the Depths: Women's Experience of Evil and Salvation,* Ivone Gebara speaks of the "dailiness of salvation." She says that resurrection is not only something that we anticipate. It is part of the daily process of "... recovering life and hope and justice along life's path even when these experiences are frail and fleeting."[10] Looking for those fleeting moments when there is food for the family meal, or medicine for someone's pain, or even a small act of caring leads us to gratitude for the mending that is possible along the way as well as at the end of our present journey. This in turn gives us daily connection to the power of resurrection and ears to hear the voice of Princess Africa Izwelethu who is buried alive, but "Still the Princess Sings" (Dube, 186). We can also hear God's "no" to suffering and oppression as we join God's "yes" to healing, peace and justice in our whole world, and right in the dailiness of where we are.

God is the God of all life and God weeps with us in the midst of the destruction of God's creation and our lives. Surely we can find courage to continue in the use of our theological and biblical imagination trying to understand the ways in which God calls us to work for the mending of creation and the restoration of justice and life. Re-imagining the Bible and our own understanding of hope and resurrection calls *now* for the mending of women's lives and for the mending of their homes and nations. It can give us the power to name the suffering while speaking of hope where there is no hope. Together, we do our theologies as a community of women of faith, not because it is easy, but because those who have been sacrificed before us call us to speak of life, and of the way our hope is full of their continuing presence in our lives!

Endnotes

1.   Mary Catherine Bateson and Richard Goldsby. (1988). *Thinking AIDS: The Social Response to the Biological Threat.* NY: Addison-Wesley Publishing Co, Inc., 10.

2. Musa W. Dube. (2001). "Preaching to the Converted: Unsettling the Christian Church," *Ministerial Formation*, Vol. 93: 43.

3. Brooke Grundfest Schoepf. (1997). "AIDS, Gender and Sexuality during Africa's Economic Crisis," *African Feminism: the Politics of Survival in Sub-Saharan Africa*, Gwendolyn Mikell, ed. Philadelphia: University of Pennsylvania Press, 1997, 311.

4. Mercy Amba Oduyoye. (1997). "Woman with Beads," *Heart, Mind and Tongue: A Heritage of Woven Word*, Elizabeth Amoah and Pamela Martin, eds. Accra, Ghana: The Circle of Concerned African Women Theologians with SAM-WOODE LTD, 7-8; Mercy Amba Oduyoye and Musimbi R. A. Kanyoro, eds. (1992). *The Will to Arise: Women, Tradition, and the Church in Africa*, Maryknoll, New York, 1-6.

5. Julia Esquivel. (1982). "They Have Threatened Us With Resurrection," in *Threatened with Resurrection: Prayers and Poems from an Exiled Guatemalan*. Elgin, Illinois: The Brethren Press, 59-63.

6. Letty M. Russell, ed. (1990). *The Church with AIDS: Renewal in the Midst of Crisis*. Louisville, Kentucky: Westminster/John Knox Press, 35-66.

7. Nyambura J. Njoroge. (2001). "A Spirituality of Resistance and Transformation," in *Talitha cum! Theologies of African Women*, Nyambura J. Njoroge and Musa W. Dube, eds. Pietermaritzburg, South Africa: Cluster Publications, 66-82.

8. Virginia Fabella. (1990). "Christology from an Asian Woman's Perspective," *We Dare to Dream: Doing Theology as Asian Women*, Virginia Fabella and Sun Ai Lee Park, eds. Maryknoll, N.Y.: Orbis Books, 7-8.

9. Elizabeth Amoah. (2002). "Tears of Compassion and Hope," a sermon preached at Yale Divinity School on Jeremiah 31:15-17 during the Consultation on Gender, Faith, and Response to HIV/AIDS in Africa, March 1, [unpublished manuscript].